Architecture and the American Dream

Architecture and the

American Dream

CRAIG WHITAKER

Clarkson N. Potter / Publishers
New York

Copyright © 1996 by Craig Whitaker

Published by Clarkson N. Potter, Inc., 201 East 50th Street, New York, New York 10022. Member of the Crown Publishing Group.

Random House, Inc. New York, Toronto, London, Sydney, Auckland
http://www.randomhouse.com/

CLARKSON N. POTTER, POTTER, and colophon are trademarks of Clarkson N. Potter, Inc.

Printed in the United States of America

Design by Abigail Sturges

Library of Congress Cataloging-in-Publication Data is available upon request.

ISBN 0-517-70378-5

10   9   8   7   6   5   4   3   2   1

First Edition

for Jennifer

Contents

FOREWORD

I AM A PRACTICING ARCHITECT, NOT A HISTORIAN; CONSEQUENTLY, THIS BOOK IS NOT an attempt to write history, but an effort to set forth a point of view. More particularly, it is the assertion that cultural values, more than any other attribute, determine how we shape our man-made environment, and how we appraise what we have built.

Many circumstances brought me to this conviction, but among them the discovery of two very disparate books stands out. Several years ago I came across Fernand Braudel's two-part history written in the early 1970s, *The Mediterranean and the Mediterranean World in the Age of Philip II*.[1] Braudel's work, in turn, brought to mind Camillo Sitte's 1889 study of Italian hill towns, *City Planning According to Artistic Principles*, which had fascinated me as an architecture student.[2]

Braudel asserted that the history of the countries bordering the Mediterranean—what happened to them over time—was less the product of short-term events, like war and natural disasters, than the outgrowth of deeper, more immutable forces, such as the environmental circumstances of climate and tide. These forces shaped a people's economy and their cultural values. Braudel also showed that once cultural values had formed, they changed very slowly, and only over many generations.

Camillo Sitte was a late nineteenth-century Viennese architect who had studied plans of dozens of densely built medieval Italian hill towns, all of which had remarkably similar features despite their relative isolation from one another. Each town had crooked streets, closed plazas, and few if any freestanding buildings. Even the statuary adorning the plazas formed consistently similar patterns. Because the towns had such picturesque appeal, Sitte thought their organization indicated some higher aesthetic truth that should be replicated in modern civic design.

Despite the complete irrelevance of his ideas to a new country like America, thinly spread across a large continent, the similarities Sitte found among these medieval cities fascinated me. Although relatively separate and self-contained, the towns were obviously the product of similar historic circumstances.

Sitte's affection for these intimately scaled towns led him, understandably enough, to disdain the "brutal ruthlessness"[3] of the cities of the New World. He believed any culture that carved up its land as America had was incapable of producing great art: simple rectangular blocks lined with small freestanding buildings were not the stuff of excellence. A vast open network of streets, few of which led to any conclusion, only reinforced his view that America's new cities had little to offer the civilized world.

Many European visitors to this country shared Sitte's opinions. Mrs. Frances Trollope, for example, in 1832 praised one of the few buildings she admired, saying that in one room its owners had demonstrated "more art and taste . . . than all Western America can shew elsewhere."[4] Her views were echoed by many American critics and architects who with great frequency turned to Europe as a source of inspiration and a model for how this country might improve upon its first hurried and ill-considered efforts.

Sitte, for his part, was less focused on criticizing America than on shaping the outcome of an enormous public works program then under way in his native Vienna.[5] Although his ideas subsequently had little impact on Vienna's redevelopment, they caused a great stir among architects and city planners elsewhere. Almost immediately after *City Planning According to Artistic Principles* was published, "Sitte Schules" began sprouting up all over Europe as students and planners rushed to embrace Sitte's vision of a picturesque modern city.

As designers approached the technological promise of a new century, however, Sitte's ideas came to be seen as antiquated. Within a decade after the book first appeared, his influence began to wane. By 1922, when the Swiss-born French architect Le Corbusier captured the public's attention with his call for a *Ville Contemporaine*—a modern city composed of isolated towers set in parklike surroundings—Sitte's vision of tightly twisting streets and small-scaled towns seemed antediluvian. Ironically, Le Corbusier, like many other architects of the time, had earlier embraced Sitte's ideas before throwing them aside.[6] Sitte, as architectural historian Sigfried Giedion put it, "had become a kind of troubadour, ineffectually pitting his medieval songs against the din of modern industry."[7]

I discovered Sitte's treatise in the 1960s at a time when the truly apocalyptic consequences of Le Corbusier's visions were first being felt in the United States. Slum clearance and urban renewal had become national policies, shaped in large measure by his thinking. These programs were demolishing hundreds of acres of older inner-city tenements and erecting stands of isolated towers in their place. The towers, set away from the street and their surroundings, often left gaping scars. The resulting carnage was causing a growing number of architects to rethink Le Corbusier's ideas. It was in this context that a thumb-worn copy of Sitte's book reappeared, and to some, his ideas once again had currency.

The book had an immediate impact on me, but for different reasons. Sitte showed that nearly identical patterns had manifested themselves from town to town for hundreds of years. Despite the existence of each village as a separate semiclosed world, the towns' remarkable similarities indicated quite clearly that many choices had been made by people who were unconscious of nearly identical decisions being made elsewhere.

Also included in Sitte's survey were Michelangelo's plans for the Campidoglio in Rome, and the changes Sansovino had made to the Piazza San Marco in Venice. Although these Renaissance designs were the work of artists celebrated for their individual genius, they grew out of earlier medieval plazas that had been on the same sites. The earlier plazas had come into being through a collaboration of artisans, patrons, and officials, many of whose names were never recorded. Dramatic and singular as the works of Michelangelo and Sansovino were, they owed much to these earlier patterns. Their work took its place among the other aesthetic decisions spanning hundreds of years that had shaped these plazas.

In reflecting on these patterns in light of Braudel's theories on the endurance of cultural values, I recalled a different but equally remarkable replication of building patterns detailed by Thomas Sharp in a small monograph on English villages. Published in 1946, *The Anatomy of the Village* demonstrated consistent patterns running through a number of tiny English hamlets, some of which were little more than two rows of buildings lining a single unpaved path.[8] These patterns were very different from the ones Sitte had found: the English villages were more open and had more greenery, and the village church was often freestanding and off to one side, rather than symbolically dominating the town, as it did at the head of an Italian plaza. The internal consistency of these English villages further reinforced the idea that common cultural circumstances would give rise to similar architectural characteristics.

Many American towns and cities also look very much alike, and they look very different from towns and cities elsewhere in the world. As I posited a link between cultural values and architectural pattern I came to believe that American values, more than any other attribute, underpin the singularity of America's architecture. Concomitantly, the link between values and pattern strengthened my belief that style—which changes quite rapidly, but which nevertheless is often used to define a culture's architecture—was not a very useful tool for understanding our uniqueness.

A repetition of particular patterns over time also undermined for me one of the most dearly held precepts of modern art and architecture: that an artist acted and created solely as an individual, or as Joan Didion put it, "the painting was the painter as the poem is the poet, that every choice one made alone."[9] On the contrary, the patterns suggested that artists in a given culture were more likely to have a shared vision than an individual one. I began to see that pattern, as the critic Sibyl Moholy-Nagy observed in 1968, "in the original meaning of 'archetype' was never, as in a work of art, the revelation of a single creative individual, producing a singular, unrepeatable configuration. It was the predominance of one communal concept over the other coexisting ones, and it repeated itself where similar conditions prevailed."[10]

This being so, the powerful forces that shape American culture must also create patterns that express themselves regardless of the style of a particular building, the period in which it was built, or the methods of its construction. This idea was serendipitously strengthened when, just after discovering Braudel and beginning to think about pattern, I saw an early spaghetti western starring Clint Eastwood. These films were so named because they had been produced in Italy (and filmed in Spain), not in Hollywood. I was unaware of this at the time, but in an early scene when Eastwood strode into some mythical western town, I knew instantly the buildings had not been designed by Americans. The town had an almost hallucinatory, dreamlike quality. Set designers had striven mightily to give it the trappings of the Old West; all the ingredients were there—saloons, hitching posts, and feed stores—but the relationship of the buildings to each other and to the land was clearly not American.

I realized that the set designers had missed other defining characteristics of an American western town. Only after I had seen the movie again did it become clear to me that the buildings were arranged to look more like the rudimentary beginnings of a European village surrounding a central plaza than an American town strung out along a main street. This divergence was not a pattern I expected American buildings to make, even in the movies.

If a culture's values do repeatedly assert themselves, even subconsciously, I believe one has a better chance of manipulating these values successfully and of using them to improve the built environment, if one is aware of them. This seems especially so in America, which since its beginnings has tried to celebrate individualism, equality, freedom, community, and renewal—often all at the same time.

Architecture and the American Dream

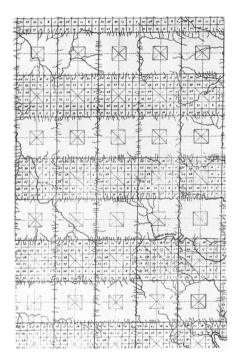

Chapter I

American Dreams

Make American Patterns

WE ADMIRE A BUILDING OR GROUP OF BUILDINGS BECAUSE THEY EXPRESS, HOWEVER subtly, certain images and ideas we have about ourselves. Conversely, when a building's appearance conflicts with these beliefs we find its architecture disquieting. The criteria we use to make these judgments are very much a product of our culture and our values, many of which are deeply ingrained.

Many American values are also unique. This country was founded on a belief in freedom, equality, and the opportunity for renewal. Underpinning this dream was a belief that physical mobility makes it possible—we can pick up stakes and begin anew. These ideas infuse our culture and, therefore, our buildings. Understanding how the dream expresses itself is indispensable to producing an architecture that reflects our uniqueness.

Can one actually describe architecture, and specifically American architecture, by evoking cultural values? As there are themes and patterns that differentiate American literature and movies from books and films made elsewhere in the world, are there themes that resonate through American buildings and cities, themes that stamp an architecture as uniquely our own, and to which Americans respond? I think there are. More important, I believe we can better express these singular values, and in so doing contribute to a built environment that is both more satisfying and more in keeping with American sensibilities.

To recognize fully our own propensities and devise ways to capitalize on

3

1. Above: Neo-Spanish hacienda, Billings, Montana.

2. Right: Japanese teahouse, Martha's Vineyard, Massachusetts. This small garden structure is used for entertainment.

them, we must also occasionally turn to the architecture of other cultures, particularly those of Western Europe. Our deep roots in European culture notwithstanding, sifting through history is always a selective task for designers. Revisiting the architecture of other epochs is a search not so much for knowledge as for patterns and forms that still seem relevant. In this regard, European examples can help to explain why certain archetypes continue to have resonance for us whereas others do not.

Americans, however, populated a new continent centuries after Europe's great cities had arisen and, in some cases, waned. Consequently, the more important source for understanding American architecture is our own beginnings and how they shaped our values. Central to these values is the dream of possibilities—of what we could become.

We Americans believe in the fundamental right to choose and thereby to express our individuality. With no sense of contradiction, we also believe in equality; we put great faith in the tenet that, although each of us is unique, we are all created equal. Most important, we believe in freedom and renewal, in the right and power to be who we want, even to change who we are—and begin again. Each of these values affects our built environment.

America also prides itself on its diversity, on being a mosaic, a house of many rooms. Because this country is a place where one is free to choose, it has welcomed new people with new concepts throughout its history. This is as true in architecture as it is for American culture in general. Starting with Pierre Charles L'Enfant, the expatriate Frenchman who in 1791 produced the plan for Washington, D.C., the country has welcomed foreign architects and their ideas. In this century alone such noted figures as Walter Gropius, Mies van der Rohe, Richard Schindler, Richard Neutra, Marcel Breuer, I. M. Pei, and Eliel Saarinen all came from abroad to live and practice architecture in America. Within recent

3. Neo-Gothic auto
showroom (later a
sporting-goods store),
Denver.

years, leading American architectural schools have selected deans from England, France, and Argentina.

We are a nation whose earliest settlers began by borrowing and adapting many architectural forms and ideas from the European culture they had just left. Certainly the best known of those who looked to Europe for inspiration in the early days of the Republic was Thomas Jefferson, who believed that European classicism and, in particular, the work of the Italian Renaissance architect Andrea Palladio were uniquely fitting models for a new democracy. Palladio's freestanding villas in the Veneto, designed in a vocabulary of Greek and Roman forms, seemed to Jefferson especially appropriate prototypes on which to build an American style.[1]

However, a single national style was never to be. In the nearly two centuries since Jefferson espoused a Palladian model we have adopted an ever-growing repertoire of different styles. As one measure of our diversity, authors Virginia and Lee McAlester list some thirty-nine identifiably distinct styles ranging from Queen Anne to Dutch Colonial.[2] As the American architect Charles Moore put it, "we, the inheritors of a hundred traditions, had our pick."[3]

A multitude of styles calls into question any attempt, based on style, to generalize about American architecture. So, too, is it difficult to make generalizations based on construction methods or the choice of materials underlying different regional styles, such as the use of adobe in New Mexico or of silvered cedar shingles on eastern Long Island. In every locale there are so many exceptions to any one norm that such generalizations are, at best, only taxonomic exercises. Because they are so stylistically different from their neighbors, a neo-Spanish hacienda in Billings, Montana (Fig. 1), a Japanese teahouse on Martha's Vineyard (Fig. 2), and a neo-Gothic auto showroom in Denver (Fig. 3), attest to our unbridled eclecticism. Exceptions like these are the norm; and they tell us

4. Above: K Street, Washington, D.C., 1994.

5. Above right: Boulevard Sebastopol, Paris, ca. 1865.

that, apart from our penchant for diversity, style reveals little about our architecture. Many Americans would agree with the English architecture critic Geoffrey Scott who wrote in 1914 that using style as a tool to arrive at some broader understanding "leads nowhere" and that even the attempt, though "flattering alike to the author and his reader," fails "to explain why the styles of architecture which [one finds it] necessary to condemn have in fact been created and admired."[4]

Although our many styles explain nothing in themselves, they quite clearly reflect our freedom to choose. For Americans the potency of that idea has had far more currency than the wish for a common style. Our right to choose is our right to express ourselves, and we cherish the opportunity. When automobile manufacturers, like General Motors' Alfred Sloan, realized in the 1920s the importance of consumer choice, they trumped Henry Ford's unchanging black Model T with "the annual model change." Ford's competitors inaugurated a profusion of styles, and the availability of different models shaped the American automobile industry as profoundly as had Ford's introduction of the assembly line more than a decade earlier.

Residential developers, too, have long understood the market appeal of offering more than one model. Nineteenth-century row-house developers, for instance, frequently offered potential buyers the choice of different trim and decoration, although the underlying house remained the same. Today many developers offer multiple styles and models even within a single small development.

The opportunity to choose a style, whether it be French Château or English Tudor, is a consumer's right demanded by every home buyer. Choosing a style— or a school or a neighborhood—is for Americans an act of empowerment. Vincent Scully has written that "many species of high quality can inhabit the same world. Such multiplicity is indeed the highest promise of the modern age."[5] This rings especially true in America.

We want to exercise our right not only to choose but also to show the world how well we are doing. Architectural historian J. B. Jackson, in a 1984 treatise on indigenous architecture, called the American single-family home "a miniature estate . . . much concerned with keeping its image honored and respected by the outside world."[6] Historian Daniel Boorstin thought that "since the image is already supposed to be congruent with reality, the producer of the image . . . is expected to fit into the image—rather than to strive toward it." Once an image is established, its owner has "to do nothing more than go about his business, avoiding scandals or any public information that might discredit the image."[7] In short, our buildings not only tell others who we are, they also supposedly describe the quality of life within; and invariably the message projected by an American building, most especially on its front facade, is that those who live or work within are doing rather well, thank you.

The jostle of competing facades, all announcing their well-being, is nowhere more evident than on K Street in the heart of downtown Washington, D.C. (Fig. 4). The real estate values in this office and commercial district push builders to fill every square foot of their lot. However, attendant restrictions, keeping the height of all buildings below that of the dome of the United States Capitol, limit the height on K Street to 130 feet. These two forces create a street of buildings that extend out to the sidewalk and are essentially the same height— circumstances which would seem to be ideal for engendering common architectural elements such as cornices, stringcourses, and other features that would have tied together a similarly scaled Parisian street, for example (Fig. 5). On K Street, however, each building strains sullenly against the restrictions, trying to establish its own identity by sharply distinguishing itself from its neighbors.

In similar fashion, main streets across America show considerable stylistic diversity, and most American downtown skylines look like smaller versions of the jagged profile of Manhattan (Fig. 6), a skyline that American writer Henry James described in the early 1900s as "some colossal hair-comb turned upward and so deprived of half its teeth."[8] More recently Vincent Scully opined that New York's skyscrapers "were all different beings . . . lifting châteaux, temples, and mausolea into the sky, their tripods smoking among the clouds."[9]

Americans, then, can and do choose from among many styles, and critics have often equated the fruits of this right with endemic chaos. "We see a babble of tongues, a free-for-all of personal idiolects, . . . where there once were rules of architectural grammar, we now have a mutual diatribe,"[10] wrote Charles Jencks recently about architecture in general. His charge, it should be noted, is one of long standing in America. The planner Elbert Peets declared in 1937, "the plain fact is that our cities have architectural indigestion."[11] Werner Hegemann and

6. Manhattan skyline.
Photograph by
Andreas Feininger
ca. 1935.

Elbert Peets argued together in 1922 that American cities were rapidly becoming a riot—a premise based on the lament that "every orchestra played its own tune" and that adjoining buildings could be "wantonly different or even obnoxious."[12] To bolster their contention the authors reprinted a cartoon that had appeared eighteen years earlier in the *Architectural Review* showing a street filled with buildings of different heights in a hodgepodge of styles. The cartoon was entitled simply, *Chaos*[13] (Fig. 7). To the vast majority of Americans, however, this seeming cacophony was the whole point: America really was a country where one was free to choose.

Many American styles originated in Europe, and many observers have reflected on the consequences of the transplantation of these styles to a new continent. They have seen a dissolution of order tending toward anarchy. Christian Norberg-Schulz, a contemporary Norwegian critic sympathetic to American architecture, believes "an obvious effect of such a transfer is fragmentation and relativization. The New World, in fact, no longer consists of integrated systems based on defined values but has become a seemingly chaotic multitude of scattered bits."[14]

This seeming disarray of styles, however, masks a deeper reality. If anarchy and chaos were truly the norm, then America's built landscape should appear so disordered that each locale would look different from any other. For the most part, in fact, the opposite is true. American cities look remarkably like one another, as do most American suburbs. Commercial strips across the country are nearly interchangeable. American suburbs in particular, despite a plethora of styles, are often remarkably cohesive architectural groupings. Parts of many cities also display a real unity, not because the buildings profess a common style, but because beneath their various styles they exhibit a conceptual similarity. Moreover, when the various features of the American landscape are compared in their entirety to similar areas in Europe, or anywhere else, they look distinctly American. They bear the mark of designers and builders who, while acting independently of each other, shared similar values and therefore made similar choices.

J. B. Jackson noted that "there are landscapes in America separated by hundreds of miles that resemble one another to a bewildering degree. Many American cities are all but indistinguishable as to layout, morphology, and architecture . . . the lack of variety in much of our man-made environment is recognized by anyone who has traveled widely in this country . . . it is true that I cannot always remember the difference between one small town and another . . . the traveler in the United States finds evidence wherever he goes of a specifically national style of spatial organization. He may not care for it, he may prefer a greater variety, a romantic confusion; but he cannot fail to be impressed by it."[15]

This similarity suggests one of the central paradoxes of the American landscape: in vigorously exercising their right to choose, Americans have often chosen the same thing. Despite our many styles, one building and one town look like another.

This similarity, however, has never led to a celebration of our uniqueness. Quite the contrary, many architects and critics have expended considerable effort, even until now, trying to improve upon "our own primitive American culture."[16] Concomitant with our architectural proclivities has been the long-

7. *Chaos*, Architectural Review, *1904*.

standing conviction that there were better alternatives. The City Beautiful movement of the late nineteenth and early twentieth century, for example, was based on a nearly messianic belief in the superiority of European archetypes and the conviction that these historic examples could and should be folded into our culture with uplifting results.

Of all the features of America's built environment that critics have decried, the most prominent and common are the gridded streets of our cities and towns.

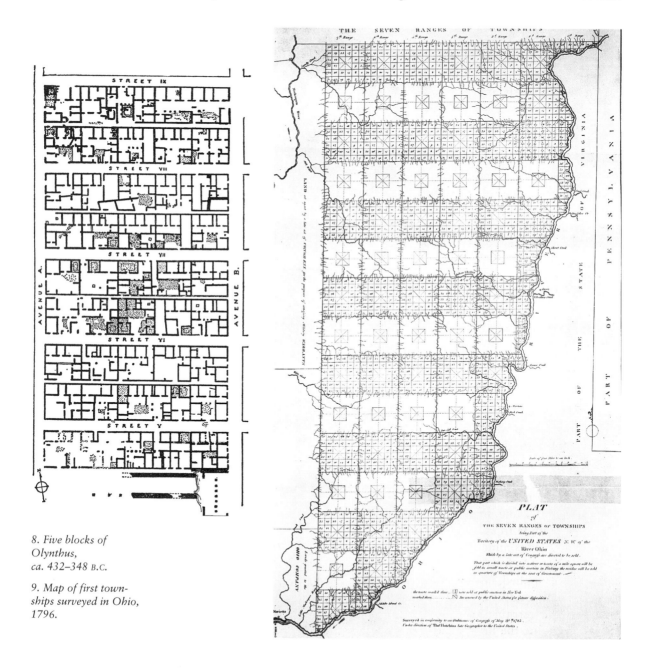

8. Five blocks of
Olynthus,
ca. 432–348 B.C.

9. Map of first townships surveyed in Ohio, 1796.

As with the host of various styles, critics have seen the grid as a dramatic manifestation of this country's lack of culture. Because there is no grand hierarchy of places in a grid—all property and all lots are the same—many critics regard the street grid as hopelessly banal. Even Jackson, who has written with great empathy about the American landscape, thought the grid perhaps "too commonplace for greatness."[17]

Gridded cities are not, of course, uniquely American. The first grids can be traced back to well before the fifth century B.C., to the designs of Hippodamus for the Ionian city of Miletus and in the layout of other Greek cities, like Olynthus (Fig. 8). The order and geometric logic of a grid intrigued a people who were deeply involved in the study of mathematics, and the Greeks used a grid often as they spread their culture across Asia Minor. The Egyptians employed a grid pattern as early as the second century B.C. in quarters built for the laborers and administrators at Kahun. That grid, however, was chosen less for its appeal to the intellect than for its usefulness in helping overseers register and keep track of those working on the tomb of King Usertesen. The potent symbol for the Egyptians was the pyramid the workers were building, not the compound where the laborers lived.

The Romans too built gridded cities across their empire. For them the grid symbolized the order and authority of the imperium. Centuries later French and Spanish military explorers built gridded settlements in the New World. For these early visitors to a new continent the order of a grid was a reassuring symbol at the edge of a vast and sometimes terrifying wilderness.

The grid also connoted order for Americans and was, as well, a sign of virtue and rectitude. Not only was the grid the pattern of choice for most new towns and cities, it was used to divide up the entire country. The Land Ordinance Act, passed by the Continental Congress in 1785, called for the platting of all unsettled and unexplored portions of America into a gigantic gridiron (Fig. 9). Jackson, in comparing America to Republican Rome, talked of "the same well kept farms, neither too large or too small, the same hardworking families, the same countryside of square fields; everything square in all senses of the word, with every good quality and every limitation associated with squareness." Elsewhere he tried to define the American landscape. "Classical is the word for it, I think; and rhythmic repetition (not to say occasional monotony) is a classical trait, the consequence of devotion to clarity and order."[18]

Gridded streets became a nearly ubiquitous feature across America, despite the many opportunities to adopt a different plan. For all its supposed ordinariness, Brigham Young, for example, thought the grid to be as much an attestation of the Mormon faith as a practical framework for a new city when he laid out a series of gridded communities across the country culminating in Salt Lake City in 1847 (Fig. 10). As for future expansion, Young said, "when [one] square is thus laid off and supplied, lay off another in the same way, and so fill up the world in these last days; and let every man live in the city for this is the City of Zion."[19]

Difficult terrain was seldom a deterrent to making a grid. Some of the streets ascending the hills of San Francisco are so steep that horse-drawn carts

10. Salt Lake City, 1870; aerial view.

could not traverse them. To this day many of the city's sidewalks have steps or deep grooves in the pavement to assist pedestrians. We like overcoming natural impediments, as attested to by the switchbacks on Lombard Street, one of the San Francisco's most popular tourist attractions (Fig. 11).

Alternatives to the grid appeared, but only infrequently. The most famous example, of course, was L'Enfant's plan of 1791 for Washington, D.C., which featured broad open allées and public buildings set at the ends of long diagonal streets. The plan could have been an avatar of civic beauty because L'Enfant prepared his design at a time when the nation had barely begun its westward trek and many American cities did not yet exist. Most surveyors and public officials heading across the continent knew of the plan, yet most still ignored it.

Occasionally, a critic, citing L'Enfant's plan as a model, would raise a voice in opposition to the nearly ubiquitous use of the grid. Even as late as 1830 one author felt impelled to issue a call for L'Enfant's ideas to be adopted in other American cities while there was still time. "It is as easy in planning a town to consult good taste and beauty as not to do it, and unless this is done now, the odds are greatly against its ever being done."[20] Nevertheless, Americans almost invariably chose a grid.

The symbol of a grid, paradoxically, is its very lack of symbolism. Precisely because all places are alike, the grid was a uniquely appropriate choice for a young democracy. Many settlers heading to the frontier carried with them lithographs of the new town to which they were headed. Pictures of block after block of unoccupied land, as in Salt Lake City, assured these pioneers that their own building lot would be no better or worse than their neighbors'. Rather than recreating the hierarchy of streets most immigrants had left behind, a grid affirmed equality and suggested a new beginning. The plans they carried were an inducement to undertake a difficult and perilous journey—a tangible promise that regardless of differing ethnic and economic circumstances, newcomers to America started as equals in the race to succeed.

Even L'Enfant's own designs for Washington show the heady effects of democracy. When he began work, L'Enfant had many great European precedents from which to draw. His father had been a court painter at Versailles, and as a young man L'Enfant experienced firsthand the radiating avenues in front of King Louis's palace as well as the diagonals of Le Nôtre's gardens behind (Fig. 12).[21] As a student in Paris he saw the beginnings of the Champs-Élysées and the great swath it was cutting through Paris. After L'Enfant had been chosen to make the plan for the new capital, he asked Thomas Jefferson to send him the plans of a number of other European cities, including those for the German provincial capital of Karlsruhe (Fig. 13).

The plans of Versailles and Karlsruhe, however, illuminate the dilemma

11. Lombard Street, San Francisco, 1995.

L'Enfant faced. The slashing diagonal streets of each clearly ended at a single point of focus: the seat of power. Any plan for a new American capital that featured only grand boulevards radiating outward from a single center of authority would have been an entirely inappropriate symbol in a country where the thirteen colonies still had considerable power, where there were grave questions about the potential tyranny of the federal government, and, moreover, where everyone was supposedly equal.

Torn between the hierarchical structure of a radial street system and the knowledge that America had created multiple seats of power, L'Enfant simply added more symbols and more diagonals (Fig. 14). In addition to the two great open allées stretching from the White House and the Capitol, and the radials intersecting these focal points, he created many other diagonal streets, all at odd angles with one another. Among the foci L'Enfant created were the National Church, the Supreme Court, and a multitude of statues and fountains, many of which were dedicated to the various states. L'Enfant spread focal points throughout the city, much as a farmer would spread seed across a field. The difference between the plan for Karlsruhe and the democratic energy of L'Enfant's plan for Washington is much like the difference between a web spun by a normal spider and one spun by a spider that has been artificially stimulated (Fig. 15).

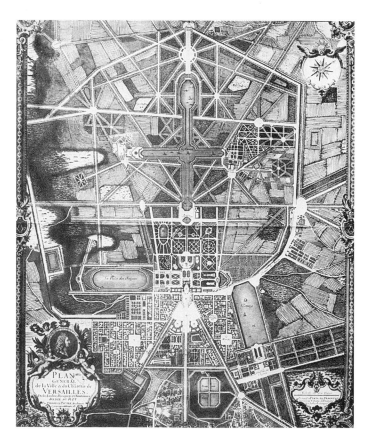

12. Plan engraving of Versailles by Pierre Le Pautre.

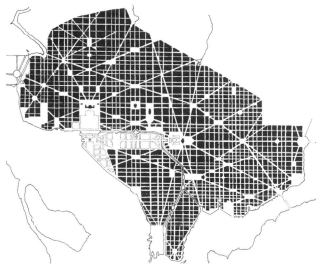

13. *Karlsruhe, after a plan from the middle of the eighteenth century, aerial view. The prince's castle stands at the center of the radial street pattern. The castle faces the proposed site of a Reformed church several blocks distant. Regional Plan Association, 1931.*

14. *Plan of Washington, D.C., by Pierre Charles L'Enfant, 1791. Note the many intersections and other symbolic foci. Note also the Mall extending from the Capitol to the Potomac River and shorter South Lawn extending from the White House at right angles with the Mall.*

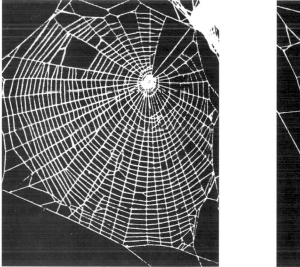

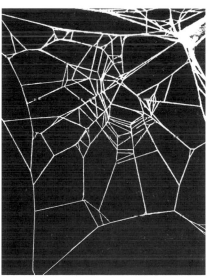

15. *Normal spiderweb, left; caffeine-induced web, right. The photographs appear in a tract on regulatory biology which describes the effects of various stimulants on web making.*

In the hope of integrating his ideas with those of the new democracy L'Enfant also underpinned his diagonals with a grid. Jefferson had been lobbying for a grid all along and had made several sketches to that effect. L'Enfant, ironically, had earlier reported to George Washington that Jefferson's sketches were "tiresome and insipid" and nothing "but the continuance of some cool imagination."[22] Nevertheless, L'Enfant added a grid to his own plan. Today the diagonals and grid seen together read like transparencies on a light table of two different cultures, one imposed uncomfortably atop the other.

Over the ensuing two centuries critics of L'Enfant's plan have frequently pointed to the splinters of odd lots and remaindered parcels left from the collision of these two different systems. Hegemann and Peets thought the sheer number of intersections alone weakened the plan: "the radial and diagonal avenues have their identity, beauty and dignity sapped away by the constant intrusion, often at very acute angles, of the gridiron streets." They also noted that it would "be mighty hard to fudge the intersections into any semblance of regularity."[23] In simple fact, it was impossible. L'Enfant could not have massaged the diagonal streets to fit the grid without bending and contorting them out of alignment, nor could he have recalibrated or reoriented the grid underneath without tearing it from its north-south and east-west axes.

Historian Paul Zucker thought it "curious that the influence of the Washington plan was not more widespread."[24] In retrospect, it is curious that L'Enfant got as far as he did. The small shards of unbuildable land still strewn throughout Washington are testament to a false hope that authoritarian symbols and patterns from Baroque Europe could ever be meshed easily with those of the New World.

Given the opportunity, Americans not only embraced the grid, they frequently erased, smudged over, and abandoned plans based on other precepts, and they did so with energy and conviction. The difficulties faced by Judge

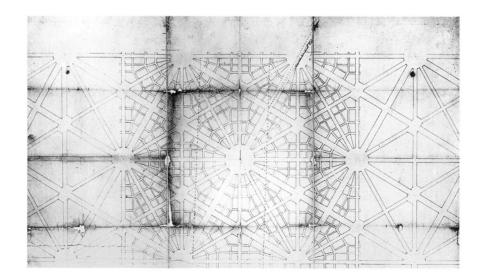

16. Plan for Detroit, by Augustus Woodward, 1807.

Augustus Woodward, a young magistrate appointed by Congress to prepare a plan for the city of Detroit, illustrate the point. Woodward put forward his plan in 1807, and unlike L'Enfant's combination of diagonal and gridded streets, Woodward's effort was an integrated mosaic composed entirely of diagonal streets and irregularly shaped lots (Fig. 16). City fathers actually built a portion of the plan, traces of which remain today at the center of the city. Each time Woodward left town, however, local officials, finding his vision "ill adapted to the situation," introduced resolutions changing and diluting the concept. Ten years after it was put forward, and as Detroit continued to grow, city officials abandoned Woodward's plan altogether in favor of a grid.[25]

Perhaps the most dramatic example of our predilection for the grid is the change wrought upon the original plan of Circleville, Ohio. First platted in 1810, the town had as its central focus a double ring of pie-shaped lots converging on a courthouse in the middle. Surrounding the entire plat was a circular ring road. The composition was intended to pay homage to the remains of great Indian mounds that had been discovered on the site, parts of which formed a perfect circle.

Veneration of the ancient past, however, soon gave way to a new sensibility. Twenty-seven years after the initial plan was adopted, the State Assembly authorized creation of a Circleville Squaring Company whose sole mission was to replat the circular streets and lots at the center of town (Fig. 17). The symbolism of the original plan had ceased, obviously, to have meaning for Circleville residents. John Reps quotes local historians who said that townspeople considered the original plan awkward and "a piece of childish sentimentalism." The central circular lawn around the courthouse was derided in particular as "a place where local pigs ran at large."[26] On reflection, it is equally obvious that had the symbolism signified anything important to the town's residents, they could easily have found someplace to pen the pigs.

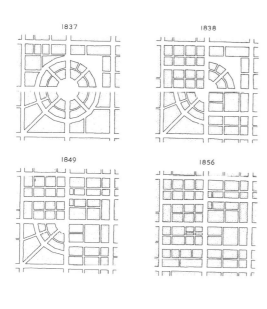

17. *Plans for the squaring of Circleville, Ohio, 1837–1856.*

18. *Plan for Llewellyn Park, New Jersey, by Alexander Jackson Davis, 1853.*

19. *Above: Levittown, New York, ca. 1950; aerial view.*

20. *Right: Japanese rock garden.*

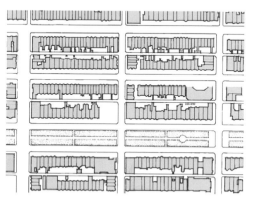

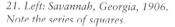

21. *Left: Savannah, Georgia, 1906. Note the series of squares.*

22. *Above: Plan for Back Bay, Boston. Typically, bigger structures were built on the corners, partially screening the back yards and alleys.*

By the mid-nineteenth century, as the industrial revolution spread across America, the grid began giving way in newly planned suburban communities to curved streets and lots. The picturesque romanticism of curved plats, like those of Llewellyn Park, New Jersey, designed by Alexander Jackson Davis in 1853 (Fig. 18), appealed to new suburbanites as an appropriate antidote to the recti-linear streets of a grimy city.[27] Nevertheless, the underlying symbolism remained largely unchanged from that of the grid. To this day the preponderance of American suburban plats have curved streets, yet the streets in most of these sub-urbs are as evenly spaced as the furrows made by the tines of a gravel rake in a Japanese garden (Figs. 19, 20), and in any given section the parcels they delineate are as equal in value as those made by the grid.

Although the grid sometimes produced exquisite results, as in Savannah's small-scaled streets and squares (Fig. 21), in the elegance of Boston's Back Bay (Fig. 22), and in the dramatic tension of gridded streets laid over the hills of San Francisco, the pervasive use of the grid and the often less than interesting plats it

*23. Via degli Strozzi,
Florence, ca. 1880.*

created seemed enduring proof to many critics of our plebeian values. Camillo
Sitte, for example, thought the grid doomed America to permanent cultural
mediocrity. In *City Planning According to Artistic Principles*, he blamed the grid
on the country's newness. "America lacked a past, had no history, and did not
yet signify anything else in the civilization of mankind but so many square miles
of land . . . wherever people are concerned merely with colonizing land, live only
for making money, and earn money only in order to live, it may be appropriate
to pack people into blocks of buildings like herring in a barrel." Sitte advocated
that future cities everywhere adapt tightly closed irregular street systems like
those in Italy that he had admired and studied. "Once the unfortunate building
lots of the block system are imposed upon our overall plan as the standard units
in real estate contracts," he warned, "then are all efforts in vain, for in a section
of town designed that way nothing meaningful can ever transpire."[28]

The historian and social critic Lewis Mumford thought America's gridded
cities even lacked order—that the grid was nothing more than a means of
exploitation: "No section or precinct [can be] suitably planned for its specific
function: instead the only function considered [is] the progressive intensification
of use . . . in urban planning, such bare surface order is no order at all."[29] John
Reps thought the grid's "lack of beauty, functional shortcomings, overwhelming
dullness and monotony, cause us to despair."[30]

Critics have also suggested that the grid came about primarily because of
expediency, particularly when it was used in towns planned by the railroads. A
grid, critics argued, was the only feasible choice for surveyors who were fever-
ishly driving property stakes into an empty plain days before track crews and
trains were to arrive bringing settlers by the carload—and occasionally bringing
entire cities as well. Reps quotes a nineteenth-century bystander in a western
town reporting that "a man . . . told me that while he was standing on the rail-

way platform, a long freight train arrived, laden with frame houses, boards, furniture, palings, old tents, and all the rubbish that makes up one of these mushroom 'cities.' The guard jumped off his van and, seeing some friends on the platform, called out with a flourish, 'Gentlemen, here's Julesburg.'"[31]

For many critics and designers, however, the principal objection to the grid was one of aesthetics. Gridded streets did little to enhance the buildings fronting them. Sitte not only wanted streets to lead to an explicit event like a plaza, but he also wanted them to be narrow and irregular in order to frame the adjoining structures along the way (Fig. 23). Straight streets, he thought, diminished a building's importance: "everything which is unusual in their layout is seen only in an indistinct foreshortened view, and a structure can never dominate the design." Charles Dickens, after touring Philadelphia, put it more simply, saying he "would have given the world for a crooked street."[32]

Yet even the curved suburban plats, which became popular in America after the Civil War, did little to alleviate these aesthetic concerns. Although Sitte never recorded his reaction to these plats, it is unlikely that he would have seen them as any improvement in American cultural sensibilities. Frederick Law Olmsted's 1873 plan for Tacoma, Washington, is a good example of the issue (Fig. 24). Even though the continuously curving streets in Olmsted's plan closed off the open views at either end, the streets themselves did not lead to any grand conclusion, and the generous radii of the curves allowed the adjoining buildings to glide by without engaging a passerby's attention. The seeming consequence of having chosen a plat of endlessly curving streets, like the choice of the grid before it, was that Americans presumably would never produce great civic design.

The plat for Tacoma also riled one of Olmsted's contemporaries, who likened the shapes of the blocks to "melons, pears, and sweet potatoes."[33] City officials presumably agreed, because Olmsted was soon replaced by a planner who executed a gridded plan.

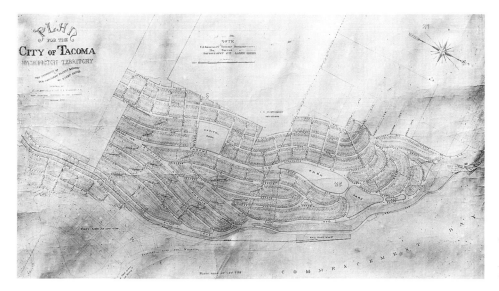

24. *Plan for Tacoma, Washington, by Frederick Law Olmsted, 1873.*

Going beyond our disparate styles and widespread use of the grid, critics have believed that Americans, because of their dislike of cities, would also never produce an architecture worthy of a great culture. In this century some critics have linked the aversion to cities with racism because so many of those now living in inner cities are minorities. Scully, for example, with some irony excoriated our penchant for getting out: "the city is *bad*; tear it down, get on the road, and be a pioneer, live in Greenwich like a white man."[34] This is a powerful notion, but the desire to leave the city preceded the problem of race, and the desire to leave will outlast it. Increasing numbers of African-Americans have also gotten on the road to the suburbs; cities from Washington to Atlanta are sprouting new, sometimes affluent, predominantly black suburban neighborhoods. Asian-Americans, as well, are creating new suburbs in parts of California, Texas, and New York.

The American antipathy to cities can be traced to the country's agrarian origins. Cities, despite having been the seat of culture throughout all human history, connote for many Americans only crowding and compromise. They suggest mutual dependence in a country that stresses independence. Although the vast majority of Americans live highly interdependent lives, the belief in independence still infuses our sense of self.

Americans have always wanted to control their destiny, and for many this means having a plot of land and a place of one's own. Moving from the city offered an opportunity to live in such a freestanding environment. Consequently, this pattern has high symbolic value and predominates throughout much of the country. It is very different from the pattern of tiny English villages that Thomas Sharp detailed (Fig. 25). The English hamlets he showed were in an open landscape where there was little danger of hostile attack, yet the tiny houses still ganged together, joined by party walls to their neighbors. In America, by contrast, settlements ranging from Plymouth to Williamsburg all had freestanding houses. A map of Fairfield, Connecticut, as it appeared in 1640 (Fig. 26), shows large lots and great distances between buildings. Settlers in towns like these lived more or less communally with their neighbors, yet the freestanding buildings are strong evidence of a passion for demonstrating, if only symbolically, a belief in independent living. These settlements all date from the seventeenth century, showing how long this sentiment has been with us. The communities were founded more than a century before Jefferson voiced his belief in the superiority of agrarian living, and more than two and a half centuries before the appearance of the automobile, which enabled many Americans to move to the suburbs, and which social critics often assert gave rise to our cities' present malaise.

We have always wanted to keep our distance from one another, even in the most trying circumstances. If there was ever an episode in American history where huddling together for mutual survival should have been appropriate it was in the California mountains during the winter of 1847. Settlers in the Donner party, unable to cross through a mountain pass before it was blocked by snow, trekked back down the slopes to the forests below to await spring. Instead of grouping together and combining forces, families chose to live quite far from one

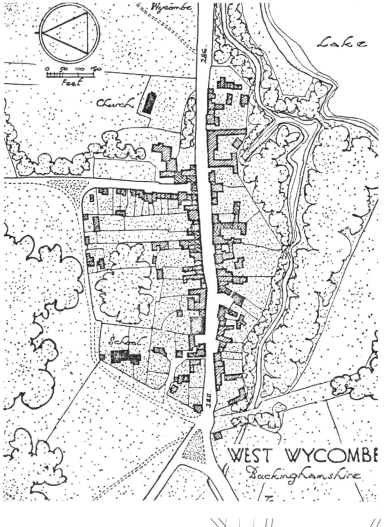

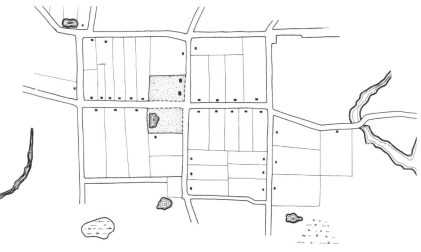

25. Plan for
West Wycombe,
Buckinghamshire,
England. The village
church, as here, is typi-
cally less prominent
than those in Italian
hill towns.

26. Plan for Fairfield,
Connecticut, 1640.
Note that buildings are
generally equidistant
from each other and
from the street.

another—even miles apart—while they endured a winter of slow starvation and cannibalism.

Many Americans, to be sure, built and lived in attached single-family row houses in cities like Philadelphia, New York, and Boston. Nevertheless, a pattern of houses joined by party walls to their neighbors never carried with it the symbolic connotation of community that it did in England, for example. Writers noted that in the eighteenth century nearly everyone, rich and poor alike, lived between party walls; even the prime minister's residence at 10 Downing Street in London is joined to its neighbors.[35] The English royalty in their freestanding palaces were the grand exception (Fig. 27). In America, by contrast, because every man is a king, every man's home is a castle. As Jackson put it, "the family holding is thus a miniature state, neither too large nor too small for its purpose . . . distinctly and forever separate. It is a territory with its own domestic hierarchy, its own ancestors, its own divinities to be venerated on special days and in special places."[36]

Historically, multifamily dwellings were an even less persuasive pattern in America than were single-family row houses. During the industrial revolution row houses became associated in the public's mind with workers' domiciles— that is, homes for people who were too poor to live in freestanding buildings.[37] It was only with great effort that developers at the end of the nineteenth century were able to convince affluent New Yorkers of the virtues of apartment living.

Even today a party wall can sometimes connote the need for support, of being unable to stand alone. Although many Americans choose to live in town houses, garden apartments, and condominiums, these arrangements still exude the faint suggestion of straitened circumstances or of dependency, as in a retirement village for senior citizens. And while attached living has long since ceased being an impoverished lifestyle, it is for many symbolically one notch below free-

27. Buckingham Palace, London; aerial view.

28. Single-family homes in Queens, New York.

standing independence. Small, tightly spaced freestanding houses, each on its own lot, in working-class Queens (Fig. 28) and freestanding mansions in Beverly Hills have much in common: they differ only in size and splendor, not in concept.

As Americans gaze out at the world from their miniature estates, they look toward the most potent symbol of all: the open road. Over the course of our history we have immersed ourselves in the road's imagery because it, more than any other symbol, has meant freedom and renewal. We have surged forth in our covered wagons and private cars; in the Wabash Cannonball, the Santa Fe Super Chief, and the Twentieth Century Limited; in sixteen-wheelers, and in mobile homes. We read "Song of the Open Road" by Walt Whitman, "The Road Not Taken" by Robert Frost, and *On the Road* by Jack Kerouac. Road movies are such common fare that we know any number of them by name.

For America's first settlers, freedom meant moving to the New World. Today, for descendants of these immigrants, freedom means the right to renew oneself by getting on the road again. Our faith in the redemptive power of the open road is very different from the perspective of voyagers in the great travel epics of other cultures. Odysseus, for instance, traced a fretful and beleaguered path back and forth across the Aegean. His trail in Homer's *Odyssey* was not the path of someone confidently in control of his destiny; it was rather like the erratic track of a fly in a bottle (Fig. 29). Desperate for shelter and succor, Odysseus spent seven of his "twenty years of woe and wandering" hidden from the gods in Calypso's cave. When he finally ventured forth again onto the open sea, he went not as a great adventurer covering himself with glory but as a rag doll being tossed about by the wrath of Poseidon.

In ages past, travel was fraught with murderous danger, as Voltaire vividly showed in *Candide*, his most popular novel. Candide witnessed every form of mayhem and dismemberment during his own odyssey. At various times he was flogged, shipwrecked, injured by falling debris in an earthquake, and almost eaten by savages.

29. Odysseus' journey through the Mediterranean.

Similarly the most enduring images in French director Jean-Luc Godard's 1967 film, *Weekend,* are of broken bodies and burning vehicles littering the highway. Godard's bodies are metaphors for the hazards of travel, as were those that Candide stumbled over on his journeys. When at length Candide returned from his wanderings, he decided that rather than setting off soon again, "we must cultivate our garden." His decision was consistent with the centripetal power of French culture in general.[38] David Copperfield made his one trip abroad, in Charles Dickens's great sentimental nineteenth-century romance, not for adventure, but to mourn. Marriage, happiness, and a career were Copperfield's in London only after he returned.

In Europe roads converge upon the city. As the old saw puts it, all roads lead to Rome. Within a city, roads also lead toward specific goals—to monuments, churches, and the palace of the king. One of the most dramatic examples of a goal at the end of a road is Charles Garnier's exuberant confection, the Paris Opera House, at the head of the Avenue de l'Opéra (Fig. 30). Built between 1861 and 1874, it is the embodiment of high culture, a grand edifice, and reason enough for any Frenchman to head toward the city.

The city was the source of enlightenment and wealth: it was where the aristocracy lived; peasants and artisans lived in the surrounding countryside. The countryside, particularly from the industrial revolution onward, served more as a source of pleasure for the well-to-do and a sign of status for those who had made their fortune elsewhere. Although not all English landowners were of the nobility, all aristocrats had estates; and when a commoner was elevated to the peerage by a grateful monarch, his title was often accompanied by the gift of a large tract of land.[39]

In America it was often the land itself, there to be conquered, that made one wealthy. Therefore, symbolically, American roads lead out of town, not to it. A maxim that proclaimed "all roads lead to New York" would seem arrogantly nonsensical to most Americans, regardless of the city's importance in the country's cultural history. But if roads symbolically lead away from a city—from a center and a place to stop—then architecture is that much more difficult to confront and enjoy. If Americans are on the open road, they are more focused on the trip than on the panorama, which, in any case, is swiftly passing.

Architecture critics have often been particularly vexed that American roads lead outward. Mumford, without citing evidence to bolster the claim, thought "movement from the center carries no hope or promise of life at a higher level . . . the expanding universe carries its separate fragments ever further from the city, leaving the individual more dissociated, lonely, and helpless than he probably ever was before." It was so difficult for Mumford to believe that mobility, along with the open road that symbolizes it, was what most Americans wanted that he argued the urge to move must be irrational, or a choice that has been forced upon us. Mobility, he contended, "provides fewer, not more opportunities for association than compulsory stability provided in the walled city."[40]

Norberg-Schulz had a similar view of the effects of mobility on society. He recognized that "technical means of communication have freed us from direct human contact, and an increasing number of people have become physically mobile." He gloomily extrapolated from this fact the prediction that the world created by such communication "would make human development impossible." Such a mobile world would not be "based on the repetition of similarities in connection with a stable system of places . . . nor would a mobile world allow for real human interaction." He then quoted the architect Christopher Alexander in support of his position: "social pathologies . . . delinquency and mental disorder—follow inevitably from the lack of intimate contact."[41] Obviously these critics felt that the far better alternative was to find a place, settle down, and stay off the road.

We often celebrate mobility in other cultures, such as the wandering exis-

30. Opera House, Paris, Charles Garnier, 1861–1874.

tence of Masai herdsmen in Kenya and the nomadic life of the North African Bedouins. We see the Eskimo's trackless pursuit of seal and whale in the film *Nanook of the North* as a noble and tragic account of a unique culture. Nevertheless, for Mumford and other critics of mobility our own open road is a symbol of adolescent escape rather than the path to renewal.

Some would argue that by believing in the open road, we deny the existence of limits. Delighting in the journey without facing its conclusion makes an American cultural staple of the perennial cartoon of the man proclaiming that the world is coming to an end. In fiction, the end sometimes arrives as an apocalypse—a fiery Hollywood holocaust like the one in Nathanael West's *The Day of the Locust* (Fig. 31). Critics would assert that today, with frontier days behind us, with our highways clogged by cars, and with the vast Pacific confronting us, we must finally stop and face reality. We must do this in order to mature as a culture and make our place in the world, architecturally and otherwise.

The country has many social ills, but the idea that mobility is among them clashes with what many Americans know to be the truth. Indeed, the journey itself often engenders camaraderie, as it does for the subjects of George Caleb Bingham's painting, *The Jolly Flat-Boatmen* (Fig. 32), as well as racial understanding, as it does for Huck and Jim on their raft in *The Adventures of Huckleberry Finn*. The journey can be an occasion for intimacy, as when Cary Grant hoists Eva Marie Saint into an upper bunk on the Twentieth Century Limited in the final scene of Alfred Hitchcock's movie *North by Northwest*. The trip can also create self-esteem, as it does for the two beleaguered women in *Thelma and Louise*.

Most especially the open road brings close friendship, as it does for Dorothy, who meets all her best pals on the Yellow Brick Road in *The Wizard of Oz*. And when Dorothy and her party encounter their only serious misadventure—we know why they have been led off the path. The Wicked Witch has snatched away the Yellow Brick Road, causing them to career into a field of poppies. In America "staying on the straight and narrow" is a goal in itself.

31. The Day of the Locust, *1975.* © *Paramount Pictures.*

32. The Jolly Flat-Boatmen, George Caleb Bingham, 1846, oil on canvas, The Manooginn Collection.

To Americans the road means progress and new frontiers, however vaguely we define the terms. Historian Frederick Jackson Turner noted that this country closed an important chapter in its history when free land ceased to be an inducement for western migration. Yet Turner also believed it "would be a rash prophet who should assert that the expansive character of American life has now entirely ceased. Movement has been its dominant fact, and unless this training has no effect upon a people, the American energy will continually demand a wider field for its exercise."[42]

Mobility in America in this century has become synonymous with the automobile, yet the causality between the two is often confused. Rather than engendering movement, as critics sometimes assert, the car is simply a facilitator, finally allowing large numbers of Americans who had always wanted mobility, and the freedom that went with it, to get on the road. The automobile is but a symbol of deeper values.

Even many environmentalists, who are implacable foes of the private car, use the open road as a symbol. Theirs is not the road of cars and traffic, but of hiking trails and bikeways.[43] The paths along the Chesapeake & Ohio barge canal in Washington, D.C., and along the Erie Canal in upstate New York are but two prominent examples of car-free pathways. They testify to movement as a motivating force in the American psyche, regardless of the means of locomotion. We have always celebrated movement, whether on Route 66 or the Appalachian Trail.

Nor do we need a grand conclusion at the end of the road to motivate us to begin the journey. Despite the lack of a glorious goal, or even any goal at all, Americans still want to make the trip. Every child who has seen *The Wizard of Oz* learns that even disappointment at the end of the road does not invalidate the journey. When Dorothy finally reaches the Emerald City, her dog Toto pulls back a curtain to reveal the wizard as a gentle fraud, and by implication, the Emerald City to be fraudulent as well. Dorothy learns she did not need to find a wizard at the end of the road—the power to return to Kansas was hers all along.

Similarly, the last scene in the film adaptation of John Steinbeck's *Grapes of Wrath* shows a long line of motley trucks. They are not on the path to glory; they're on the road to Fresno, filled with sharecroppers and their belongings, people who hope for twenty more days of farm labor. Ma Joad cautions her family not to be overly optimistic: "Maybe twenty days' work and maybe no days' work. We ain't got it till we get it." Director John Ford's final shot shows the trucks, starkly outlined against the sun, wobbling onward. Ma voices her conviction that "We keep a comin.' We're the people that live. They can't wipe us out, they can't lick us, and we'll go on forever, Pa, 'cause we're the people."

Because the actual end of the trip means little to us, we show our lack of interest in it in many ways. On any given night, on selected streets across America, mock solemn parades of teenagers may be seen cruising slowly back and forth in their cars as spectators gather to watch. The procession of cars has no specific beginning or end, nor does it have any particular relationship to the architecture around it. When the crowd thins out, the cars simply "pull a 180" and, with tires screeching, start back in the opposite direction.

The long line of cars sketches a very different pattern from an evening paseo in a South American village, for example, where men, their faces lit by torches, stroll in a long line around the central plaza as women promenade in the opposite direction. The two groups move slowly in the flickering light, one inside the other, tracing the outline of the square and the buildings that surround it.

Those on the American road make as much effort to be seen as do those living alongside it. On Van Nuys Boulevard in Los Angeles, where automobile "cruising" supposedly began, the vehicles rumbling slowly past admiring onlookers may be floridly painted, filled with stereo equipment, and occasionally even lit on their undersides.[44] The scene on these streets is much like the one in Pasadena on New Year's Day when crowds gather to view a long line of flower-bedecked floats gliding through the streets in the Rose Bowl parade. Those riding the floats, like those in their cars, want to be noticed—as badly as do the gentry on Sunday who parade in their long line of buggies in Orson Welles's 1942 movie, *The Magnificent Ambersons,* or the carriage drivers Henry James wrote of at the turn of the century, "who were driving on the vast featureless highway, to and fro in front of their ingenious palaces."[45]

So strong is our belief that those in motion are worth watching that movement need sometimes only be implied. In Huntington, West Virginia, for example, when teenagers run low on gas money, some will simply sit in their trucks with the engine turned off and "cruise" without moving.[46]

Neither the participants nor the spectators care where a procession starts or finishes so long as everyone is seen. If the parade has a reviewing stand, the judges, like the onlookers, are just somewhere along the way. Nobody marks where floats, buggies, or custom cars join any procession or where they will drop away, only that they pass. Who knows where the Easter Parade begins or ends?

These values illustrate the architect's dilemma: imagine a long line of wagon trains standing in front of a large monument on the trail. The column may be at an appropriate spot in the journey, but we do not want our progress impeded. In America monuments do not belong in the same picture with wagons—or with vehicles of any kind (Fig. 33). Earlier travelers would never have blocked the road. Even if they had, surely someone would have climbed down from the driver's seat by now and taken a sledge to the impediment so that those who followed would have an easier trip.

At its best, American architecture stands to one side, ennobling but not impeding the journey of the Joads who believe that "the river, it goes right on." In America it is not the goal that gives meaning to the path, it's the obverse. The open road is the great symbol that pulls all things and all goals, even architectural ones, into its wake.

Given then our many styles, the exuberance with which we proclaim to passersby how well we are doing, the pervasiveness of our gridded streets, our desire for independence, and the overarching symbolism of the open road, the great task in American architecture is to use these attributes to ennoble the journey as well as to create a sense of community along the way—rather than to hope we will someday change who we are.

33. Wagon trains on a frontier Main Street, ca. 1880s.

Chapter 2

Front Door

A man must ride alternately on the horses
of his private and public nature.

RALPH WALDO EMERSON
"Fate," *The Conduct of Life*

Back Door

WE EXPRESS OUR PUBLIC IMAGE ON THE FRONT OF OUR BUILDINGS, AND MORE THAN
most cultures we put great stock in how well others think we are doing.
Americans have always wanted to put a gloss on things; we are the nation that
invented advertising and public relations. We invest great effort and expense in
our front doors and front yards. We like to impress the world with how well the
king is faring in his castle; we want to keep up with the Joneses.

The backs of our buildings are just as important to us, precisely because
they lead to domains where image is not a priority. The American back yard is
often the obverse of the front: a place to store what we do not want the world
to see. Nathaniel Hawthorne thought there was "more truth . . . in the back
view of a residence, whether in town or country, than its front. The latter is
always artificial; it is meant for the world's eye, and is therefore a veil and a
concealment. Realities keep in the rear."[1]

The back yard is often a private sanctuary where we can be at home with
nature. In America, rock gardens, birdbaths, and vegetable patches are usually
behind the house, not in front of it. Many of the earliest settlers in the New
World were seeking an earthly paradise; for many today the back yard is that
small Edenic preserve. One American has said, "I don't know what the people
of Paris want. But what they have is a very small amount of open space that is
theirs and a lot of public amenities . . . we have much more individual lifestyles
. . . we have our own park. It's right out back."[2] Taken together, front and

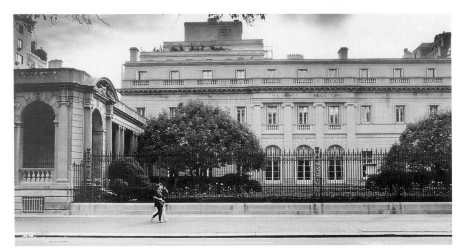

34. Above: The Frick Mansion, New York City, Carrère and Hastings, 1914.

35. Right: House, Route 36, Ohio. Note all windows are equal size—except for the living room picture window.

back create a dichotomy, a tension between our public and private selves, that dictates how we present ourselves to the world and how we shape our architecture.

In addition to demonstrating on the outside of their buildings how well they are faring, Americans will often reveal to passersby aspects of their private lives within—and they expect others to do the same. In America a grand estate is much more likely to be surrounded by an iron fence than a high wall. Better to give a glimpse of the luxury within, as at the Frick mansion on Fifth Avenue in New York City, for example, than to hide it altogether (Fig. 34). Similarly, in an American suburb, as Boorstin noted, "when we look out our own picture window, . . . we are apt to see our neighbor himself. But he too is apt to be doing nothing more than looking at us through *his* picture window."[3] Because a large picture window offers a view of life inside the house, in many small towns it is considered unneighborly to keep one's drapes permanently closed; the drapes should be open, at least some of the time. In other words, it is culturally ambiguous to have a picture window but not to let us see inside (Fig. 35).

The dichotomy between front and back, public and private, frequently extends to the inside of our buildings. In many American homes a hallway or entry foyer will connect the front door directly to the more formal and public rooms where we craft our image—the living room and dining room. Behind these areas, at the back of the house, are the family room and the eat-in kitchen where we lead our personal and informal lives. Expensive antiques, coffee-table books, and objets d'art are on display in the living room, while the toys, news-papers, and television set are kept in the family room. In the nineteenth century, those who could afford it might have two sitting rooms, the more formal of which was sometimes known as the bishop's parlor. Even in a two-room seven-teenth-century colonial house, a parlor for receiving guests was often differenti-ated from the "keeping room," where most of the domestic chores took place.[4]

The dichotomy between the public and private face is much less noticeable in other cultures; often it is absent altogether. A typical American corporate headquarters building, for example, might feature a dramatic atrium or a tree-filled lobby near the front entrance. Directly contiguous will be large meeting rooms, an auditorium, and important offices where the corporation and public interact. Smaller offices and manufacturing areas are some distance behind these areas and well out of sight. Conversely, in a Chinese office building, the em-ployees' kitchen might well be in full view of everyone, directly adjacent to the front lobby.

An American school will frequently feature decoration or other architec-tural features around its front door. Inside the entrance, sports trophies or chil-dren's art will be on public display, while the back doors will lead to the playground. In a French school, by contrast, visitors might cross a courtyard, which is also used for children's play, to get to the front door.

The dichotomy between front and back also has little resonance with many Native Americans. The Crow, for example, historically made no distinction between public and private places. They believed the whole earth was commu-nally owned—one large back yard, in a sense. On the Crow reservation in Montana it still makes little difference that from a front window one might look out onto old cars and pieces of machinery stacked (sometimes quite neatly) in what the rest of America would call the front yard. Because everyone is a mem-ber of the tribe—everybody is already named Jones, so to speak—there is much less need to maintain a public face.[5]

Despite the Anglo-Saxon roots of much of our culture, the American dichotomy between front and back diverges from British sensibilities. One telling difference can be seen in the organization of rooms in a typical eighteenth-century London row house. Summerson noted that most dwellings were rela-tively narrow, their dimensions being a function of the cost of supplying each house with utilities and services.[6] The more dwelling units per given length of street, obviously the lower the infrastructure cost per unit. Summerson, however, without explaining why, described the remarkable propensity of English builders of the period—at great effort and expense—to raise the level of the street in front of London's more luxurious homes (Fig. 36). Builders would construct a road-

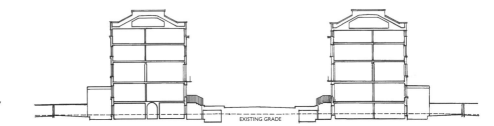

EXISTING GRADE

36. Typical elevated residential street, Bloomsbury, London, eighteenth century.

way by first erecting parallel retaining walls. They would fill the trench between the two walls with dirt and then cap it with a paved carriageway and sidewalk. The houses were set back from the road, connected to the sidewalk by a bridge from the front door. Although the ground floor of the house thus appeared to be one full level below the street, it was actually nearly at grade. Full-sized windows allowed sunlight into this lower floor.

The considerable cost of constructing elevated streets made sense only because of the deeply rooted values of a society structured by class. All Englishmen were worthy citizens, all could enter directly from the street, and all deserved full-sized windows. Yet one class of Englishmen still lived above the servants working in the basement. The architectural consequences of class were succinctly expressed by the popular 1970s British television series *Upstairs Downstairs*. By the same measure, back yards have never had the same appeal for the British; from inside a row house it would have been the servants who had better access to the rear yard. Frequently, the back of one row house directly abutted the back of another, and when a back yard did exist it was often a slum of servants' housing and stables directly accessible from the lower floor.[7]

Just as we often organize a building's interior to differentiate between public and private spaces, we design a building's exterior to make the same distinction. So important is the symbolic message transmitted by the front of a building that sometimes the shape and exterior massing of even the simplest house will derive entirely from its front elevation. The Cape Cod saltbox, for example, bigger in front than in back, rises up to greet the road, then slides quietly away behind, its distinct profile and the decoration around the front door being its only architectural features (Fig. 37). Because the front of a building is where we create a public image, it is where we put most of our decoration and architectural effort. In Europe, as elsewhere, important buildings have glorified fronts, but in America we celebrate and exaggerate the front of nearly everything from the grandest public building to an ordinary roadside stand (Fig. 38).

Intricately carved door surrounds, brass carriage lamps, wrought-iron railings, the corporate logo, and Christmas lights are always in front. We put more formal foundation planting, more azalea bushes, more Japanese maples, and often more lawn in front than in back. As architects Kent Bloomer and Charles Moore have pointed out, we may want the front facade of our house to be sym-

37. *Above left: Solomon Richardson House, East Brookfield, Massachusetts, ca. 1748.*

38. *Above: Ice-cream store, Route 27, East Hampton, Long Island.*

39. *Winslow House, River Forest, Illinois, Frank Lloyd Wright, 1893; front facade, above; rear facade, right.*

40. Model for
National Football Hall
of Fame, Venturi and
Rauch, 1967.

metrical, but we almost never put the same architectural stricture on the back (Fig. 39).[8] Architects frequently describe this dichotomy by saying a building has a Queen Anne front and a Mary Ann behind.

We frequently exaggerate the front of a building, not as an inducement to enter into an even more splendid interior, but as a substitute for any interior grandeur at all. The front often becomes an end in itself. Venturi and Rauch's entry to the National Football Hall of Fame competition, for example, proposed a little building set beneath a huge electronic billboard (Fig. 40). Similar to the signs in Times Square, the billboard was to transmit plays and other data across a parking lot and picnic green. The architects explained their entry by citing as one precedent the partially false-fronted facades of Gothic churches.[9] However, the rose window in the front of a Gothic cathedral promises a sublime architectural resolution within the building. The proposed Hall of Fame would have housed small alcoves filled with photographs and old football jerseys. The museum was to have been tiny, reason enough in America to exaggerate, and the billboard above the front door was well in keeping with the attenuated columns and other rhetorical devices we regularly employ to make small buildings look bigger.

The Greek Revival style that swept across America in the early decades of the nineteenth century provided us with many such stylistic devices. The Arcadian forms epitomized the rational democracy espoused by a new Republic, and the image of the Acropolis was an appropriate metaphor for a country that was to be a city on a hill. The Greek Revival style had another equally important attribute, however: it allowed newly prosperous citizens to demonstrate how well they were doing by dramatically increasing the importance of the entrance. The Greek Revival front porch at Rose Hill in Geneva, New York, aggrandizes and brings into focus what would otherwise be only a large rambling two-story clapboard house (Fig. 41). Similarly, the facade of one Greek Revival house on Martha's Vineyard (Fig. 42) shows that, to its builder at least, the overscale columns themselves were a far more important stylistic attribute than equal spacing between them.

41. Left: Rose Hill, Geneva, New York, 1839.

42. Below: House, Martha's Vineyard, ca. 1835.

43. Model for State Capitol, Richmond, Virginia, Thomas Jefferson, 1786.

So strong was the focus on the front of the building that some historians think the style should more accurately be called the Roman Revival, as Thomas Jefferson showed when he modeled his designs for the Virginia State Capitol after the Maison Carré, a Roman temple in Nîmes, France, which he had seen and admired during his European travels (Fig. 43). The Maison Carré's distinctly different front and back were typical of Roman architecture, whereas most Greek antecedents, like the Parthenon, would have been identically colonnaded on all four sides.

Even today the exaggerated fronts of a house in Miami Lakes and a small office building in Daytona Beach, Florida (Figs. 44, 45), carry on a long American tradition of overstatement. Likewise, Venturi's frequently published study for a tiny house behind an enormous neoclassical front is a paradigm of a little building trying to look big (Fig. 46). Venturi demonstrated that, as fashion dictated, exaggerated fronts could range anywhere from Egyptian Revival to McDonald's Modern, showing that many different styles lend themselves to aggrandizement in America.

The best-known image of American overstatement is George Washington's porch at Mount Vernon (Fig. 47). Ironically, despite being at the back of the house, this Georgian colonnade has been emulated in thousands of buildings across America, usually in front. As architect Robert A. M. Stern noted, the loggia "quickly became the front porch of the nation."[10]

The front door in America has symbolic importance even if the door itself is seldom used. In Houston, Texas, for example, the absence of a zoning ordinance has resulted in one type of apartment complex organized like a large two-story doughnut around a garden, swimming pool, or other amenity.[11] The shape of the building acts as a barrier between an enclosed semiprivate world at the

44. House, Miami
Lakes, Florida.

45. Office building,
Daytona Beach,
Florida.

46. Plans and facade
studies for house pro
ject, Venturi and
Rauch, 1977.

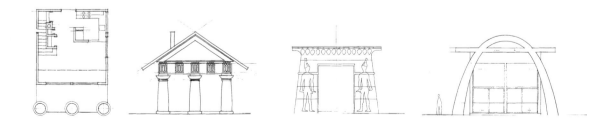

47. View of rear porch
at Mount Vernon,
Fairfax County,
Virginia, 1757–1787. A
symmetrical rear facade
is rare in America.

48. Apartment
complex, Houston.

49. Storage sheds,
White Marsh, Virginia.

50. Parade on Main Street during Sweet Pea Carnival, Bozeman, Montana.

center and an unzoned city outside. In one such complex entrances to the individual apartments directly face parking lots along both sides of the building. Nevertheless, all the architectural features are clustered around one largely unused overscale front door (modeled after Mount Vernon) that faces the street (Fig. 48). In similar fashion, the clapboard facades and front doors of what appear to be small cottages in White Marsh, Virginia (Fig. 49), are actually three long lines of storage sheds with doors along the sides.

The relationship between the front door and the rest of the building is much like the relationship between Main Street and the rest of the town. Main Street was always a small town's public face to passing travelers. It was where we traditionally put our best architectural efforts, often exaggerating the size of buildings. The main street of Bozeman, Montana, is a grand example (Fig. 50). Some of the two- and three-story buildings facing the street are nearly fifty feet high, creating interior rooms much higher than are needed by the stores, law offices, and other businesses occupying these spaces. Immediately behind Main Street are the smaller one- and two-story structures typical of the rest of the city.

Our proclivity toward concentrating the decorative elements at the front is not a recent phenomenon. In colonial days it often seemed appropriate to a frugal people with meager resources to put expensive clapboards on the front of a freestanding house and to face the rest of the dwelling with shingles (Fig. 51). "Houses built of both wood and brick have only the wall towards the street made of the latter," noted a visitor to New Brunswick, New Jersey, in 1750. "This particular kind of ostentation could easily lead a traveler who passed through the town in haste to believe that most of the houses are built of brick."[12]

Even today the practice of using different materials on the front and on the sides remains common enough to go largely unnoticed (Fig. 52). When the front of a building is grand, and where it is supposed to be, our cultural bias filters out the rest, including what we are not supposed to see. We do not focus on the unadorned brick side walls and small windows of Louis Sullivan's Bayard Building in New York City, for example, although they are clearly visible (Fig. 53). Sullivan treated the front like a "taut screen dropped to define a public space."[13] The rest of the exterior has no architectural value at all.

Large enclosed suburban shopping malls frequently use the same cultural filter to play down their back doors. Inside a mall, the front doors of the stores face inward toward an enclosed pedestrian street. Back doors either flank a service corridor or face directly out onto the parking lot (Fig. 54). From the merchants' perspective this is fine because the front doors of the stores attract customers who are already inside the mall. For those on the outside, however, the view is of buildings bristling with blank walls and loading docks interspersed occasionally with entries into the complex. To alleviate the visual chaos, many

51. Below: House, Edgartown, Martha's Vineyard.

52. Bottom: House, Columbus, Ohio.

53. Bayard Building, New York City, Louis Sullivan, 1898.

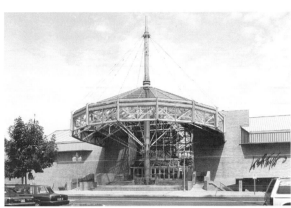

54. *Above left: Back doors, Lane Shopping Center, Columbus.*

55. *Above right: Super front door, shopping mall, Danbury, Connecticut.*

56. *Left: False fronts, Utopia, Texas.*

shopping centers have begun creating super front doors—overscale entrances big enough to hold shoppers' attention as they proceed to the front entrance from the parking lot (Fig. 55).

When some effort has been made to focus our attention on the front, we actually like seeing the unadorned portions of the building. We understand the dialectic, as with fake-fronted western stores where what we are not supposed to see is almost always clearly visible (Fig. 56). Similarly, we do not mind seeing the backs and sides of buildings surrounding tiny Paley Park in Manhattan (Fig. 57), designed by Zion and Breen. An earlier building on the property had been connected to its neighbors by party walls that were several stories high and bare of

57. Paley Park, New York City, Zion and Breen, 1967; plan, left; aerial view, right.

decoration. These walls were never intended to be seen, nor were the backs of the buildings beyond the rear of the property. Their unsightliness actually adds to the tableau because the waterfall at the rear of the park and the new walls bounding it are tall enough to hold our eye. If what we are supposed to see dominates, we enjoy the tension of being reminded of the rest.

(Paley Park's critical success spurred the New York officials to instigate a city-wide program of vest-pocket parks. Very few of these parks were architecturally satisfying, however. Waterfalls or enclosing walls would have been prohibitively expensive, so even the best of these small parks lacked focus. With nothing to draw one's eye from the back doors and side walls of adjoining buildings the parks seemed little more than landscaping on a vacant lot.)

We are often fascinated with the reality that lies behind the image. Pleasure in the tension between what we should and should not see partly explains why the Tweed Courthouse building directly behind New York's City Hall (Fig. 58) is still standing, although it was originally slated for demolition. The building's bulk and style are so similar to City Hall's that they impinge upon City Hall's more important symbolic purposes. Yet the two buildings together give a front door–back door picture of how New York once actually functioned. The mayor gave speeches in front while the judges disposed of of society's ne'er-do-wells behind. The appeal of the two buildings together is not dissimilar to the opening shot of the weekly program *Meet the Press,* which shows wiring, unlighted falsework, and cameras around an illuminated set. The foreground is bright enough to hold our attention, yet we like knowing how the operation actually works.

The dichotomy between front and back, between image and reality, draws many Americans to film-studio lots to see how movies are made. We want to view the fake buildings and props—we want to examine the truth behind the fantasy. The tension between what we should and should not see is sometimes essential, as in one scene of pure pandemonium in the Marx Brothers movie *A Night at the Opera*. A horrified audience watches as Harpo swings through the stage rigging, raising and lowering sets to expose the backstage area. Downstage a tenor (who is European) continues to sing as if nothing unusual were happening while behind him a painted backdrop depicting a small bucolic village changes to the deck of a battleship—and the police tear back and forth across the stage trying to catch Harpo.

Poet Gwendolyn Brooks put the dichotomy well in "a song in the front yard":

> *I've stayed in the front yard all my life.*
> *I want a peek at the back*
> *Where it's rough and untended and hungry weed grows.*
> *A girl gets sick of a rose.*[14]

To go behind the scenes to the back yard, however, is to enter a private realm. This domain, whether lavishly decorated or unadorned, is important to us because it is private. Back yards have their own code of behavior; to talk over a

58. City Hall, New York City, Mangin and McComb, 1811, in left foreground; behind it, the Tweed Courthouse, John Kellum, 1872.

59. *Residential subdi-*
vision, Nantucket.

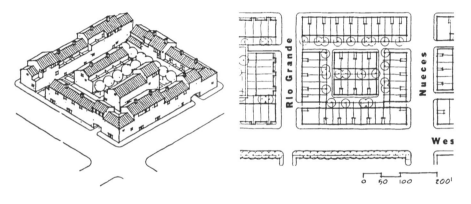

60. *Town House*
Maze, Austin, Texas,
Venturi and Scott
Brown Associates,
1983–1985.

61. *Model of Getty*
Museum, Los Angeles,
California, Richard
Meier, 1991. © Jack
Pottle/Esto.

back fence is to say things one might not say in public. Strangers, even trades-people, come to the front door, but if the back door is easily accessible, friends and neighbors will habitually use it. To be invited to a back-yard barbecue is to be invited to a private party or a family affair. By contrast, when we notice some-one staging an event in the front yard, we surmise it must be a block party, an effort to raise money for the Little League, or some other quasi-public gathering.

Because one's own back yard is private, scrutinizing the neighbors too closely in their back yard is regarded as an invasion of privacy. As author Joel Garreau observed, "Americans go home to their back yard and they fence it in and they feel safe."[15] Any behavior that calls that feeling into question is there-fore disruptive—such as a person peering into a back yard, even if he is doing so from a public street.

America's urban highways and railroad lines frequently cut through back yards because land at the rear of the property is typically less expensive than right-of-way in front of a house or down the middle of a street. The trade-off to lower land costs, however, is that train passengers and motorists have a more discomfiting trip past disproportionate numbers of raw rear walls and private rear yards. The Merritt Parkway in Connecticut, which passes some of the most expensive residential real estate in the northeast United States, eliminated this discomfort by extensive planting along the road. The vegetation hides the abut-ting back yards, leaving both driver and homeowner to enjoy separate domains.

Even when we can easily look into a neighbor's back yard from our own front yard, we are still intruding upon a private realm. When architects and plan-ners fail to observe this demarcation between front and back, the results seem chaotic, as in a new subdivision on Nantucket where the front doors of many houses face the neighbors' back doors (Fig. 59). This juxtaposition of front door and back door diminishes the front door's value, as happens in one town-house proposal for Austin, Texas (Fig. 60). A similar problem compromises Richard Meier's Getty Museum complex in Los Angeles. The group of buildings, remi-niscent of freestanding temples on the Acropolis, will appear dramatic from the base of the hill, but will seem less well organized from within the grounds, again because of front doors facing back doors (Fig. 61).

In the movie *Rear Window*, Alfred Hitchcock brilliantly exploited our ambivalence toward being able to see our neighbors' private doings. Even though James Stewart is watching from within his own home as events unfold in the apartment across from him, we are torn between squeamishness over his voyeurism and admiration of his discovery of a murder (Fig. 62). It is only his apprehension of the murderer that excuses his behavior.

Because back yards for Americans are private and personal realms, other than requiring rear-yard setbacks, municipal zoning ordinances generally leave people's back yards alone. Camillo Sitte thought back yards and interior courts should actually be planned and zoned. It was an intriguing idea, one that had already been tried in Hamburg, Germany, where municipal regulations were keeping inner courtyards open for communal use.[16] But the idea had little rele-vance to Americans who cherished the privacy of their back yard.

*62. Above: Director
Alfred Hitchcock on
the set of* Rear
Window, *1954.*

*63. Above right:
Common area in block
bounded by Houston,
MacDougal, Bleecker,
and Sullivan Streets,
New York City.*

One rare exception is a communal courtyard lined by shade trees and low fences in the interior of a small block bounded by Houston, MacDougal, Bleecker, and Sullivan Streets in Manhattan's Greenwich Village (Fig. 63). In the 1920s residents cut out a long narrow strip from the block's existing back yards and paved it. The abutters to the strip retained ownership, but dedicated the area to common use and shared in its maintenance. Each owner, however, still retained an enclosed back yard adjoining the common area. The decision not to eliminate these private rear yards has enabled the common area to endure for more than sixty years despite periodic attempts to eliminate it. Those in favor of carving up the strip and returning it to the abutters have been beaten back each time by those arguing that nobody has been denied a back yard. Everybody still has an adjoining private domain of his own; the common area is a bonus—an addition to one's back yard, not an alternative to it.[17]

Whether a back yard is a place to put trash, a small garden paradise, or something in between, Americans' belief that it is theirs to do with as they will has sometimes led to unlikely confrontations, as, for example, in New York between trustees of the Metropolitan Museum and supporters of Central Park. The museum has its front door on Fifth Avenue, but the body of the building sits in the Park. In recent years each time the museum has announced plans for expansion, vociferous cries of protest have arisen from park supporters. The new additions were all planned for sides of the museum not facing the street, sides having no clear boundary with Central Park. The trustees thought the additions were in their own back yard, so to speak, and should have been considered as such, but the protesters obviously saw these expansions as a further breach in the levee already opened by the museum itself (Fig. 64).

More frequently, confusion over where back-yard rights end and front-yard responsibility begins stems from a denial that each side or facade of a building may actually have a different symbolic role. This denial has been especially prevalent among modern architects who have tended to see buildings as sculptural objects to be viewed in the round. As Venturi argued, they have "emphasized the freestanding, independent building even in the city—the building which is an isolated pavilion rather than one which reinforces the street wall has become the norm."[18] Facades that are different in front and back connote to some Modernists a passive acquiescence to society's dictates. To be accused of "facadism," or producing false fronts, is still a serious charge in some architectural quarters. A grand front contrasted with a bland behind means both must have been tacked on to the building from without, rather than emanating from within. By contrast, quite similar facades on all sides suggest that a building's character arises more from its intended use and the designers own personal vision and sense of form.

64. Central Park, New York City, ca. 1960. Note the Metropolitan Museum extending into the park at top center of photograph.

65. Art and Architecture Building, Yale University, New Haven, Connecticut, Paul Rudolph, 1963; front view, above left (the Yale Art Gallery by Louis Kahn, 1953, is in the foreground); alley view, above right.

One dramatic example of this expression is the Art and Architecture Building at Yale University by Paul Rudolph (Fig. 65). The building's four facades are nearly identical in their massive scale and enormous window size, although only two sides face the street. The other two facades can be seen only by traversing back yards and rear alleys.

By ignoring the differences between front and back, architects and planners have sometimes muddied otherwise noble intentions. Clarence Stein, for example, in his famous 1928 plan for a suburban housing project in Radburn, New Jersey, turned the fronts of the houses toward a park and the backs toward the street (Fig. 66). Stein and his colleagues had realized that the automobile was becoming a permanent feature of American life. They also realized cars were dangerous to pedestrians.[19] Consequently, they planned Radburn to keep automobiles at the periphery of the community. The barriers between cars and people were the dwellings themselves. Stein sited the houses around small cul-de-sac streets. Motorists parked their cars, then went through the houses to fingers of green space behind, which, in turn, were connected to larger parks, an elementary school and a community swimming pool. For years, the most frequently photographed feature at Radburn was a pedestrian underpass allowing children to walk from home to school without crossing the street (Fig. 67). Statistics kept at Radburn and other so-called garden cities showed how few pedestrians had been injured or killed by cars.

At Radburn the kitchens were on the side of the house facing the driveway and the street, Radburn's only hard-surfaced areas. With mothers able to supervise from a kitchen window, many children played on the street side of the house, even though most of the play equipment was in the park behind. Residents came to feel the street side was "the back"; consequently, they reasoned that it was perfectly appropriate to perform other back-yard functions there as well. Years later Stein wrote good-naturedly of real estate agents who, when showing houses at Radburn, would go up and down the street before a prospective buyer arrived, asking neighbors to take laundry off their street-side clotheslines.[20]

Stein recognized that what we normally think of as the front of the house had become symbolically ambiguous.[21] However, what eventually happened on the other side of the house—the side facing the park—demonstrates even more dramatically our front door–back door sensibilities. On the park side each owner maintains his or her own yard, which extends from the house out to a commonly

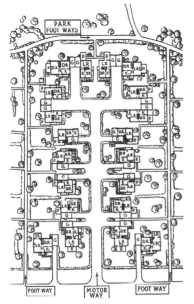

66. *Above left: Plan for typical cul de sac street, Radburn, New Jersey, Clarence Stein, 1928.*

67. *Above: Pedestrian underpass, Radburn.*

68. *Left: Yards at rear of houses abutting footpaths leading to park, Radburn, 1986.*

owned sidewalk. For the first forty years of Radburn's existence covenants specified what could or could not be built or planted in these yards. As soon as these covenants expired, however, residents began marking off their domains with pickets, chain-link fences, and hedges. Even though Stein had meant these areas to be used more like typical front yards, outdoor furniture and barbecue equipment began to appear. Within months the yards on the park side looked like any other American back yard (Fig. 68). The salient feature at Radburn today is that everyone now has two back yards and no front yard.

A low-rise town-house project in Philadelphia's Society Hill has engendered a similar confusion. The buildings' front doors face a central court, which is entered from the street through a single secured entrance. Many of the rear facades abut the street (Fig. 69). Intermittent recesses in these facades create small, private, walled courtyards, which can be partially viewed from the street through slatted gates. At first the courtyards seem to be front yards, but they are actually back yards, adorned, like Radburn, with outdoor furniture and barbecue equipment. They create an uncomfortable dynamic for passersby, who on any given summer Sunday morning, cannot know whether a knock at the gate might be answered by someone reading the funny papers in his pajamas. The courtyards are back yards—but they're on the wrong side of the house.

Frank Lloyd Wright, on at least one occasion, also forgot the difference between the symbolic realms of front and back. As an adjunct to his theoretical Broadacre City plan of 1935, thought by many critics to be an accurate prediction of what American suburbs would soon become, Wright proposed cluster units consisting of four separate dwellings, each on its own lot, backed up to a cruciform party wall (Fig. 70). On the rooftop level every unit had a private deck for cookouts and other outdoor functions. The seeming value of this novel arrangement was that, from inside the house or on the deck, one could look out at a large expanse of lawn without seeing his or her immediate neighbors. Wright later proposed this arrangement for several unbuilt projects and a prototype of

69. Rear facade, Society Hill town houses, Philadelphia. Slatted wooden gates offer passersby a partial view of the courtyards within.

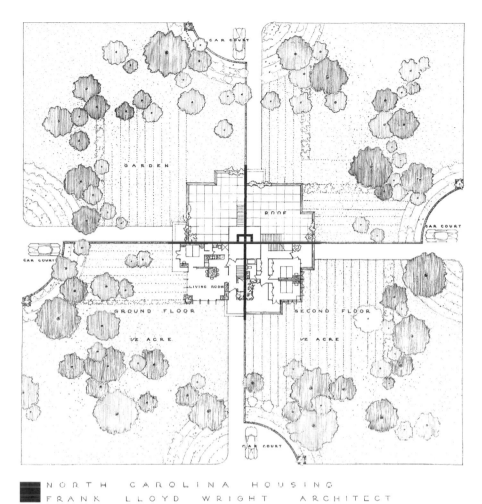

NORTH   CAROLINA   HOUSING
FRANK   LLOYD   WRIGHT   ARCHITECT

*70. Cluster housing,
Frank Lloyd Wright.*

the cluster was actually constructed in Ardmore, Pennsylvania, but the idea never really captured the public's fancy. Wright had ignored a basic American convention of private space: no American, after choosing to live in the suburbs, wanted to rub his backside up against three strangers, as in Wright's design, while being forced to hold his barbecues in the front yard, or on the roof.

Many multifamily housing projects have assaulted the dignity of their users by eliminating the privacy of a back yard, even though densities were low enough to have included one. Such was the effect of Greenbelt, Maryland, built in 1935 as part of the Federal Suburban Resettlement program (Fig. 71). The lack of a back yard often escaped the attention of critics. Fresh Meadows, in Queens, New York, is such an example. Mumford thought Fresh Meadows to be "probably the best looking piece of architecture in the metropolitan area."[22] Without back yards, however, this development, like Greenbelt, has the aura of a military barracks—an apt analogy in that barracks are usually freestanding

71. Greenbelt, Maryland, Hale Walker, planner; Douglas D. Ellington and R. J. Wadsworth, architects, 1935; aerial view.

structures surrounded by public space. Barracks have no back yards because, for soldiers living together, privacy is neither desirable nor encouraged.

The differing roles of front and back are important not only in our residences but in our commercial buildings as well. In most retail establishments, the customer's end of the building is in front, where signs and displays draw him toward the store. Consequently, locating loading docks and trash bins where customers will not see them is a key component of any plan. Inside a store, especially in smaller establishments, the cash register and the cashier's watchful eye are positioned near the front door to ensure that merchandise does not leave without being purchased. For these reasons a back door, if there is one, is usually locked.

One developer of a small shopping center on the Hudson River waterfront in New Jersey who ignored these imperatives found his design summarily overridden by the tenants. Thinking a splendid view of Manhattan just across the river would enhance his mall's marketability, the developer sited the backs of his stores against the shore, with a rear door set in a large expanse of glass, opening out onto a long wooden deck above the river (Fig. 72). At the opposite end of each store, another door and an identical expanse of glass face the parking lot.

Because customers arrived from the parking lot, most merchants soon blocked off the doors facing the river, leaving the back of the shopping center, despite its view, as a mélange of blank, unattractive facades. For a while the owner of a pizza parlor was a single exception. He placed his ovens and kitchen behind a counter against one wall in the middle of the store. The door to the deck offered customers who had already paid at the counter a view of Manhattan while they ate. An art gallery later joined the pizza parlor in opening a rear door—presumably because paintings are difficult to remove undetected, even from a gallery with an unlocked back entrance. The rest of the merchants, however, locked the back door and painted over the glass or boarded up the back to hide changing rooms, storage areas, and staff bathrooms.

Back doors and back yards seldom figure prominently in an architect's equation, simply because they hold less interest than the front. Consequently, their potential for disruption, as in the shopping center on the Hudson River, is often realized only after the fact. Such was the case with New York City's most ambitious postwar zoning initiative, promulgated in 1961, just three years after completion of the Seagram Building (Fig. 73) on Park Avenue by Mies van der Rohe. The ordinance relied heavily on the Seagram Building as a model for future development.[23]

72. Shopping mall, Edgewater, New Jersey; view of back doors facing the Hudson River.

73. Opposite: Seagram Building, Park Avenue, New York City, Mies van der Rohe, 1958. Note the open excavation on the block to the north. Ezra Stoller © Esto

74. Above: Une Ville Contemporaine, Le Corbusier, 1922; perspective.

75. Left: Seagram Building, Fifty-third Street facade. The five-story wing in the left foreground extends to the sidewalk, aligning with the building to the far left. Ezra Stoller © Esto

In the two decades preceding the Seagram Building, many of America's architects and public housing officials had come to embrace Le Corbusier's "tower in the park" model for large urban housing projects (Fig. 74). Even though Le Corbusier had meant his towers to be office buildings, the idea seemed to lend itself to apartment houses, particularly because attendant swaths of greenery and open space could be used for local recreation.

Towers in the park, however, created formidable problems. They required large tracts of land, and even in a depressed inner-city market these entailed a considerable expenditure of public funds. Bureaucracies had to be created to buy property, demolish buildings, close streets, and build each project. The process created political problems as well, because even after the original residents had long since been dispossessed, a sour residue of hostility toward the project—and to the politicians who had approved it—sometimes lingered in the community.

The Seagram Building appeared to offer a solution to these problems. Architects, urban designers, and public officials alike saw that open areas could now be constructed on a single city block using a Modernist "tower in the park" approach. One could even build on less than a city block; the Seagram Building was actually a "tower in the plaza." The elegance of this mutation of Le Corbusier's original theories was immediately apparent. Public officials

76. New York City, Commissioners' Map of 1811. Collection of The New-York Historical Society.

could still promote progress and a modernist architectural vision, but they no longer needed to alienate large numbers of voters by being directly involved. Government could take an entirely passive role by shifting responsibility to the private developer, who would be a lightning rod for any adverse political reaction. So powerful was this allure that, in large measure, the aesthetic vision behind the Seagram Building drove the overhaul of New York City's zoning resolution.

The new ordinance encouraged developers to build towers in plazas in exchange for permission to erect bigger buildings. This bonus quickly led to a rush to "piazzafy" Manhattan. In the fervor that followed, many architects and city officials overlooked the subtlety of Mies van der Rohe's design. Critics have frequently described the Seagram Building as a freestanding tower, but that is not what it is. The lower floors push out behind the tower to align with the adjoining buildings along the street (Fig. 75). These floors partially block the side walls and rear yards of adjacent buildings from view, much like a mother hiding dirty children behind her skirts.

This configuration was possible because the Seagram Building was an office tower. Unlike an apartment building, it did not need windows in all habitable rooms, nor did it need a rear yard for sunlight. When Mies's prototype was employed elsewhere, however, particularly in residential towers, these buildings

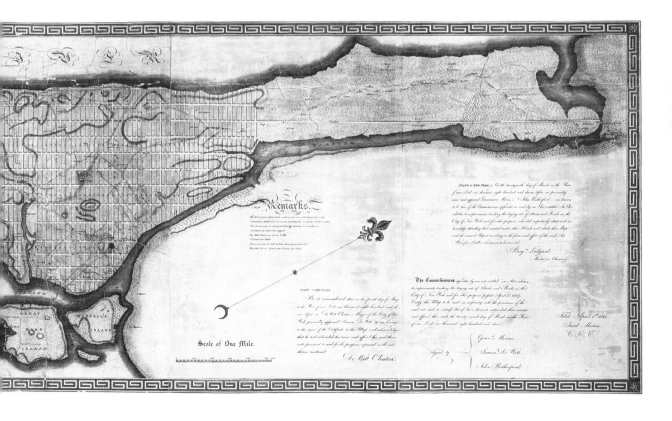

77. Back doors,
Thirteenth Street,
New York City.

had to be pulled away from the adjoining structures to let in sunlight. Over the next three decades a surge of new apartment construction tore many New York streetscapes apart: freestanding towers exposed hundreds of raw side walls and back yards that were never meant to be seen. The unintended impact of the ordinance makes the Seagram Building, arguably, the most influential structure built in New York City during the twentieth century. In 1994, under growing pressure from the public, the City Council eliminated the plaza bonus in most neighborhoods.

An inability to anticipate the often disruptive effects of the back door has affected New York in other subtle and unanticipated ways. At the beginning of the nineteenth century, with the city growing rapidly northward, city fathers decided to map all remaining open land from Greenwich Village to 155th Street. The Commissioners' Map of 1811, as it was called, divided Manhattan into an enormous grid (Fig. 76). Because most traffic would travel in a north-south direction, parallel to the long axis of the island, the commissioners planned 100-foot-wide avenues in that direction and narrower 60-foot-wide streets running east and west, from river to river. Because some traffic would move back and forth across town, the narrower streets were periodically augmented with wider ones: Fourteenth, Twenty-third, Thirty-fourth, and others.

Wider crosstown streets naturally attracted more commercial users. As businesses grew, so did a need for larger stockrooms, storage areas, and loading

docs for incoming inventory and outgoing garbage. In time, retail establishments on the wider streets began buying property on the street behind them,
pushing through to create loading areas and back doors for their buildings.

Thus, as an unintended consequence of the commissioners' plat, the narrower streets adjoining the wider crosstown streets came to have more back
doors. Not surprisingly, these adjacent streets are typically dirtier and less interesting, with longer stretches of blank walls. Fourteenth Street, for example, has
been a major shopping street for many years. Consequently, Thirteenth and
Fifteenth Streets are less attractive (Fig. 77), and the property values are relatively lower than those on Twelfth and Sixteenth Streets, just one block away.
This is true of other wider crosstown streets as well.

Duany & Plater-Zyberk's much acclaimed 1983 plan for a resort community in Seaside, Florida, uses a similar pattern of stores extending through an
entire block—and encounters equally intractable problems (Fig. 78). Some of the
back doors of the stores at the center of town face the front doors of the surrounding houses, diminishing their appeal.

Front doors are not only where we put our architecture but also where we
look out at the world. We want to watch the procession passing by as much as
we want to be noticed by it. Whether from the grand porch of a hotel in Saratoga
Springs, New York (Fig. 79), from a picture window in a suburban tract house,

or from a small-town veranda (Fig. 80), the front of the building is where we wait for the postman, greet strangers, and wave at the passing parade.

The front porch, in particular, is an American institution. Although it arrived in this country via the porticos of Greek Revival architecture, the front porch quickly embedded itself in the culture, as did the porch rocker from which we dispensed wisdom, and the porch swing where boy courted girl.[24] Neither quite public nor entirely private, the front porch was a place to watch the world pass by, a zone where both neighbors and strangers could interact, and a place to spend a rainy day (Fig. 81).

Even as the front porch has waned in popularity, those on the Gothic Revival houses in Oaks Bluffs on Martha's Vineyard still seem appropriate features more than 130 years after the tiny dwellings were built. During the summer these porches, particularly the ones that face a main drag, are filled with people who have come to the island ostensibly to get away from the noise, crowds, and automobiles they sit watching. Similarly, the hotel porches on Miami Beach are

79. Above: The United States Hotel and the Worden, Broadway, Saratoga Springs, New York, ca. 1900. Both hotels were demolished after World War II.

80. Left: Elm Street, Lumberton, North Carolina, ca. 1910.

81. *Right: Front porch. The narrow width, symmetry, and Carpenter Gothic trim of this solitary cottage are typical of the cottages in the Campground, Oak Bluffs, Martha's Vineyard.* Stephen Dohanos, Saturday Evening Post.

82. *Below: Hotel front porch, Miami Beach, 1994.*

filled with people year-round, even though many are within fifteen feet of heavily trafficked streets (Fig. 82).

In America houses almost always face the road. Even though car windows and air conditioning have long since made the motorist anonymous, the symbiotic relationship between a passing traveler and those at the side of the road is still very real. Throughout the country, despite large tracts of land to build on, many houses continue to cling to the road. In rural areas houses are often much closer to the road than can be explained by the cost of removing snow or the expense of longer utility runs. Power and telephone companies in Montana, for example, offer several hundred feet of free installation—a distance from the road greater than that at which many people site their homes. A journey along the interstate highway system reveals houses built close to the road well after a highway's completion—in plain view of a thundering stream of traffic (Fig. 83). Although the back yard is a private realm, across America the front door and the front yard face the public—they face the road—and because they do, they have other consequences as well.

83. House abutting Interstate 70, western Pennsylvania.

Chapter 3

From House

*The road will, as it were, get out of breath trying to catch up
with the huge number of front doors that it must serve.*

LE CORBUSIER
Oeuvre Complète, 1934–1938

to Road

FRONT DOORS AND ROADS GO TOGETHER IN AMERICA. BECAUSE FRONT DOORS ARE
where we meet the world and tell it how well we are doing, the closer we can
bring the world to our front door the more easily we can convey the message.

Since the invention of the automobile, however, the connection between
front door and road has often posed an architectural dilemma. Front doors
generate activity, thus it follows that the more front doors there are, the more
life they will bring. But more front doors mean more streets, and more streets,
since the automobile, have meant more cars. Not only are cars potentially dangerous, as Clarence Stein and others had by the late 1920s come to understand,
but across America the growing network of new streets and highways seemed
to augur the dissolution of traditional pedestrian-scaled cities and towns.

As auto-related injuries grew and the car's power for disruption
increased, architects and planners began trying to segregate people from cars—
a difficult task, indeed, because to separate the two it seemed necessary to
break the historic bond between the front door and the road. In the past sixty
years attempts to create auto-free zones, view corridors, greenways, and
pedestrian-only streets have all derived from three premises: the car is bad; an
active, pedestrian-oriented environment is good; and if one can simply find the
right formula one can create an active front-door environment without streets
and cars.

By 1961, however, Jane Jacobs had demonstrated indirectly just how strong the link was between front doors and vehicular streets. She noted in *Death and Life of Great American Cities* that there were more bookstores in Greenwich Village than on the Upper West Side of Manhattan.[1] This disparity had come about, she reasoned, not because fewer readers lived on the Upper West Side but because Greenwich Village was a more interesting place to stroll. Jacobs thought the appeal of the Village derived in part from its irregular street pattern and shorter blocks, attributes that encouraged people to shop and browse. Shorter blocks meant more corners, and because corners were visible retail locations, they were ideal spots for stores, some of which sold books.

More street corners mean more streets, however. A comparison of the net buildable area in Greenwich Village and that of the Upper West Side bears this out. The Village has considerably less productive land per acre and more asphalt dedicated to vehicular streets. It is also the most pedestrian-friendly area in New York City—suggesting, ironically, that under the right conditions vehicular streets actually increase rather than diminish the potential for pedestrian activity.

Rockefeller Center, begun in 1931, is an even better example of the humanizing power of a vehicular street (Fig. 84). The complex, covering nearly three full blocks between Fifth and Sixth Avenues in mid-Manhattan, would have seemed oppressively large had not its principal designer, Raymond Hood, reduced the scale by inserting a narrow vehicular street in the middle of the complex parallel to the avenues.

At the time the project was announced, upscale New Yorkers were loath to wander west of Fifth Avenue into a part of the city still brimming with tenements, seedy bars, and the Sixth Avenue elevated transit line. Consequently, Hood designed the complex so that the principal pedestrian entrance from Fifth Avenue is a long allée lined with shops. The walkway leads to a sunken plaza, and then to the most important building in the complex, 30 Rockefeller Center. But to get to this building pedestrians must cross Hood's new vehicular street.

Given the client's original brief to the architects, which stressed the importance of attracting shoppers into the complex, extending a pedestrian-only walkway directly to the Center's most important building might have seemed like the perfect solution. Such a design would have consigned vehicular traffic bound for 30 Rockefeller Plaza to the building's side entrances. The appeal of a car-free connection from Fifth Avenue—at a time when separating cars and people was becoming an increasingly popular idea—makes the decision to insert a new north-south vehicular street all the more remarkable.

In retrospect one can see that a pedestrian-only allée would have diminished the symbolism of the front door to 30 Rockefeller Plaza, which faces the plaza, and by forcing taxis and limousines to drop off passengers elsewhere, would have dampened activity around the entrance. Jane Jacobs thought Rockefeller Center's extra street produced a "fluidity"[2] that came from offering more choices—more choices essentially meaning more front doors and the opportunities they bring.

The synergy between vehicular streets and front doors has, however, escaped the attention of many architecture critics. The eminent historian Sigfried

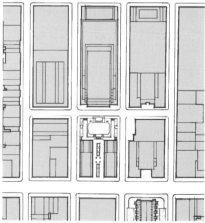

84. Rockefeller Center, New York City, Reinhard and Hofmeister; Corbett, Harrison and MacMurray; Hood and Fouilhoux, 1931–1940; site plan, left; aerial view, above. Regional Plan Association.

Giedion, for example, in 1941 ignored entirely the insertion of an extra street at Rockefeller Center, suggesting that "nothing new or significant can be observed on looking over the site. The ground plan reveals nothing."[3] Architectural historian William Jordy went even further, suggesting in 1972 that Rockefeller Center would actually have been improved "by the elimination of the private roadway."[4]

Many architects also miss the interrelationship between front doors and streets. Steven Izenour, one of the authors of *Learning from Las Vegas,* recently compared the differences between the Strip as it existed in the 1960s and the Strip it has since become.[5] The growing popularity of Las Vegas has resulted in many changes, one of the biggest of which has been a dramatic increase in both pedestrian and vehicular traffic. To alleviate the congestion, Izenour and architectural historian David A. Dashiell III suggested a study of several measures, including depressed cross streets, more through-traffic lanes, alternative access roads, and the limiting of cars during peak periods.

All of these alternatives, however, would weaken the connection between cars and the businesses that depend on them. If, in particular, automobiles were limited to other roads—presumably those leading to the "ill-kept backsides"[6] of the buildings—front doors would start following the cars. As front doors moved, so would the neon signs. The Strip would dim, sapped of its energy by front doors relocated elsewhere. Americans, like the characters in Hunter Thompson's novel *Fear and Loathing in Las Vegas,*[7] want to arrive by car. It matters little how slowly traffic on the Strip is moving—we are there because we want to see neon lights blotting out the stars. If we wanted a faster ride or a look at the night sky, we would have headed out along a dark desert road instead.

It is the abundance of vehicular streets, particularly slow streets, that gives scale and character to areas as diverse as Boston's Beacon Hill and Miami's Coconut Grove. Gramercy Park in Manhattan, one of New York's lesser-known treasures, shows the capacity of even one extra block-long street to give focus to a neighborhood (Fig. 85). Gramercy Park, a tiny square evocative of the residential squares in London's West End, derives its ambience in large measure from the many front doors ringing its perimeter. The front doors, in turn, are the product of an extra vehicular street: Lexington Avenue, between Twenty-first and Twenty-second Streets, splits in two.[8] The extra street is similar in concept to the pattern James Oglethorpe created in 1733 to bring life to the small park squares in his renowned plan for Savannah, Georgia. Despite these examples it is, nevertheless, still apostasy for a twentieth-century architect or planner to stand before an audience and suggest that the path to a more human scale is through the creation of more vehicular streets.

Rather than advocating more vehicular streets, two decades ago many American architects and planners actually began pressing for their elimination. In particular, they urged the closing of selected downtown commercial streets to vehicles in a number of towns and cities. Free of automobiles, these pedestrian streets would supposedly revitalize flagging retail establishments, making them more attractive to shoppers who were then heading for the suburbs. Selected

streets took on new life as granite cobbles, trees, and benches replaced the asphalt paving.

Now some of the same municipalities are ripping out these features and returning the streets to automobile traffic.[9] The reasons for the unpopularity of auto-free streets are instructive. As the concept initially spread, merchants and building owners would frequently petition local government to close a particular street. A closed street, however, meant that merchants had to schedule deliveries after shopping hours, a solution that drove up costs. Alternatively, they could open up service areas behind the stores with access to a vehicular street. Frequently they chose the latter option. Meanwhile, pedestrian-only streets were exacerbating an already short supply of parking by eliminating parking spaces in front of the stores. Not infrequently, as in Ithaca, New York, and at Lincoln Road Mall in Miami Beach, a municipality after closing a street would alleviate the shortage of parking by building garages on adjoining blocks. These new parking structures when added to the merchants' service areas only increased the blight, making traffic-free streets seem like anomalous islands in a sea of back doors and garages.

This isolation is vividly apparent in the small town of Cape May, New Jersey, which in 1971 removed the cars from a three-block-long commercial street, ostensibly to preserve the community's Victorian character (Fig. 86). An all-pedestrian street is not evocative of a late nineteenth-century seashore village, however, and Cape May paid a heavy price for its decision. Flanking the pedestrian-only street are two wide vehicular streets complete with diagonal parking spaces, trash cans, and the general ambience of a late twentieth-century low-density strip mall (Fig. 87). For every block of ersatz Victoriana, Cape May got two blocks of what it had sought to avoid. Some merchants, needing to attract shoppers from their cars behind the pedestrian street, installed back entrances, despite the security problems and the expense these entrances entailed.

Front doors and streets engender activity, and in America they also mark

85. Gramercy Park, New York City; the plan, above; front doors, above left.

86. *Pedestrian street,
Cape May, New Jersey,
1993.*

87. *Adjoining vehicular
street, Cape May,
1993.*

the boundary of the public domain. As we expect a front door to face the street, we assume that a street is public, unless it's clearly marked otherwise. So strong is the link between front door and road that when facing a front door that's not on the street—as in a shopping mall, for example—we have trouble believing we are standing in a truly public place; it seems more likely that we have passed into some semiprivate environment beyond.

Conversely, we do not want back doors to face the public domain. Our conviction that back doors open onto the private realm of a back yard is so deeply ingrained that it overrides even the most dogged architectural efforts to suppress it. A short stretch of esplanade on the Fells Point waterfront in Baltimore, bordered by the back yards of adjoining houses, demonstrates this propensity. The rear facades of the houses have been made more front-like by the addition of new porches and architectural detail (Fig. 88), and a decorative metal fence separates the yards from the abutting brick path. Front-like facades on one side and boat moorings on the other indicate that the path is public. Nevertheless, as one strolls along the esplanade, one has a lingering sense of having invaded someone's back-

88. *Pedestrian walk-way, Fells Point, Baltimore. Note the architectural detail on the rear facades of the houses.*

89. *Houses along Pacific Coast Highway, Malibu, California.*

yard privacy. At any moment a door will be flung open, people will spill out headed for their boat, and they will have primacy and superior rights.

In California, state law makes all ocean beaches public. In communities without streets to delineate a boundary, however, homeowners abutting the beach often seek to privatize it. The front doors in exclusive communities like Malibu will often face the Pacific Coast Highway or a street, and back doors will abut the beach. Houses stand shoulder to shoulder along the street like Roman legionnaires, forcing people seeking the ocean to traverse long unbroken phalanxes of fences, walls, and buildings (Fig. 89). Homeowners make every effort to discourage frequent public access to the water because they know some members of the public who do get to the beach—absent a street to mark the boundary of their domain—will occasionally wander into these exclusive back yards.

Our belief that back yards are a private realm and that we face the public only at the front door has rendered several recent regional planning policy initiatives ineffective. For example, as businesses left older urban maritime and industrial waterfronts, drawn to larger out-of-town sites with better highway access, municipalities began reclaiming their waterfronts for new uses. As an enticement to the public, many cities also began requiring commercial and residential developers to dedicate portions of the waterfront to parks, marinas, and other recreational uses. This policy grew from a realization that without public intervention many waterfronts would soon become a series of private enclaves.

This seemingly unassailable policy sometimes ran afoul of deeper values, however, as the New Jersey side of the Hudson River shows. Developers on the Hudson River waterfront typically wanted to exploit their best asset—the view of Manhattan. To keep these views exclusive to those who were paying large sums to live along the river, developers invariably fenced their projects to keep the public out. As this pattern became apparent, the state of New Jersey responded by requiring a thirty-foot-wide walkway open to the public at the water's edge to be built as part of any new project. But as soon as the legislation passed, developers in project after project began showing remarkable ingenuity at subverting the law's purposes. Some ignored the requirement altogether; others disguised public walkways by installing gates, adding barbed wire, or letting the weeds grow (Fig. 90). In one large project a developer even constructed the required public walkway *inside* his building. The new law actually exacerbated the problem, creating a series of flawed projects, some of which caused bitter confrontation and litigation.[10]

What had emboldened developers to bar, or at least discourage, public access to the waterfront was the orientation of their projects, all of which had their back yards facing the river. Whatever the rules, these back yards seemed private. Otherwise law-abiding condominium residents, lacking a street to separate them from the river, began actively lobbying local officials not to enforce mandated public access through their new back yards. Meanwhile, the state of

90. Entrance to pedestrian walkway, Roc Harbor, North Bergen, New Jersey, 1993.

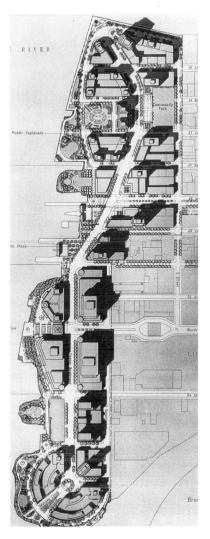

91. Site plan for Queens West, Queens, New York, Gruzen Samton and Beyer, Blinder, Belle, 1994.

92. Battery Park City Esplanade, New York City.

New Jersey pressed for design changes, and several public interest groups went to court.

New Jersey is not an isolated example. Oblivious to the problems this policy had created, New York City, for example, in 1993 enacted waterfront legislation quite similar to New Jersey's statutes, even though the lack of streets defining the public realm creates the same potential for conflict. At Hunters Point where a large proposed project along the Queens side of the East River (Fig. 91) will force strollers to pass through a sizable number of back yards directly abutting the river. The Battery Park City esplanade in New York (Fig. 92) has a similar unintentional ambiguity. Absent a street, most buildings bordering the waterfront esplanade have their front doors elsewhere. Battery Park City partially overcomes this ambiguity with its great density—the sheer number of people partially dilutes the esplanade's aura of exclusivity and privacy.

93. Vehicular street ending at the Boardwalk, Atlantic City, New Jersey.

Atlantic City's famous ocean boardwalk, abutted directly by buildings selling to boardwalk strollers, seems an exception. However, the narrow vehicular streets that terminate at the boardwalk would be illegal today in most jurisdictions because fire trucks and other emergency vehicles cannot turn around at the end. But if the streets were widened to provide turnarounds, many of the buildings on the boardwalk would have to be razed.

Because most smaller boardwalk stores have no vehicular street access, merchants carry their garbage to bins located at the ends of the streets (Fig. 93). Larger casinos and hotels have multiple front doors, some facing the boardwalk, others facing the street. Their garbage is usually collected from along these streets as well. In short, the pedestrian boardwalk has inexorably led to a permanent jumble of front doors, back doors, and trash on the streets leading to it.

Without a street to mark boundaries, the ambiguity about whether an area is public or private increases as density decreases. The town of Seaside, Florida, mentioned earlier, is a good example of this phenomenon (see Fig. 78). Laid out along a Gulf Coast shorefront highway, Seaside has been much praised for its sense of community: similarly scaled wooden houses, tin roofs, and picket fences all signal their owners' shared values. The only structures on the ocean side of the road when the first residents moved to Seaside were elegantly scaled pavilions leading down to the beach. Between the pavilions were large open areas of sand and beach grass. These "special districts" were reserved for future development.

Now shorter-term rental units are filling these tracts, their front doors facing the road and their back doors facing the beach. This layout, as in Malibu, blurs the boundary rather than marking the beach as clearly public. The units at Seaside sit on dunes above the beach, creating some sense of separation between themselves and the bathers below. Nevertheless, the owners of these units will eventually see the Gulf more as their private preserve than an amenity to be shared equally with those living on the other side of the highway.

94. *Front doors facing the park, Oak Bluffs, Martha's Vineyard.*

95. *Houses facing Chesapeake Bay, Oxford, Maryland.*

In contrast to Seaside, houses on the Campground in Oak Bluffs on Martha's Vineyard (Fig. 94) project a clear sense of community. The Campground's parks belong to everyone: where the greensward begins and ends is not at issue because a narrow road creates a boundary between park and houses. The houses, quite naturally, have their front doors facing the street—and the park.

This pattern also creates a narrow public waterfront park in Oxford, Maryland, where a tiny lane separates single-family houses from a grass strip along Chesapeake Bay (Fig. 95). On a much larger scale the Lake Michigan shoreline in Chicago (Fig. 96), one of America's great waterfronts, has a similar pattern of parks and buildings separated by streets over much of its length. So vivid is the image of Chicago as a city of skyscrapers pressed tight against the sweep of Lake Michigan's shoreline that noted planner Kevin Lynch wondered who, when drawing Chicago, would not start with a simple green line down the

96. Lakefront, Chicago, Illinois, ca. 1930. The image of the city pressed against a broad public waterfront is strong enough to overcome the many facilities sited in the public land, including extensive rail yards, arterial highways, a municipal football stadium, and a convention center.

middle of the page.[11] The separation this line implies would be much less obvious if Lake Shore Drive and other waterfront streets did not clearly delineate the boundary between city and lakefront. In all of these examples the public and private realms are clear: front doors are on one side, the public realm is on the other, and a street lies in between.

Because of the power of vehicular streets to define public places, my firm, in a 1992 urban-design commission for the redevelopment of the Hudson River waterfront in Hoboken, New Jersey, proposed creating new blocks similar to existing ones simply by extending Hoboken's grid and adding a street to run along the river the length of the city (Fig. 97).[12] An esplanade and park on one side of the street and front doors on the other give activity and security to the waterfront and make back-yard encroachment impossible, regardless of the kinds of development projects that are later proposed.[13] The vehicular roadway will clearly define the public realm, but stop signs and traffic lights on the new street will discourage through traffic. Half of the waterfront plan has been passed by municipal officials, the rest is still under discussion.

South Beach in Miami, perhaps more than any other American example, demonstrates the proposition that front doors and streets mark an area as public—and back doors without streets do not. Ocean Drive on South Beach is, for much of its length, a boundary between the beach and the mostly Art Deco hotels facing the water (Fig. 98). The rehabilitation of these hotels and the consequent resurgence of the district's economy have been major success stories in Miami over the past decade. Ocean Drive is crammed with cafés and verandas; people spill back and forth across the street from front doors on one side to Ocean Park and the beach on the other.

A different arrangement of buildings elsewhere along the drive demonstrates how powerful the synergy between front doors and streets really is. At the

southern end of the beach a large stand of apartment buildings erected after the Second World War looms into view on the outboard side of the street (Fig. 99). These newer buildings have their front doors on Ocean Drive, but their back doors face the Atlantic. Behind these buildings pedestrian traffic diminishes even though the beach remains public. More importantly, the rehabilitation of the older buildings on the inboard side of the street also drops off, as does the intensity of pedestrian activity. Miami Beach succeeds only where its front doors face the beach—and Ocean Drive.

Although drivers have little hope of parking in front of the hotels and cafés on Ocean Drive, the steady parade of cars attests to our desire to drive past the front doors. For this same reason pedestrian streets, like the one in Cape May, seem symbolically awry because even if there are few parking places we still want to be able to drive past the stores. A street may be crowded and narrow, the parking places few—but it is the symbolism that matters. Cars near the front door not only suggest activity, they bespeak important comings and goings within. F. Scott Fitzgerald noted in *The Great Gatsby* that on party night at Gatsby's house "the cars are parked five deep in the drive, and already the halls and salons and verandas are gaudy with primary colors."[14]

The closer the car can come to the front door, at least temporarily, the better we like it, which is one reason why the work of the British architect Sir Edwin Lutyens has had considerable resonance for Americans. Lutyens designed a number of English country houses with grand gravel driveways leading straight to the front entrance (Fig. 100). These driveways imply the presence of a feature that is absent from most American homes—a butler in livery ready to receive a steady stream of guests as they step from their large, highly polished automobiles. The imagery also suggests chauffeurs who then drive the vehicles away to car barns hidden from view elsewhere on the estate. Frank Lloyd

97. Opposite: Model of proposed plan for Hoboken, New Jersey, Craig Whitaker Architects, Wilday & Dupree, Landscape Architects, 1992. The lighter buildings represent new development.

98. Left: Ocean Drive, Miami Beach.

99. Below: Ocean Drive; view looking south. Note the apartments on the beach side of the street.

100. *Entrance, Grey Walls, Gullane, Scotland, Edwin Lutyens, 1900.*

101. *Above: Model Home for* Ladies' Home Journal, *Frank Lloyd Wright, 1900. The scheme suggests a porte cochere is within the grasp of any American who can afford $7,000 for a house.*

102. *Right: Trinity Episcopal Church, Burlington, Vermont.*

*103. Nehemiah Homes,
East New York, New
York City, 1985.*

Wright sometimes employed a porte cochere to create the same ambience
(Fig. 101). The porte cochere brought the car closer to the front door, and in
Wright's schemes there was also a garage in back in which to store the car. Occasionally in America a porte cochere will even be used to bring us closer to God
(Fig. 102).

We differentiate between getting to the front door by car and needing to
store the vehicle there. Permanent parking elsewhere is the implied promise of
the porte cochere. We never see, or even think about, the White House car-pool
areas, for example. We see only the well-appointed dignitaries disembarking
under the porte cochere that dominates the north facade of the building.
Conversely, we sense that a housing project is for low-income people simply
because the front yards have been compromised by concrete parking pads, and
the car owners have no place else to store their vehicles (Fig. 103).

Long-term storage of the car, usually in a garage, is a back-door function.
Therefore, when garages swung around and attached themselves to the front of
many modern American suburban houses, the symbolism became confused. As
Scully put it, "the twentieth-century house was to draw [the road] into its huge
garage and to enshrine its bug-eyed creatures there."[15] More important, this
enshrinement frequently occurred at the front of the house. The large amount of
space needed to store a car (or cars), relative to the overall size of the house,
meant that a back-door function now dominated the front facade. Very few
architects have successfully resolved this ambiguity.

Le Corbusier seemed to have solved the problem in his villa at Garches,
built in 1927, which is partly why the building—and particularly its front
facade—has fascinated American architects. The facade contains a front door
and a garage door as well as a service entrance (Fig. 104). Le Corbusier even
directed the axis of the entrance driveway directly toward the service door rather
than the front door, a formulation that seems very strange to an American eye
(Fig. 105). The power of the facade derives in part from two entry doors symmetrically located but placed at different elevations and with different-sized

104. Top: Front facade of Villa Stein, Garches, France, Le Corbusier, 1927.

105. Above: View from the front gate of Villa Stein.

106. Right: Front facade of Villa Stein.

107. Left: Garage sale, Columbus, Ohio.

108. Below: Winkler Goetsch House, Okemos, Michigan, Frank Lloyd Wright, 1939. Despite the prominence of carports in many of Wright's buildings of this period, cars never appear in the photographs.

canopies. The tension in the facade depends, however, on our ability to suppress the knowledge that after the photographer leaves, groceries, tradespeople, and trash will once again pass through the service door, and the garage door will probably be open a good amount of the time (Fig. 106).

Despite our best efforts to ameliorate its impact, an open garage door facing a suburban street still reveals to the world the cat litter, bicycles, and lawn food that we think should be stored in back. A garage sale in America means the sale of personal belongings a homeowner no longer needs (Fig. 107). Several communities with the political muscle to enforce regulations have actually begun limiting the number of hours a day during which garage doors facing the street may remain open.

Frank Lloyd Wright in his "Usonian" houses of the 1930s and 1940s—a time when ownership of a car still suggested modernity and relative affluence—sometimes put a carport adjacent to the front door. But cars seldom appeared in photographs of the house because their presence would have suggested owners unable to store it elsewhere (Fig. 108).

Robert Venturi is nearly unique among American architects in that he has tried to give symbolic meaning to the garage. Venturi centered and highlighted the garage door in one project and, in another, used expensive paving on the garage floor. More typically, Americans put their best architectural features not on or in the garage, which serves a back-door function, but where the car comes to rest in the driveway. We celebrate arrival as a two-step process—exiting the car and entering the house. Homeowners may use lamps, paving stones, hedges or railings to mark where the car comes to rest, in addition to putting decorative features around the front door (Fig. 109).

On larger suburban lots the garage is sometimes entered from the side of the house, a solution that eliminates the symbolic dissonance between front and back, yet allows direct access to the house from the street, leaving the back yard free of a garage. Venturi chose this option in an unbuilt project he designed for owners living at the end of a long lane who, wanting to subdivide their property, would otherwise have regularly passed open garage doors (Fig. 110). Cheek walls push the garages farther from the front facade and increase the apparent size of the houses. A garage entered at the side of a house, however, necessitates more driveway and a relatively wider lot because a car must turn to enter. Wider lots mean greater land costs and longer utility runs, thus garages on the side of the house are more typical of higher-priced subdivisions.

Walt Disney's theme parks also hide their garages, yet still suggest that cars can get to the front door. The Disney experience has bedazzled us since the original complex opened in Anaheim, California, in 1955. Charles Moore wrote that

109. House with lamp at the driveway, Columbus, Ohio.

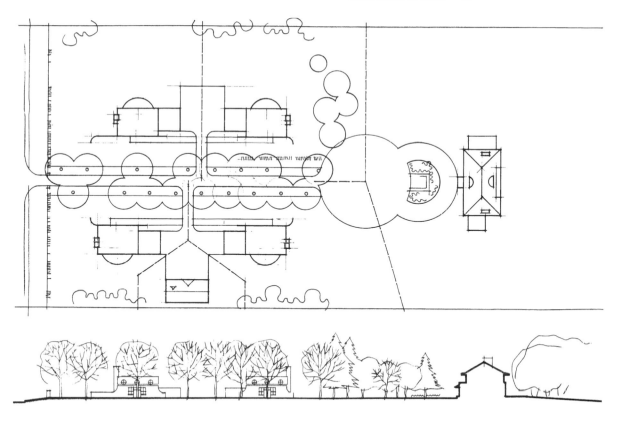

110. Subdivision proj-
ect, Philadelphia,
Venturi and Rauch,
1972; site plan, top;
sections, above.

Disneyland® was one of the better examples of planning in America in this century,[16] and developer James Rouse thought it was "the greatest piece of urban
design in the United States today."[17] As in a gigantic mall, the action at
Disneyland begins only after one has left the parking lot. The first stop in all
Disney parks is Main Street, U.S.A., the park's centerpiece (Fig. 111). The architectural detail and miniature scale of the buildings pull the street together into a
cohesive whole, evoking an image of small-town America. Sidewalks, curbs, and
asphalt paving indicate that Main Street, U.S.A., is a vehicular street, but just as
in the photographs of Lutyens's driveways and Wright's carports, cars are elsewhere. The only vehicles on Main Street, U.S.A.—or anywhere in the park—are
the trolleys and trams carrying visitors.

In addition to the illusion that cars can get to the front doors at Main
Street, U.S.A., there is the sense that back-door functions have vanished. The
stores and exhibits at Disneyland are stitched together so that "back doors"—the
pipes, gears, garages, storage barns, and employee locker rooms required to
make the park go—are hidden from view (Fig. 112). These backstage functions
consume enormous amounts of land, yet because they are never seen, they never
intrude upon the fantasy. Restaurants, rides, and souvenir shops are all serviced
invisibly from behind, while the public meanders through a world bounded by
front doors.

*111. Main Street,
U.S.A., Walt Disney
World. Used by permis-
sion from Disney
Enterprises, Inc.*

Walt Disney World® in Florida disguised its back doors even more completely than had Disneyland. Instead of using gates and fences to hide service
functions, Walt Disney World installed tunnels that snake through the park
behind and beneath the exhibits. Food, merchandise, garbage, and employees all
move back and forth through these tunnels to pop up at their appointed destinations. Mickey and Goofy appear magically from around corners and through
small doors, then disappear as the script dictates, leaving the public in an her-
metically sealed all-front-door world.

Walt Disney World's service tunnels seemed to confirm what many planners had already believed long before the park opened—that tunnels were a prac-
ticable solution for real cities. As early as 1910 Eugène Hénard, the chief
architect for the city of Paris, was vigorously promoting what he thought modern cities would soon become: buildings sitting atop a veritable catacomb of service tunnels (Fig. 113).[18] Hénard produced prototypical sections showing trams,
garbage wagons, and coal carts coursing under the streets, hidden from view in
their own separate rights-of-way. So strong was the intellectual appeal of these
conduits as tools for shaping cities that some twenty years later pipes-and-wires
advocates were suggesting that urban design was simply the art of deploying
infrastructure. In the 1950s architect Victor Gruen actually proposed a network
of service tunnels, which was never built, for the center of Fort Worth, Texas.[19]

112. Right: Service gate, Disneyland. Used by permission from Disney Enterprises, Inc.

113. Below: Section of multilevel street of the future, Eugène Hénard, 1910.

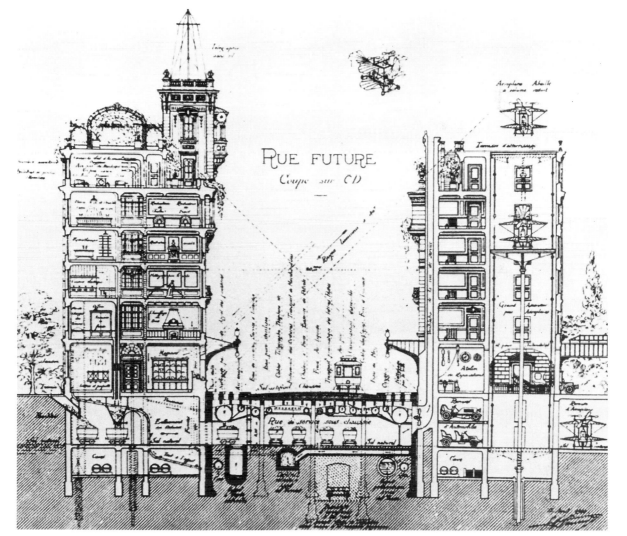

RUE FUTURE
Coupe sur CD

When Walt Disney World opened, interest in service tunnels flared anew. Again nothing came of the idea because the capital costs were such that service tunnels were truly feasible only in the very densest cities—and at Walt Disney World. For the rest of the country they were "megastructural" fantasies. Moreover, the real issue was not eliminating back-door functions, as Disney's front-door-only world suggested, but locating them where they were least disruptive, where our cultural values expect them to be. Also lost in the enthusiasm for Disney's tunnels was the knowledge that many American cities already had a much cheaper tool for linking back-door functions to the street—the alley.

Alleys, which were a common feature in many American towns and cities up until the Second World War, may once again bear consideration, because they offer solutions to a host of newer problems. Alleys allowed Americans to watch the passing parade from their front door while leaving less attractive functions to be serviced in back. Truck deliveries and off-street garbage collection could take place in the alley; carriage houses, horse barns, and, later, garages could also be located there.

Alleys have a symbolic role: they are to streets what back doors are to front doors. As the street's antithesis, alleys evoke the imagery of America's darker side. The obligatory fistfight in a western movie might erupt through the front door of a saloon onto a dusty main street, and the final gunfight—the showdown between good and evil—might also take place on the street, but a knife fight usually occurred in the alley. "Alley cat" is not a term of praise. American alleys are seen as slightly sinful places, a bit risqué, like the alley speakeasies and the Tin Pan Alley music of Prohibition days. The caption of a 1946 cartoon showing Harry Truman as a battered Little Lord Fauntleroy beset by bullies reads in part:

> *Look at little Truman now,*
> *Muddied, battered, bruised—and how!*
> *Victim of his misplaced trust,*
> *He has learned what good boys must.*
>
> *In the alley after school,*
> *There just ain't no golden rule.*[20]

Even when gated, alleys seem risky to Americans because we greet the public at our front door. Gaining access to a house from an alley seems like jumping a person from behind. This image endures, even though from a burglar's perspective there will probably be more people to give alarm—eating, doing homework, or watching television—at the back of the house than at the front. In keeping with the alley's image, a homeless man in the film comedy *Down and Out in Beverly Hills* wreaks havoc on an affluent family that takes him in from an alley behind their house where he has been foraging through the trash. At the end of the film the man leaves by the same route.

Paradoxically, despite the alley's indecorous reputation, Americans view certain buildings on the alley as rather luxurious adjuncts to a main house. Guest

114. Washington
Mews, Fifth Avenue,
New York City.

cottages, mews houses, studios, and cabanas all connote opulence or, at the very least, the means to support a second mortgage.

Alley buildings beget an architectural complexity often missing in America. If the "real" front door is at the front of the lot, where it should be, then without symbolic dissonance an alley building can have its own front door, plus a garage door, a place to put the trash, and a back gate from the house, all in the same facade. It can be, like Le Corbusier's villa at Garches, a tapestry of many parts.

Like a Scottish tartan, alleys create a more complex weave of building scales along the street—a play within a play. Washington Mews, just off lower Fifth Avenue in New York, for example, is a vestigial lane of two-story alley buildings set among much taller apartments (Fig. 114). Washington Mews is an anomaly in the Manhattan grid sitting on a deep, irregularly shaped block sandwiched between Lower Manhattan's earlier patchwork of grids to the south and the Commissioners' Map of 1811 to the north. The carriage houses on the alley, which once served adjoining town houses, are now tiny residences and offices for New York University, giving the alley its front door–back door character. The change in scale between street and mews was noticeable even when the alley buildings were surrounded by four- and five-story row houses. But today, like a diminutive Christmas display in a department store window, the tiny buildings elicit delighted surprise from those who come upon them for the first time. A sudden change in scale is also integral to the architectural character of many other older urban neighborhoods, like Back Bay in Boston and Georgetown in Washington, D.C.

Beyond their architectural possibilities, alleys also have economic implications. Narrower lots mean cheaper infrastructure costs per house. A block of single-family homes bisected by an alley with garages on it, for instance, can accommodate more lots than a block without an alley but with driveways along-

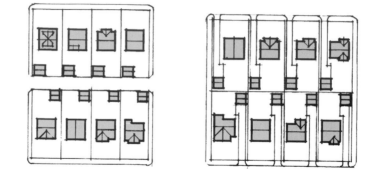

115. Blocks with and without alleys. Even if the garages in the block without alleys on the right were attached to the houses and entered from the street, the total square footage of driveway paving would still exceed that of the alley.

side the houses. Additional land costs for the alley and its extra paving costs are offset by eliminating the expense of individual driveways (Fig. 115). Alleys also provide rights-of-way for unattractive overhead utility lines that many communities find too expensive to bury.[21]

In addition, alleys facilitate trash storage and removal. Manhattan, one of America's dirtier urban areas, has few alleys. The commissioners who prepared the city's official map in 1811, believed that future prosperity depended upon having a large amount of salable land whose owners would pay real estate taxes. Consequently, these officials designated more than two-thirds of the mapped area as private property and left less than one-third as public streets, sidewalks, and parks. In 1811 the plat seemed a perfect blueprint for a robust young metropolis.

To obtain this high ratio of private to public property, the commissioners omitted all alleys; back yards pushed up against other back yards. That simple decision meant New Yorkers would forever bring their groceries in through the same front door they would later use to take out the garbage. Consequently, New York will always be relatively dirtier than cities with more alleys.

Finally, alleys eliminate the ambiguity over where to put the back door—a choice that may seem obvious but in reality is not. In the 1850s, for example, officials of the Illinois Central Railroad prepared a standard gridded plat of lots and blocks to be used at every new depot stop (Fig. 116). Because the plan had little variety, it is still used by critics to demonstrate the banality of American gridiron planning. Yet, the plan did have a simple rhythm of streets and alleys. Streets were wider and had names, alleys were narrower and without names. From these two clues alone settlers knew to face their front doors toward the street and their back doors toward the alley.

By contrast, confusion over the issue mars the rhythm of James Oglethorpe's otherwise masterful plan for Savannah. In the north-south direction, Savannah's through streets alternate with streets interrupted by small squares. In the east-west direction the rhythm of streets and alleys is more complex. What at first might seem to be an alley terminating at each square is actually a street. Fearful, perhaps, of how alleys might have looked when viewed from the parks, Oglethorpe simply widened them into streets (Fig. 117).

The lots on either side of these widened alleys were all reserved for public

116. *Illinois Central Associates' standard town plat, ca. 1855.*

117. *Four of Savannah's twenty-six squares, 1994. Note how the building pattern on blocks with alleys differs from the blocks without alleys.*

buildings. But there were not enough public structures to fill these sites, which compared to other parcels were quite large. Consequently, as Oglethorpe's pattern was repeated, lots on either side of the widened alleys were subdivided, and many now contain several buildings. Not surprisingly, front doors of the buildings abutting the park face the park, but around the corner some buildings front on the widened alley while others face the opposite direction. Several small blocks have become a potpourri of front and back doors (Fig. 118).

Despite its virtues, Americans came to see the alley in the 1950s as an anachronistic feature of a pre-automotive past. In some cities big landowners, despite the unseemly appearance of truck loading docks on a street, petitioned officials to close existing downtown alleys so that a new building could cover more of the block. In the suburbs, having a garage on the alley meant carrying one's groceries across the back yard. This too came to seem like an antiquated arrangement, especially when in the alternative one could drive a gleaming new car directly from the street into an attached and heated garage.

Nevertheless, alleys may once again be an answer to societal demands, particularly in new suburban developments seeking to serve a changing market. Deep and lasting demographic changes are taking place in America. At one end of the spectrum, families are smaller and there has been a dramatic increase in single-parent households. At the other end, the number of unrelated people sharing a single house is increasing. Health costs are keeping the elderly in their homes longer, while many college and high school graduates, who once would have left to start their own households, are returning home as "boomerang" children. Most suburban communities built since World War II did not anticipate these changes. Three- and four-bedroom houses constructed for nuclear families provide neither the room nor the privacy for what may soon be a different standard household unit. It is difficult to remember whether the senior Nelsons in the 1950s television series *Ozzie and Harriet* had parents of their own, but if they did, they certainly lived elsewhere. When the Nelson children finished school, they too were expected to have their own domiciles.[22]

Faced with a larger household, a suburban homeowner can reconvert the family room, add a new wing, or buy a larger house. Grown children might be housed in the basement, if there is one, but grandparents usually remain aboveground. These options all entail disruption, however, and none offers grown family members their own front door, as an alley building would. One can build on an alley without changing the existing house; one can even construct a separate rental unit with its own address and access through the alley to a street. Most important, because alleys increase the number of possible front doors on a given lot, they can also dramatically increase the density.

Railroads and electric trolley lines enabled Americans to live in the earliest suburbs. Automobiles later let them shop and work there as well. Computers now offer the choice of working at home. Growing numbers of Americans are running small businesses from an extra bedroom or the basement; some 22 million Americans now have home offices.[23] When a business outgrows the home, the next move is often to an office above the stores on Main Street or to a suite in an outlying office park. Many of these same businesses could well operate from a small alley building—if there was one. The resulting mix would create variety in lower-density areas, like the mix that Jane Jacobs found so important to urban neighborhoods like Greenwich Village.

One might expect that the American propensity for having front doors face the road and back doors face a private domain would translate into orderly towns and cities, but this has not happened. Because we are most interested in a building's relationship to the street, it is the road itself that dictates how we organize ourselves on the land rather than vice versa. This can clearly be seen on a night flight across America by looking down at patterns of light shaped like strange galaxies. From brightly illuminated downtowns, lights spread outward clinging to major highways and streets. In even the smallest town, from the small lighted clusters marking shopping-mall parking lots, high school football fields, and main streets, the lights diminish outward until only barnyard poles and an occasional illuminated roadside sign are left. As the next town slides into view the diffuse spots of light coalesce along the road once again. By contrast a flight over England reveals sharp-edged, brightly lit chunks of developed land. Compact towns and villages abut darkened farms and forests. The English landscape rolls on like some gently undulating quilt, a tidy tapestry of light and dark.

Our history and our cultural values make it likely that however the American landscape may change in the future, we will design our buildings to reflect our public and private lives, style them to show our individuality, and face them along the road to meet the world. The great value we place on freedom, equality, and renewal also dictates what we will continue to look for from the road as we pass by.

118. Front doors adjoining back doors, Savannah.

Chapter **4**

The heavens themselves, the planets, and this center
Observe degree, priority, and place,
Insisture, course, proportion, season, form,
Office, and custom, in all line of order.

WILLIAM SHAKESPEARE
Troilus and Cressida

All in a Row

IN AN AMERICAN SUBURB OF MANY STYLES, OFTEN THE ONLY COMMON DENOMINA-
tors among buildings are their similar size and similar setback from the road.
These, and occasionally the roughly equal spacing between buildings, may be
the only architectural threads tying a composition together. These similarities,
so prevalent as to go often unnoticed, are essential counterpoints in a culture
that extols the individual.

As different styles celebrate our uniqueness, so common setbacks celebrate our equality. We may all be different, we may each be king of our own
castle, but we all agree to line our castles up at the same distance from the road.
Mandated front- and side-yard setbacks are common enough requirements in
America to be nearly ubiquitous. Except in densely built downtown areas, they
are a feature of nearly every municipal zoning ordinance in the country.

From our earliest days we have wanted to line up along the road while
also keeping some separation from our neighbors. William Penn, for example,
having witnessed the plague of 1665 and the Great Fire of 1666 in London,
prescribed freestanding, regularly spaced buildings in his original plan for
Philadelphia. "Let the houses be built in a line, or upon a line, as much as may
be . . . let every house be placed, if the person pleases, in the middle of its plat,
as to the breadth way of it, that so there may be ground on each side for gardens or orchards, or fields."[1] The spaces between the dwellings were intended
to reduce the spread of contagion and fire; but whether Penn consciously con-

sidered the symbolism or not, equally spaced buildings and common setbacks also connote equality and community. Because all dwellings would be the same distance from the road, all would share equally in the experience of a New World.

In the right context common setbacks lend majesty to an architectural assemblage. Henry James intuited this when he wrote *The American Scene* in 1907, following a visit to America after having lived many years in London. He was especially taken with the appeal of the widely spaced white clapboard houses of Litchfield, Connecticut. James found them to possess a certain grandeur, quietly proclaiming to passersby, "we are good, yes—we are excellent; though we know it very well we make no vulgar noise about it. We just stand here in our long double line."[2]

Individualism and regard for community are equally important values to Americans, and we want both to be expressed simultaneously. This, in great measure, is the underlying appeal of the three churches on the Green in New Haven, Connecticut (Fig. 119). Two of the churches are similarly styled Federalist brick buildings with different steeples, and the third is a Gothic Revival structure built of stone. We know that the different styles and different steeples are products of our religious pluralism, but we also know intuitively that similar bulk, similar setbacks, and equal spacing between churches express a sense of common purpose that Americans believe transcends religious differences. It is also important to the composition that the Gothic Revival stone church is not located in the middle. Had it been, flanked by Federalist brick churches on either side, the stone building would have seemed to be the center piece and more important than its neighbors. This placement would have been more hierarchical—and far less satisfying.

Likewise, the appeal of three adjacent houses on Martha's Vineyard emanates from the same cultural values (Fig. 120).[3] Turrets, different roof pitches, and the slightly different architectural treatment of each house signify

119. Opposite: Three churches, New Haven Green; aerial view, 1976.

120. Three houses, Edgartown, Martha's Vineyard.

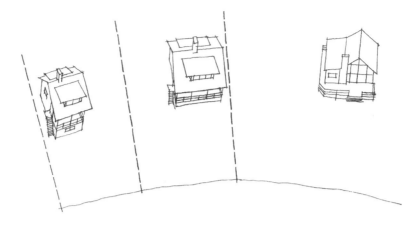

121. *Three houses, Lindbergh Lake, Montana. The two on the left are by Craig Whitaker Architects, 1991. The one on the right was preexisting.*

individuality, while the shingles, similar spacing, and common setbacks from the bluff connote equality and a common view of the world. As with the churches on the New Haven Green, had the turret on the near house been instead on the middle house, at the center of the composition, the grouping would have been more of a triptych, an A-B-A rhythm, and therefore less equal.

Equal setbacks and similar spacing between buildings seemed such important values that on a Montana lakefront my firm sited two small houses eccentrically with respect to their lots so they would be equidistant from each other and from an existing cabin next door (Fig. 121). The three houses together suggest the beginning of a community.

Common setbacks and equal spacing can sometimes offset even considerable differences in bulk, as evidenced by a stand of equally spaced houses on the bluffs of Nantucket (Fig. 122). This particular grouping would have been more satisfying had all three houses been of comparable size. Nonetheless, the equal spacing between dwellings ameliorates the dissonance of a one-story house next to two taller ones.

In this vein, roughly equal spacing between buildings, together with front doors that are the same distance from a common road, would dramatically improve the quality of many of America's new, and seemingly ubiquitous, office parks. Garreau wrote about buildings of nearly identical size, surrounded by asphalt parking lots, that these developments often comprise. The number of parking spaces for any given building is related to that building's square footage. Developers seek to avoid the expense of garages, so a building's size is dictated by the amount of surface parking the site will provide. Yet, even without garages, the office buildings cover a greater percentage of the lot than do houses in many American residential suburbs.[4] But unlike the underlying order in these suburbs, the office complexes often appear extraordinarily chaotic. The buildings, frequently strewn about at the whim of their designers, exhibit little sense of anything beyond sprawl and visual discord. This in turn suggests that sprawl is really a result not of lower density or of the automobile per se, but of the lack of an organizing idea that would bespeak community.

122. *Left: Three houses, Nantucket.*

123. *Below: Houses, Duke of Gloucester Street, Williamsburg, Virginia.*

Creating a sense of community was clearly in Francis Nicholson's mind when he crafted the legislation creating Williamsburg, Virginia, in 1699. He explicitly decreed that houses were to "front alike" on Duke of Gloucester Street, with each building to be set back six feet from the street.[5] Actually, the homes in Williamsburg are not aligned perfectly, but vary by as much as several feet with respect to the road (Fig. 123). This small diversity actually heightens the sense of community. A narrow range of setbacks, rather than one single line, suggests that the owners of these freestanding houses have voluntarily made a similar choice. Slightly differing setbacks show that free men can still arrive at a common decision without being forced by some superior authority to toe a common line.

Although there is much to be admired in John D. Rockefeller Jr.'s restoration of Williamsburg begun in 1926, the buildings that constitute a new shopping area at the west end of Duke of Gloucester Street do not align with the street, but are randomly recessed, suggesting a genteel suburban mall rather than a colonial town.[6] Elbert Peets thought the setbacks "a preposterous travesty on

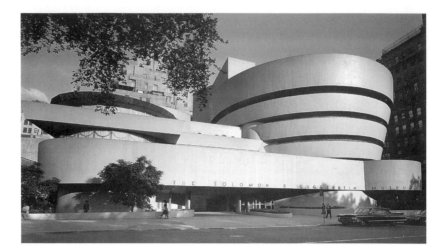

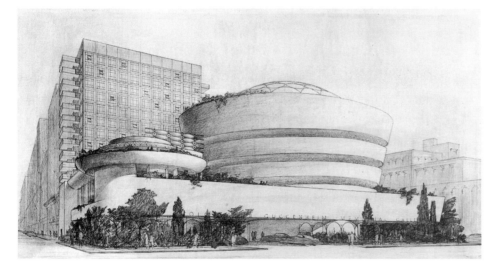

124. *Top: Guggenheim Museum, New York City, Frank Lloyd Wright, 1959; view from Fifth Avenue looking southeast.*

125. *Above: Guggenheim Museum; perspective study, 1943.*

126. *Right: Guggenheim Museum; perspective study, 1944, view looking northeast.*

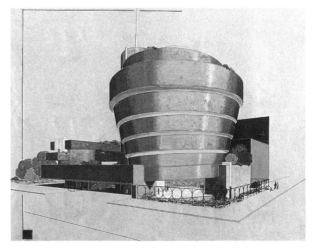

eighteenth-century planning. There is no design value in these weak deviations from alignment, merely an affectation of unmechanicalness which, since we know it is not modern, we are intended to assume it is colonial. Emphatically it is not."[7]

Buildings that are aligned along the street not only seem equal, they also subordinate themselves to the road. By being equidistant from the street and from each other, the buildings pay deference to those who are moving back and forth in front of them. In New York, as in many American cities, setbacks are less of an issue because most buildings press directly against the sidewalk. This is particularly so for most larger buildings lining Manhattan's major avenues. Few of these structures have spaces between them; most share party walls and are built to the property line. Consequently, it is the solidity of the blocks themselves, rather than the setbacks and spacing between individual buildings, that creates a sense of common purpose. Thus we remember buildings that occupy an entire blockfront and are distinctive in form, but which simultaneously smooth our trip past their front door.

Frank Lloyd Wright's grandly idiosyncratic Guggenheim Museum in New York is illustrative (Fig. 124). The conventional view of Wright's masterpiece holds that he simply ignored the building's context, willfully disrupting the existing wall of buildings lining Fifth Avenue opposite Central Park. On the contrary, the evolution of the design over many years suggests that Wright was acutely aware of his surroundings.[8] So as not to interrupt the wall entirely, at one end of the block-long structure Wright squared the roof of the administration offices, which in an earlier version had been curved (Fig. 125). The roof creates a segue from the flat-faced adjoining buildings to the curves of the museum, much like a transition in jazz from the dominant theme to a riff. At the other end of the museum Wright recessed the corner of the building in one iteration (Fig. 126). The recess was later dropped in favor of a corner that aligned with the rest of the facade. In the final design a gigantic visitor's lounge protrudes from the corner. The lounge, not essential to the museum's operation, was later converted to a reading area. Nevertheless, the suspended shape does what it is supposed to do on the exterior of the museum—it returns our eye to the wall of buildings that follows, so we can continue the trip.

Likewise, Frank Gehry's office for the Chiat Day Mojo Advertising Agency on Main Street in Venice, California, might at first appear to be an outrageous jumble of unrelated shapes (Fig. 127). Yet the diverse elements are roughly the same height, and their bulk echoes the scale of the other buildings along the street. The binoculars in the center of the complex, by Claes Oldenburg and Coosje van Bruggen, are spaced equally between two flanking wings, giving the composition an internal rhythm of solids and voids. The convex side of the binoculars faces outward, forming a porte cochere that hides the ramp to a basement parking garage behind. The three parts, each in its own fashion, press amiably against the sidewalk, aligning together like three friends pushing up to the bar. We allow for their stylistic differences because by their alignment they suggest community.

Conversely, a series of buildings that are very much out of line with each other will seem chaotic. One building stepping in front of its neighbors often signals instability and impending change. A new addition tacked on to the front of a building, in a line of buildings, is solid evidence that the owner has stolen a march, and, unlike his neighbors, is probably selling merchandise to the passing crowd (Fig. 128). We employ front-yard setbacks precisely because they preclude one house from taking advantage by being closer to the road. The lure of the road is strong, however, and the resistance to it weak enough that the results are sometimes risible, as with a tiny freestanding barbershop pressed eagerly against the sidewalk in a residential neighborhood in San Luis Obispo, California (Fig. 129).

A homeowner who intrudes upon a front-yard setback with anything other than trees and bushes is frequently viewed unfavorably. For instance, a low ornate brick wall in front of a suburban house in Columbus, Ohio, is seen by some neighbors as an act of self-aggrandizement (Fig. 130). Even though the brick wall is thoughtfully scaled and designed, it interrupts the continuity established by the other front lawns and therefore calls into question the implied equality that similar setbacks connote.

The front lawn itself is an expression of community. As author Michael Pollan put it, "maintenance of the lawn becomes nothing less than civic obligation. The failure to maintain one's portion of the national lawn—for that is what

127. Chiat Day Mojo offices, Venice, California, Frank O. Gehry & Associates, 1985–1991.

128. Beauty parlor,
Crown Street, New
Haven, Connecticut.

129. Above:
Barbershop, San Luis
Obispo, California.

130. Left: Front-yard
garden wall, Columbus,
Ohio.

131. Flag officers' houses, Army War College, Washington, D.C., McKim, Mead and White, 1908.

it is—is in many communities punishable by a fine. Our lawns exist to unite us . . . and so across a continent of almost unimaginable geographic variety . . . we have rolled out a single emerald carpet of lawn."[9]

Thomas Jefferson, for all his talent, never grasped the symbolic equality and sense of community projected by buildings with similar setbacks. Many Americans find Philadelphia's eighteenth-century buildings all pressed against the sidewalk to have great character. Jefferson, however, said, "I doubt very much whether the obligation to build a house at a given distance from the street contributes to its beauty; it produces a disgusting monotony, all persons make this complaint against Philadelphia, the contrary practice varies the appearance, and is more convenient to the inhabitants."[10] Yet Jefferson's complaint about Philadelphia does underscore a dilemma. Equality may have strong cultural roots, but if everything is truly equal, then it is also enervatingly the same. Jefferson might not have complained about McKim, Mead and White's National War College in Washington, D.C., because similar setbacks and spacing between the officers' quarters express a sense of shared purpose appropriate to a military enclave (Fig. 131). The identical houses demonstrate, however, that the price of repetition is conformity, which is the enemy of individuality. This is a fine line indeed, because in the civilian world this aesthetic suggests the dull repetition of public housing or a company town, which Jefferson certainly would have found objectionable (Fig. 132).

The difficulty of suggesting equality without creating boredom has become much sharper since Jefferson's time. Large twentieth-century developments, such as the famous Levittown tracts of small houses, many times possess a numbing similarity. Built after the Second World War, these projects—on Long Island and in suburban Philadelphia—feature thousands of nearly identical homes. Aligned in long rows, the houses suggested that the residents, like those in many public housing projects, had lost their American right to choose (see Fig. 19). When the first Levittown opened, some critics thought the robotlike conformity of the dwellings was the apotheosis of suburban malaise, both culturally and architecturally. Even though the sociologist Herbert Gans subsequently demonstrated that the political views and societal values of Levittown residents were similar to those of most Americans, the architectural afterimage has remained.[11]

Detesting the uniformity of suburban developments like Levittown, many American architects have gone to the other extreme. In an effort to suggest diversity they have scattered buildings, creating riotous irregularities (see Fig. 59). In many projects, when the budget allows, architects have opted for an "easy diversity,"[12] not only making each building's facade quite different, but placing each building differently on its lot—all to hide their underlying similarities. This diversity tilts the delicate balance between individuality and conformity too far in the other direction. While wildly different setbacks may reinforce individuality, they do so by substituting chaos for the sense of community that comes from common setbacks.

Over time, the Levittowns have changed, and the relentless similarities have blurred. Many houses have acquired dormers and family rooms; some now sport different colors or different siding materials; and others have different arrangements of trees and bushes in front.[13] The lesson of these changes is that ownership and the concomitant right to display one's own taste to the world—if only eventually—more than compensate for the initial stigma of having a house identical to one's neighbors. Underneath the changes, most of the houses remain roughly the same, as does the spacing between them, but because their facades are different, the houses now bring the competing values of individuality and community more into balance.

Yet even as stylistic differences have emerged, the long unvarying rows of houses still leave the impression that one is not moving through a community, but passing what Venturi has called "infinite consistency."[14] Without variety, the open road stretches to the horizon, lined by identical buildings—a point somewhat in keeping with the one Jefferson made some two centuries earlier.

132. Company homes on Railroad Avenue, Occum, Connecticut; photograph 1940.

The fundamental way to ameliorate this sameness is by creating occasional breaks between groups of buildings. Whether they be parks, plazas, parking lots, or simply unbuilt greensward, these breaks relieve what Le Corbusier depicted as an endless line of American buildings strung out along the road (Fig. 133), and what to Henry James gave "the eternal impression of things all in a row and of a single thickness," of "the merciless law of thinness, making too much for transparency, for the effect of paucity, . . . resembling the attempt to play whist with an imperfect pack of cards."[15] In a culture of the open road these occasional holes, or breaks between buildings, are essential mitigation.

For many Americans these open areas have value not because they are places to go to, but simply because they exist. Precisely because so many Americans already have a park in their own back yard, or at least a suggestion of one, we tolerate, despite our egalitarian tendencies, Gramercy Park in New York (see Fig. 85) and Louisburg Square in Boston (Fig. 134), which are closed to the public. We can still look in as we go by. In the same vein, architectural historian Spiro Kostof noted the sign in front of the central park in Sausalito, California, that warns passersby: "This Park Is for Your Viewing Pleasure. Do Not Enter."[16]

By the end of the nineteenth century, even in Europe, many civic spaces had lost much of their original purpose as marketplaces and gathering spots. Camillo Sitte, writing at the time, continued passionately to promote plazas for modern cities, but he knew that "we cannot alter the fact that marketing has withdrawn more and more from the plazas . . . we cannot prevent the public fountains from being reduced to a merely ornamental role; the colorful, lively crowd stays away from them because modern plumbing carries the water much more conveniently directly into house and kitchen . . . the life of the common

133. Sketch, Le Corbusier, 1935: "The single house by the road is what Americans dream of, an endless line of houses is what they get."

134. *Louisburg Square, Boston.*

people has for centuries been steadily withdrawing from public squares, and especially so in recent times."[17]

In America plazas always had much less intrinsic reason for being, at least as a place to go. As we have seen, Americans were usually elsewhere—on their front porch, in the back yard, or on the road. Robert Venturi stated that "Americans feel uncomfortable sitting in a square: they would rather be working at the office or home with the family watching television."[18] Charles Moore wondered trenchantly, "where one would go in Los Angeles to have an effective revolution of the Latin American sort . . . if one took over some urban open space in Los Angeles, who would know?"[19]

Even though the plaza in front of Mies van der Rohe's Seagram Building in New York does get considerable use, one of the great pleasures the plaza offered when it first opened in 1958 could only be experienced by driving past it without stopping. As one traveled up Park Avenue, the nearly solid phalanx of buildings opened suddenly to reveal a tall tower sitting well back from the street on its own low podium. Then just as quickly the view closed again, prompting Vincent Scully to call the plaza a "hole in the wall."[20] At night during the Christmas season the plaza glowed. Small evergreen trees sat in the plaza's pools, their white lights dancing in the reflection. For some it was a place to sit, but for many the plaza's real value was simply that it was there.

The ambience of the Seagram Building plaza depended as much on the surrounding buildings as it did on the tower itself. The symmetry and strong frontality of Mies's building echoed the same characteristics in McKim, Mead and White's earlier Italianate Racquet and Tennis Club directly across the street (Fig. 135). Like the Seagram Building, the Racquet Club covers an entire block-front. The masonry-clad structure, opposite a bronze-and-glass tower, creates an architectural tension, suggesting as Reyner Banham put it, an Old World quality that "is quite un-American—the formal good manners" of two courtly gentlemen nodding hello.[21]

Largely unnoticed at the time, but equally important to the composition, were the walls of the nondescript masonry buildings framing the Seagram Building plaza on its other two sides. These buildings did not last long, however. The block directly to the north was soon cleared for a new office building, but no new construction on the site yet obstructed the view of the Seagram Building when the most famous photograph of the tower, taken by Ezra Stoller, started circulating in the architectural press (see Fig. 73). Ironically, just as a proscenium arch in the theater makes us believe in an invisible fourth wall between us and the stage, Stoller's photograph made us believe in a building on the cleared block where none existed. Soon thereafter a large glass curtain–walled tower was built on the site, its great bulk and similar architectural treatment diminishing the uniqueness of the Seagram Building next door. More importantly, the new building's stepped-back shape lessened the sense of enclosure around the plaza.

Several years later, changes in New York's Zoning Resolution began encouraging the construction of buildings like the Seagram Building in high-density neighborhoods throughout the city. This legislation provided the final coup de grâce to the Seagram "hole in the wall" when plans were filed for a tower and plaza on the block immediately south of the Seagram Building. By this time the Department of City Planning had begun to understand the damage being done in lining up plaza after plaza: no longer would plazas, like the one in front of the Seagram Building, stand in counterpoint to blocks filled to the sidewalk with buildings. Consequently, to re-create the wall of buildings about to be torn down, the Department requested that a five-story extension be added facing the Seagram plaza on the north side of the property. Although the gesture was well meaning, the five-story structure was not high enough to enclose the plaza, and the similar height and character of the newer tower made the Seagram Building no longer unique (Fig. 136).

Park Avenue's felicitous hole-in-the-wall is now gone. In its place is an amorphous sequence of three buildings set back at varying distances from the street. Ironically, the critical success of the Seagram Building, its instantaneous status as an architectural icon, sowed the seeds of its demise. In the present cacophony of Park Avenue, it is difficult to recall the majesty of the earlier composition. It is even difficult to remember why anyone once thought the Seagram Building so important.[22]

The lack of attention paid by architects and planners to the lesser actors—the other buildings around the Seagram Building plaza—belies Venturi, Scott Brown, and Izenour's argument that most Modern theorists and architects have seen space and its creation as "sacred," and as the "essential ingredient" separating architecture from other art forms.[23] Their observations may apply to building interiors, but exterior rooms, like the Seagram Building plaza, have all too often been ravaged by Modern architects.

New York's Paley Park is another notable hole-in-the-wall. This small park is also worth just as much to passersby as to people who stop. The park's focus is an incongruity—a waterfall where none could possibly exist (see Fig. 57). The delight in discovering this cascade depended as much on the configuration of the

135. Above: Racquet and Tennis Club, New York City, McKim, Mead and White, 1917; view from Fifty-second Street, looking past the Seagram Building.

136. Right: Seagram Building, photograph ca. 1978. Note the five-story wing wall on the adjacent building and the ambiguous relationship of the two towers.

137. Fifty-third Street, New York City, looking north. Paley Park is at the left.

other buildings along the street as it did on the design of the park itself. For people walking along Fifty-third Street between Fifth and Madison Avenues, a tiny grotto opened unexpectedly, then disappeared just as quickly. One caught only a glimpse of a waterfall between the flanking buildings.

As with the Seagram plaza, however, the subsequent destruction of the frame around Paley Park revealed how much the park's pleasures depended on its context. Within a few years of its completion most of the buildings east of Paley Park were razed to make way for an office tower. This newer building, with its truncated shape, sits back from Fifty-third Street in a plaza of sorts, which extends to within two doors of Paley Park. Although Paley Park remains untouched—from within it looks as it always has—the surrounding streetscape has a profoundly different character. The setback of the tower weakens the sense of enclosure around the park, and the new plaza, which has its own waterfall, destroys the uniqueness of Paley Park's cascade two doors away. The little buildings between the two waterfalls look like forlorn and forgotten props left over from an earlier production (Fig. 137).

That Paley Park's appeal has been lessened raises the largely unexplored issue of desecration by imputation—damaging a composition without actually touching it. In the past quarter century we have learned to value our historic buildings and to save many of them, but we have not had any sustained success in preserving the context surrounding this architecture. Hundreds of important American buildings survive, encircled, like Independence Hall in Philadelphia (Fig. 138), by environments their creators could never have imagined. We have learned to save the foreground, but not the rest of the picture.

We have also wreaked havoc on the context by indulging our desire to repeat the prototype. Both Paley Park and the Seagram Building were critically acclaimed, and therefore copied. In retrospect we can see that each should have been treated as a grand exception, because exceptions have value only so long as they remain unique. When the Seagram Building opened, there was considerable debate over whether it was proper to celebrate a company that sold whiskey.

Now it seems clear that the debate more properly should have focused on how, in a democratic culture, to restrain surrounding merchants from similarly celebrating themselves.

This debate raises the issue of "spot zoning." America's zoning laws treat all property within a given district equally. Each owner has the same rights as his neighbors. A church or museum may seem unique because it is not surrounded by other churches or museums, but it could be. To save a composition like the Seagram Building—one office building surrounded by other office buildings—we would first need to find some compromise in our zoning laws between equality and uniqueness.

Central Park functions as a unique and gigantic hole in the middle of Manhattan Island. Although the park is heavily used, it too sustains many more people simply by its presence (see Fig. 64). Its complexity is contained within a simple rectangular shape, the consequence of Frederick Law Olmsted's decision to insert the park into an already platted street grid instead of reshaping the abutting streets to fit a preconceived design. Central Park's rectangular shape contributes to its greatness because of the easily understood tension between it and the surrounding wall of buildings. The park's full majesty, like the former glory of the Seagram Building plaza, is comprehensible largely because of its perimeter—we know the hole only because of the wall around it. Olmsted could not have imagined the tall buildings that now border Central Park, yet their presence makes the park grander not only from within but also as we travel around its perimeter. Another measure of Olmsted's genius lies in the transverse roads he designed to cross the park at approximately ten-block intervals. Without these connections, the two sides of Manhattan would have been cut off from each

138. Independence Hall, Philadelphia, Andrew Hamilton, Edmund Wooley, 1732–1748; aerial view. The greensward surrounding the building was first proposed in 1937.

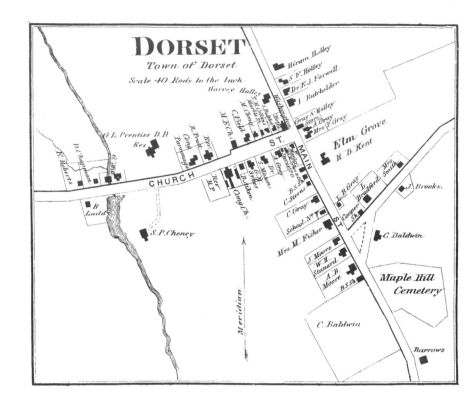

*139. Right: Map of
Dorset Green, Dorset,
Vermont; Beers Atlas,
1869.*

*140. Below: Dorset
Green; view toward
houses opposite the
green on the far side of
the state highway.*

other for more than two and a half miles. However, had these roads not been depressed one full level below grade, they would have cut the park into separate areas, at great cost to our perception of it as one large single room.

While Central Park, the Seagram Building plaza, and Paley Park are holes carved out of the most densely built city in America, more typically holes, or exterior rooms, are formed by groups of freestanding buildings like those bordering many colonial New England town greens. One such example is the New Haven Green, discussed earlier in this chapter. The three churches in the middle of the green are made more special by the surrounding buildings (see Fig. 119). Vincent Scully wrote that bordering the green "each house stood free on its own plot of ground, defining the central room as ships moored around it, not as a wall."[24]

The New Haven Green is a great square, but its shape is less important than the scale and character of the buildings facing it. This is true of most outdoor rooms, as evidenced by the tiny green in the town of Dorset, Vermont. Dorset derives much of its charm from a somewhat eccentrically shaped hole at its center. Rather than outlining a square, the buildings describe a long, narrow rectangle (Fig. 139). Bordering the rectangle is the town's principal street, which splits into two separate roadways leaving a long, grassy, lozenge-shaped strip in the middle. This median strip, called the Dorset Green, is flanked on three sides by white-painted, dark-shuttered clapboard frame buildings housing a general store, residences, and a small inn. The citizens of Dorset regard the elongated patch of greensward as the heart of town, although in reality it is little more than a traffic divider. The median strip does not stop traffic or even divert it greatly, although motorists do slow down when they pass. The tight grouping of the buildings, their close proximity to the street, and a T-intersection with a state highway at one end of the green cause this deceleration, but because drivers pass the green at a slow speed, they mark this patch of grass as the center of town.

From the perspective of motorists passing through Dorset on the state highway, the hole made by the green takes on a different character. As one enters town, the spacing of the houses along one side of the highway becomes tighter (Fig. 140). Suddenly, on the *opposite* side of the road, the narrow aperture of the green opens to view, then just as quickly is gone. Even when passing through Dorset without stopping, we get a quick glimpse of the town, and we experience a sense of place and motion simultaneously.

Author/architect Witold Rybczynski shows that starting with a village green, and the important buildings grouped around it, the spaces between buildings and the distance these buildings sit from the road create a subtle order in American Colonial towns that tells us which buildings are most important. He cites Woodstock, Vermont, as an example of how this order creates a "design that proceeds not from a predetermined master plan, but from the process of building itself . . . with individual builders adapting as they come along."[25]

Sometimes a single break between buildings gives focus and character to an entire street. A large Italianate house, for example, set well back from the road between two smaller houses, performs this function nobly on a Martha's

Vineyard street. The large residence acts as counterpoint, reinforcing the sense of common purpose shown by the other mostly Greek Revival houses aligned closer to the street (Fig. 141). The setback is convincing because both house and yard are bigger than others along the street. As if in quiet agreement, the two houses flanking the setback sit slightly closer to the street than their neighbors, heightening the sense of release the setback provides.

By its grandeur this large house has earned the right to step back. It exhibits, as James would put it, "an unmistakable manner, the quiet assurance of a position in the world."[26] (This presence, in part, is why the house was once the subject of a *New Yorker* magazine cover, even though in the illustration the house has been shorn of its context.) Had the house not been much bigger than its neighbors, however, the setback would have been irritating, highlighting the conundrum frequently posed by populist politicians like William Jennings Bryan and Huey Long, who were fond of reminding voters that America is a land where "every man is king, but no man wears a crown."

It is the resolution of the conflict between two mutually exclusive cultural values—of trying to be better while remaining equal—that dictates our positive reaction to some holes and our negative response to others. For example, on an otherwise typical suburban street in Bethesda, Maryland, a single house fronted by a large semicircular drive is set farther back from the road than its neighbors (Fig. 142). The lot, unlike the one on Martha's Vineyard, is approximately the same square footage as the neighbors', and although this house has only a single story, it is roughly the same square footage as those abutting it. Because its

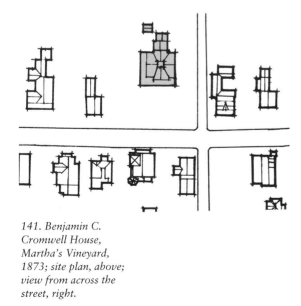

141. *Benjamin C. Cromwell House, Martha's Vineyard, 1873; site plan, above; view from across the street, right.*

neighbors are its equal, the recessed house appears to be trying to wear the crown, and that annoys passersby. One neighbor called it "uppity."[27]

The negative critical reaction to Lincoln Center in New York City when it opened in 1966 is somewhat analogous to the neighbor's response to the recessed house in Bethesda. The focus of Lincoln Center is a plaza bordered on three sides by three very similar freestanding buildings (Fig. 143). The middle building, the Metropolitan Opera House, sited at the rear of the plaza, is only slightly taller and little different in bulk and shape from the New York State Theater on the south side and Avery Fisher Hall on the north. The fountain in the center of the plaza, surrounded by the bland classicized arcaded facades of the buildings, is not big enough to dominate the composition. The Metropolitan Opera was designed by Wallace K. Harrison, the New York State Theater by Philip Johnson, and Avery Fisher Hall by Max Abramovitz. After considerable disagreement as to which structure should dominate the composition, the three architects arrived at a quintessentially American solution: agreeing only that each building would have twenty-foot spacing between the columns and be clad in travertine, they decided to go their separate ways, each working independently on his own building.[28] Because the buildings at Lincoln Center are so similar we question their arrangement. The middle building steps back portentously, yet it provides no climax to validate the hole, no waterfall or grand Italianate house, no Palazzo del Senatore, as at the back of Michelangelo's Campidoglio in Rome (Fig. 144). Lincoln Center seems very American because its parts are nearly equal, but it is and less successful because this lack of hierarchy brings the appropriateness of the setback into question.

142. *House set back from the street on the left, Bethesda, Maryland.*

143. Above: Lincoln
Center, New York
City, 1962–1968.

144. Right:
Campidoglio, Rome.

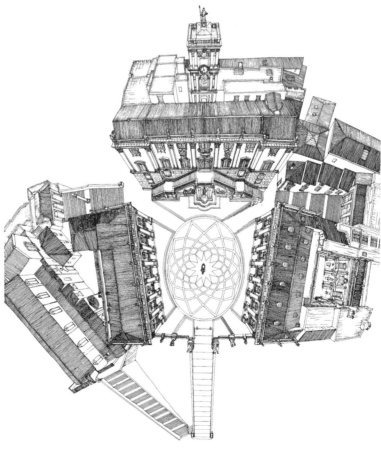

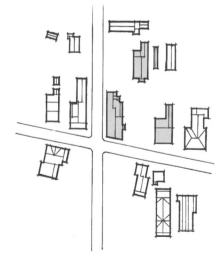

145. *Above: Three houses, Edgartown, Martha's Vineyard. The plan, above left; view from street, right.*

146. *Left: Middle house, Edgartown; view from street.*

Charles Moore, Gerald Allen, and Donlyn Lyndon wrote approvingly of a hole in the streetscape of Edgartown on Martha's Vineyard, which, ironically, succeeds for passersby despite being composed of three nearly equal parts. The hole is a space between two houses, both of which front an important street facing the harbor (Fig. 145).[29] Between them is a third dwelling set well back from the other two. Moved to the rear of the lot by a former owner, this relocated house is roughly the same size as its neighbors, but its setback does not seem to be an attempt at self-aggrandizement. The owner's idiosyncratic decision to eliminate his back yard left his house so far from the street that we have difficulty viewing all three dwellings simultaneously (Fig. 146).

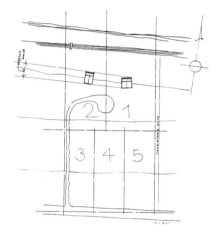

147. Wislocki and Trubek houses, Nantucket, Venturi and Rauch, 1971; view from road, above; site plan, right.

This is not the case for three nearly similar small houses on Nantucket. Venturi and Rauch designed the first two houses in 1971 (Fig. 147). Although they are stylistically similar, these houses are clearly different. Rather than being sited parallel to the shore, the two stand at a slight angle to each other, suggesting that their separate owners, though they have much in common, do not entirely agree on the best view. Since their completion, a third house in a similar style by another architect has been constructed behind and to one side of the first two (Fig. 148). Had this third house been differently styled, and had it been positioned directly facing the water behind the first two, the composition would have created a pleasing three-house "hole"—two houses closer to the water flanking a third one. As is, however, the tension of the earlier composition has been vitiated; the three houses together are more a competitive jumble than a community. The third house, because it is similar to the first two, should have lined up alongside them on the beach.

Likewise, Moore, Allen, and Lyndon discussed in some detail the relation-ship of two identical houses on Martha's Vineyard that were placed at different distances from the road (Fig. 149).[30] The vague disquiet they felt with this com-position is similar to one's reaction to the third house on Nantucket and to the middle building at Lincoln Center. The American mind-set is culturally condi-tioned to question why, when buildings are essentially the same, they do not line up. Since they were completed, the pair of houses on Martha's Vineyard have become less similar. An enclosed room under the porch of one house and different trim colors on the second house demonstrate the owners' desire to make the two seem different. Ironically, had one house not been closer to the road to begin with, the urge to obfuscate the original composition might have been lessened.

148. Third house, Nantucket; photograph 1993.

149. Two houses, Edgartown, Martha's Vineyard, photograph ca. 1973. Since then the trim on the left-hand house has been painted a darker color, and the right-hand house has acquired an enclosed room under the second-story balcony.

150. *The Royal Naval
Hospital, Greenwich,
England, Christopher
Wren, 1696–1716;
aerial view.*

151. *The Royal Naval
Hospital; view toward
the Thames.*

152. House, Atlantic City.

It matters less that a focal point at the back of a hole is bigger or smaller so long as it is a different size. We find the rhythm of two bigger buildings flanking a smaller one to be appropriate, as with Christopher Wren's Royal Naval Hospital on the river Thames (Fig. 150). To preserve the Queen Mother's view of the river from her smallish house, designed by Inigo Jones, Wren split the naval hospital into two separate L-shaped wings, creating a slot in the middle through which the Queen Mother could see the river. The Royal Naval Hospital appears frequently in American architectural treatises, in part, one suspects, because the Queen Mother's desire for an open vista is so consonant with our own values. Even large important buildings should not block our view; it should remain open and seemingly endless (Fig. 151).

Like the slot revealing the Queen Mother's house, what is at the back of a hole needs to be special, to have some intrinsic reason for calling attention to itself. Occasionally the shape or decoration on a tiny building performs this function, setting it apart from its neighbors. Sometimes large differences in size or scale will be all that are needed to make any small building interesting. A tiny house in Atlantic City set between two hotels, for example, tells us the story of an owner who was either a valiant holdout in a real estate assemblage or a poor negotiator (Fig. 152).

Breaks or holes between buildings invite us to stop if something is of interest, but they do not otherwise slow us down. For example, San Francisco's City Hall, by Bakewell and Brown, sits at the head of a broad forecourt (Fig. 153), the centerpiece of a composition that critic Henry Hope Reed called "the most important architectural ensemble in America."[31] From adjoining Franklin Street the forecourt unfolds as a grand hole-in-the-wall, yet City Hall seldom comes to mind when we conjure up images of San Francisco. The axiality of the composition and the staid neoclassical quality of the design seem out of character in a city better expressed by cable cars and fog-enshrouded views of the Golden Gate

153. Above: City Hall, San Francisco, Bakewell and Brown, 1912–1915, with the War Memorial Veterans Building at left and the War Memorial Opera House at right, Arthur Brown Jr., 1932. The center court was designed by Thomas Church.

154. Right: Noah Porter Gate, Yale University campus, New Haven. The walkway terminates at the colonnaded porch of the Commons, two blocks away.

Bridge. Unless we are headed for City Hall, we forget it after we have passed by it on Franklin Street, as is true for most holes we pass on the road.

Similarly, when one drives into downtown New Haven on Elm Street an impressively gated allée leading to the heart of the Yale campus opens on one side of the street. The allée culminates at an imposing neoclassical hall by Carrère and Hastings two blocks away (Fig. 154; also see the top left of Fig. 119). From inside the campus the composition seems stable and enduring, more Old World than New—a path leading to a goal.[32] When Elm Street and the solid wall of buildings on the other side of the street are included, however, the effect reverts to a more recognizably American grouping. For thousands of motorists who pass by every day, the gate poses a choice: they can enter Yale or, by figuratively leaning against the buildings opposite, keep on going. The allée does not force them onto the path—they can still choose to pass it by.

Until recently the principal gate onto the campus of Ohio State University in Columbus extended the same choice to passersby on adjoining High Street (Fig. 155). Composed of two pairs of pylons flanking a wide brick walk, the gate is one of many entrances onto the campus. This entrance has particular symbolic importance because it links a large open grass Oval, which is the center of the university, to High Street, the city's most important commercial thoroughfare (Fig. 156). Unfortunately, a new university art center by Eisenman/Trott Architects sprawls out onto the walkway, severing the symbolic connection and dissipating much of the gate's meaning as a break in the rhythm of the street (Fig. 157).

155. *Ohio State University, Columbus; aerial view, ca. 1960. Note the large grass Oval, which is the center of the university. Note also (at the bottom of the photograph) the entrance to the university from High Street.*

156. Top: Entrance gate to the Oval from High Street; photograph ca. 1950.

157. Above: Wexner Center, Eisenman/ Trott, Architects, 1983.

Instead of offering passersby a clear choice between stopping and continuing, a break in the streetscape can confuse by the inappropriateness of its location, as does the plaza directly across the street from the main entrance to I. M. Pei and Partners Jacob Javits Convention Center in New York City. The plaza offers passersby the choice of continuing or stopping—but in the wrong place. The entrance and the plaza opposite are the same size, and their architectural treatment clearly marks them as part of the same complex (Fig. 158). The center's front door presses forward to the street, pushing our eye to a hole on the other side of the street where nothing is happening—the reason we want to stop is inside the convention center itself.

Sometimes a hole-in-the-wall can be made more interesting simply by the presence of a freestanding building within it. Very ordinary buildings cast in the role of an event within a hole take on a special aura. Henry James noted his surprise at the simple appeal of the First Presbyterian Church on lower Fifth Avenue in Manhattan (Fig. 159), for example, calling it "one of those decent and dumb American churches which are so strangely possessed of the secret of minimizing, to the casual eye, the general pretension of churches."[33] Like many others of its

158. Jacob Javits
Convention Center,
New York City, I. M.
Pei and Partners,
1980–1986; front
facade, left; site plan,
below.

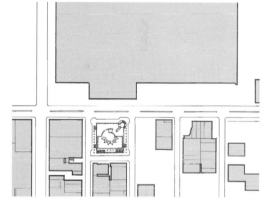

159. First Presbyterian
Church, New York
City, Joseph Wells,
1845.

160. *State House, Columbus, Ohio, Henry Walter, Alexander Jackson Davis, William Russell West, Nathan B. Kelly, and Isaiah Rogers, 1839–1861; aerial view, ca. 1950.*

size and style, this Gothic Revival church by Joseph Wells is not particularly memorable. The church grounds, however, which occupy an entire blockfront, are adjoined by taller buildings. The church itself, while not freestanding, is surrounded by lawn on three sides, becoming an event in the middle of a hole. The south transept, later designed by McKim, Mead and White, and a parish house by Edgar Tafel on the other side, make the church seem even more special. These additions, like the lower floors of the Seagram Building, hide the blank side walls of the row houses behind the church. The church, like the prototypical American house in the middle of its own lot, presides over its own separate domain.

The State Capitol in Columbus, Ohio, is also an event within a hole made by the wall of buildings surrounding the square. Henry Walters's edifice sits like a large somber jewel in the middle of Capitol Square, its neoclassical facade enhanced by the more ordinary buildings around it (Fig. 160). A similar cast of supporting buildings is the implied promise of Frank Gehry's Walt Disney Concert Hall in Los Angeles (Fig. 161). The model photographs do not show the building's context: the freestanding hall, set on its own block and surrounded by gardens, will be seen from one direction against a backdrop of office towers at the edge of the city's central business district and, from the other direction, against the less exuberant shapes of the Chandler Pavilion.

A border of simple buildings is essential to this structure's presence. If other equally interesting buildings start to surround the concert hall, the hall's distinctiveness will diminish. As we pass it on the road we will come to think of the concert hall as an enthusiastic eccentricity rather than an event in a hole or a jewel in the crown. Holes like this one remain unique features in the built environment only so long as they are different from their neighbors. In turn, a hole will remain different only so long as the neighbors surrounding it honor this distinction by lining up together around it.

161. Model of Walt Disney Concert Hall, Los Angeles, Frank Gehry, 1995.

Chapter 5

Gates and

We passed Port Roosevelt, where there was a glimpse of red-belted ocean going ships, and sped along a cobbled slum lined with the dark, undeserted saloons of the faded-gilt nineteen hundreds. Then the valley of ashes opened out on both sides of us.

F. Scott Fitzgerald
The Great Gatsby

Unintended Pauses

Paired objects abound in the American landscape. "Two" and "twin" are such often used words in our lexicon that we take their frequency for granted—more than forty places in America begin with these words. Two of anything connotes balance; one object may be the reciprocal of the other, but not the better. Two similar objects also connote equality, and in an American context this evokes a democratic ideal. Consequently, we can use this potent symbol in the built environment to mark and make more meaningful our journey.

Paired buildings exist everywhere in the country. A two-family house in Columbus, mirror-image beach houses on the New Jersey shore, and twin houses in Philadelphia are such common formulations that we take their symbolic equality for granted (Figs. 162, 163, 164). When Robert Venturi expressed interest in the ambiguous relationship of two wings of an apartment house in Rome—"are they one building split or two buildings joined?"[1]—his choice of examples reflected as much an American interest in the tension between two equal parts as it did the actual architecture of the building (Fig. 165).

Venturi has called for a greater expression of "dualities,"[2] meaning for him two more or less equal parts woven into a larger, more complex whole. Yet often the larger whole is simply two of anything. If two signals unity and equality, no larger construct is needed, as Venturi and Rauch themselves showed in their entry to the Brighton Beach Housing Competition (Fig. 166) and in their

133

162. *Top left: Two-family house, Columbus, Ohio.*

163. *Top right: Twin beach houses, New Jersey shore.*

164. *Above left: Twin houses, Philadelphia.*

165. *Above right: Apartments, Via Parioli, Rome, Luigi Moretti, ca. 1960.*

two houses on Nantucket (see Fig. 147). These architects have not been alone in elevating a two-building composition to high art, as Mies van der Rohe's Lake Shore Apartments in Chicago, or Philip Johnson's Pennzoil Plaza in Houston, Texas, attest (Figs. 167, 168).

On occasion, however, paired buildings project a mixed message. The World Trade Center in New York City is one example (Fig. 169). Here the American desire to be the best conflicts directly with the desire for equality. Aspiring to be the world's tallest buildings, the twin towers end in a dead tie. By contrast, Oscar Niemeyer's two towers for the senate and assembly staff at Brasília express a different symbolism. Unlike an American formulation of sepa-

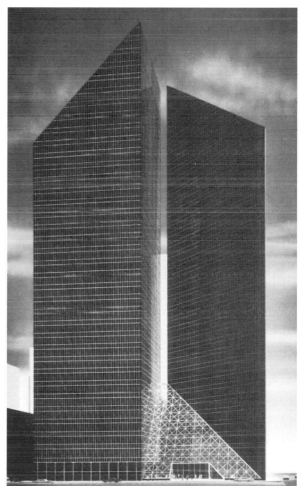

166. Top: Model of Brighton Beach
Housing, Venturi and Rauch, 1968.

167. Above: Lake Shore Drive
Apartments, Chicago, Mies van der
Rohe, 1951.

168. Right: Model of Pennzoil
Place, Houston, Philip Johnson,
1974.

169. *Right: World Trade Center, New York City, Minoru Yamasaki and Associates, Emery Roth and Sons, 1970–1977.*

170. *Below: Assembly Chamber and Senate House, Brasília, Oscar Niemeyer, 1956–1960. The towers rise above a broad plaza on the roof of the senate and house chambers.*

rate but equal, these towers, connected by aerial bridges, express both the separate identity and the mutual interdependence of the Brazilian government's two legislative branches (Fig. 170).

Two American flags together diminish the iconic power of each banner while, ironically, heightening the interest in the overall composition, as in Jasper Johns's *Flags I* (Fig. 171). We are drawn to the relationship between the two, as with Diane Arbus's photograph of twins, a picture which suggests stories across time and space that we can only imagine (Fig. 172). Two separate objects in the landscape create a similar tension that celebrates less the objects than the space between them. When this void between objects contains a path, it in turn brings attention to the persons on the path. If this focus occurs at an appropriate point in the journey the objects become milestones—reasons to pause and reflect, however briefly. This is true at the Grove Street Cemetery in New Haven. The pair of Egyptian columns at the entrance designed by Henry Austin mark the boundary between life and death (Fig. 173).

171. Above left: Flags I, *Jasper Johns, 1973 screenprint; published by Jasper Johns and Simca Print Artists, Inc., © 1996 Jasper Johns. Licensed by VAGA, New York, NY.*

172. Above: Identical Twins, Roselle, New Jersey; *photograph by Diane Arbus, 1967.*

173. Grove Street Cemetery, New Haven, Henry Austin, 1848.

174. *Above: Delaware Bay Memorial Bridge, 1969.*

175. *Right: Thaddeus Kosciusko Bridge, New York State Thruway.*

Two identical suspension bridges over the Chesapeake Bay show the considerable power of similar objects to elicit a moment of reflection, even though we pass over the spans, not between them (Fig. 174). The bridges create a simultaneous sense of past and future. Traveling high above the water in one direction, we share knowledge with those on the opposite span that each of us has seen things as yet unseen by the other. After the first span was completed, a large illuminated wreath was hoisted to the top of the bridge every Christmas. When the second span opened, the wreath was retired, ostensibly for safety reasons. In reality, the Delaware River and Bay Authority had correctly concluded that a wreath on each bridge would be symbolically confusing.[3] To a lesser extent, a pair of matched bridges on the New York State Thruway performs a similar function as the Delaware Memorial Bridge, offering passing motorists a concomitant sense of separation and connection (Fig. 175).

When we pass between paired buildings or objects in America , rather than over them, the pause or moment of reflection they engender is pitted against an equally strong desire for swift and uninterrupted progress. An extended pairing of trees or columns frequently seems static and stifling in an American context, as does the tight spacing of the columns and structural bays of a typical nave church. In the twelfth-century church of Sainte-Madeleine in Vézelay, France, for example, the architecture faithfully mirrors the rhythm of the medieval community that built the edifice (Fig. 176). As a religious procession moved up the hill

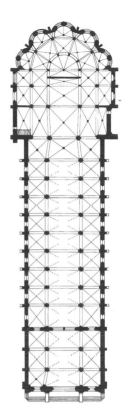

through town, each step forward was linked to the preceding pause. The cadence of the celebrants—a step, a pause, then another step—gave equal weight to moving and stopping. Inside the church the muffled steps and monodic chanting resonated against the paired columns, echoing a solemn celebration as old as Christianity (Fig. 177). The church was actually lengthened at one point in time, presumably to attenuate the drama of the procession.

In an American culture of speed and freedom, this rhythm seems slow and alien. The twentieth century, in particular, with its jazz, pinball machines, and video games, has its own very different beat. We reserve the slower cadence now for few events beyond policemen's funerals, the bride's entrance to a formal church wedding, and the changing of the guard at Arlington National Cemetery.

One might expect to find paired columns more often in American churches because of the slower, more reverent procession they connote, but even in church the columns must compete with other expressions of American spirituality. Of the two dominant traditions in Western ecclesiastical architecture—the church as

176. Above left: Vézelay, France; aerial view.

177. Above: Sainte-Madeleine Church, Vézelay, 1096–1131; plan. Note the three-bay elongation of the nave.

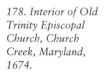

178. *Interior of Old Trinity Episcopal Church, Church Creek, Maryland, 1674.*

179. *Above: Interior of First Unitarian Church, Madison, Wisconsin, Frank Lloyd Wright, 1949–1951.*

180. *Right: Interior of First Unitarian Church, Rochester, New York, Louis I. Kahn, 1963–1964.*

181. Santa Maria di Montesanto and Santa Maria dei Miracoli, Piazza del Popolo, Rome, Carlos Rainaldi, 1662–1667, finished by Carlo Fontane and Lorenzo Bernini.

a path to the altar of God, and the church as a room where the faithful gather in the presence of God—Americans often choose the latter. In this variant the body of the church, the room in which the service is held, is more important than the procession. The interior columns of the Rocky Hill Meetinghouse in Amesbury, Massachusetts, for example, push away from the aisle to engage the second-floor balcony on three sides, emphasizing more the room than the altar or the aisle leading to it. In a similar fashion Old Trinity Episcopal Church in Church Creek, Maryland, features a meeting room void of interior columns altogether (Fig. 178). With no columns to lead us to the altar, the room itself becomes the focus.

An explicit path leading to God symbolizes submission. For at least some Americans, this architectural expression of submission to the Deity echoes the acquiescence demanded by a British king. Although a dominant center aisle tightly flanked by columns remains the organizing element in many Roman Catholic and Anglican nave churches, it is less common among other denominations. Quaker celebrants face one another, for example, and Mormons often treat the body of the tabernacle as a large assembly hall. Among this century's more famous examples of Jewish and Protestant ecclesiastical architecture that treat the church as a room rather than a path to God are Frank Lloyd Wright's Elkins Park Synagogue in suburban Philadelphia and his Unitarian Church in Madison, Wisconsin (Fig. 179). Both houses of worship feature a self-supporting roof with no interior columns. Wright was fond of likening the form of the Unitarian Church to two hands pressed together in prayer, sheltering the congregation.[4] Again, Louis Kahn's First Unitarian Church in Rochester, New York, has a nondirectional, square meeting room (Fig. 180). The large columnar structure supporting the clerestory roof rises from behind four concrete-block screen walls, which define the room. The center is completely open.

Because paired columns or paired objects enforce a measured pace, the deliberate and purposeful pauses they suggest conflict with our penchant for unimpeded mobility unless they mark a transition from one circumstance to another. This is the case with the twin churches by Rainaldi and Bernini on the Piazza del Popolo in Rome (Fig. 181), which have resonance for many American architects. The churches suggest a moment of hesitation—a gate or portal through which we must pass before we continue on to the Holy See. Yet the gate is permanently open, which is also important in an American context; it does not constitute a real barrier to block our progress.

Because the churches are nearly identical, they confer importance on the street that lies between them. (Ironically, the shortest route to Saint Peter's and the Vatican is the Via di Ripetta, to one side of the churches.) Although the liturgical trip to the altar—the path to the goal that dominates most European ecclesiastical architecture—is manifest within each church, the redundancy of matching facades subordinates the buildings to the street. Each church may offer salvation, but when the offer is doubled, it becomes less important than the Via del Corso, running between them. The street is a goal in itself—the road to salvation. The churches are mileposts marking the last leg of a pilgrim's journey; they function much the way paired columns might act between two rooms in an American house (Fig. 182). The real barrier has been breached; we have already entered the front door, and are simply passing from one function to another within. So too in Rome we have already passed the city gates and are standing in the Piazza del Popolo. The churches are only a symbol: we cannot be stopped by them, and thus their effect seems more American than Italian Baroque.

In America identical elements purposefully placed on opposite sides of a public street to demarcate a transition are more rare because of our tradition of

182. Columns flanking the doors between parlor and dining room, Old Merchant's House, New York, attributed to Minard Lafever, 1832.

183. *Above: Lions flanking the front steps, Public Library, New York City.*

184. *Left: Horses, Arlington Memorial Bridge, models by Leo Friedlander, late 1920s. A second pair of horses (not shown) frames the Lincoln Memorial from the approach road to Rock Creek Park north of the bridge. The two pairs are connected by a great arc of stone steps leading down to the Potomac River. (Because the horses face the memorial, their backsides create an awkward arrangement for motorists entering Washington on the bridge.) Photograph by Paul D. Spreiregen.*

property rights. What is plausible in a theocracy, like twin churches, seems less so in a capitalistic democracy, if only because two owners on opposite sides of the street have little reason to look alike in a culture celebrating individualism. Additionally, landowners, if they can avoid it, will not develop a project dedicated to a single use on property severed by a public street. Thus, the symbolism of paired elements finds more frequent American expression in public icons like the lions guarding the steps of the New York Public Library (Fig. 183) or the horses marking the entrance into Washington, D.C., over the Arlington Memorial Bridge (Fig. 184).

Paired elements like these that mark a transition have considerable power because they remind us of our mobility, of how easy movement is in this culture. Unlike a medieval European city where heavy gates barred outside invaders, or where gates within a city segregated one group from another, American gates, particularly those on public roadways, are only symbolic. There are no walls

185. Above: Soldiers and Sailors Memorial Arch, Hartford, Connecticut, George Keller, 1885.

186. Right: Admiralty Arch, London, Austin Webb, 1910. The roadway through the arch extends from Buckingham Palace at the far end of Saint James's Park, beyond the photograph in the lower left, to Trafalgar Square, upper right.

adjoining the Soldiers and Sailors Memorial Arch, for example, on the grounds of the State Capitol in Hartford, Connecticut (Fig. 185). The memorial's only purpose is to remind people passing through the arch of those who have served their country. By contrast, London's Admiralty Arch, sitting athwart the road from Buckingham Palace to Trafalgar Square at one end of Saint James's Park, is both a marker and a subtle barrier (Fig. 186). The two side arches of the three-span structure are open to the public, but the middle arch was reserved for the king. In America such hierarchy would not long endure. "Open up that middle span," we would demand, "especially the middle span, and let everyone through."

The desire for unimpeded progress is why many Americans have different

187. Far left: Drive-Thru Tree, Leggett, California.

188. Left: Gateway Arch, Saint Louis, Eero Saarinen, 1967. The Old Courthouse, on axis with the arch, was the site of the Dred Scott trial.

reactions to the famous redwood tree in Drive-Thru Tree Park in Leggett, California (Fig. 187), and Eero Saarinen's towering Gateway Arch on the banks of the Mississippi River in Saint Louis (Fig. 188). The redwood tree clearly signals that not even nature can stop an American. The Gateway Arch, however, which signals the beginning of the West, bestrides an esplanade that ends abruptly at the Old Courthouse, two blocks from the river. Had the arch instead straddled interstate highway I-70, which crosses the river two blocks south of the monument, Americans would have instantly grasped the meaning of road and arch together. In its present location the arch at best transmits a muddied message.

189. *Above: Arc de Triomphe de l'Étoile, Paris, J. F. T. Chalgrin, 1806–1836.*

190. *Above right: Washington Arch, New York City, McKim, Mead and White, 1892.*

In appearance the Arc de Triomphe in Paris and the Memorial Arch in Washington Square by McKim, Mead and White, at the south end of Manhattan's Fifth Avenue, are nearly identical. In reality they perform very different symbolic functions. The Arc de Triomphe sits in a *rond-point* at the confluence of twelve streets (Fig. 189). This is a place where people really stop, a spot where French politicians hold ceremonies and place wreaths. The Memorial Arch in Washington Square, on the other hand, marks a transition only (Fig. 190). The arch is a pause between the end of an important street and the beginning of a park—people want to go through the arch, not to it. A carriageway once ran through the opening of the arch. In the 1950s, Robert Moses, in his capacity as New York City highways commissioner, sought to link Fifth Avenue to Lower Manhattan by demolishing the arch and extending Fifth Avenue through the park. The ill-conceived plan did not succeed. So strong was the appeal of the arch as something to pass through, however, that the first response of opponents to the proposal was not to stop the project but to narrow the roadway so that it would fit through the arch.[5]

Freestanding gates occasionally appear in American movies, as in the 1980 film *Days of Heaven,* where a solitary gate marks off the boundaries of an enormous wheat farm. There are no fences to keep us on the path or force us between the gateposts—a seemingly absurd proposition. Nevertheless, the gate is an entirely recognizable American symbol. It evokes both the claim to property on a new continent that is too large to fence, and a concomitant belief that in America one is free to cross any boundary or barrier and keep on going. Another free-

191. *Left: Entrance portal, Yellowstone Park, Montana.*

192. *Below: Gate, Ringwood Manor, New Jersey.*

standing gate appears in the 1992 movie *Thunderheart*. This gate marks the boundary of a sacred Indian burial ground, but because there are no walls around the cemetery, the dead remain joined to the living.

A large stone gate standing alone on the Montana prairie marks the northern entrance to Yellowstone Park. The gate stops nothing: grass bends to the wind as people and bison move freely back and forth across the invisible boundary (Fig. 191). Nevertheless, the purpose of the gate is immediately clear to all who know the size of Yellowstone Park. The large stone arch, rendered small in the open prairie, testifies to the grandeur of a great natural preserve, and to the even greater promise of the new continent that spawned it.

Similarly, the gates from the old New York Life Building, standing free in a new setting at Ringwood Manor, New Jersey, quite hauntingly call forth the American conviction that we can re-create ourselves simply by moving from one place on the earth's surface to another (Fig. 192). By passing through a gate, by crossing an arbitrary line, we can change who we are. Rather than signifying exclusion, the gate signifies opportunity and renewal.

The artists Christo and Jeanne-Claude's *Running Fence* in Sonoma and Marin Counties, California, was, while it stood, the reciprocal of this belief (Fig. 193). In 1976, after four years of effort, the Christos gained permission to erect twenty-four and a half miles of white nylon sail marching across the hills and over the horizon. The only breaks in the temporary eighteen-foot-high fence were for occasional roads that gave viewers access to the work of art.

Unlike the Great Wall of China, the Christos' fence was conceived of as

193. Running Fence, Sonoma and Marin Counties, California, Christo and Jeanne-Claude, 1972–1976.

only a momentary barrier, one which American cultural sensibilities would never permanently allow. The installation's great power came from the audacity of its premise—that one could cordon off vast open spaces in a country dedicated to the belief that its people could never be bounded. Not surprisingly, many Americans who saw the fence reacted simply by wanting to pass through it to the other side.

At one end the fence disappeared into a copse of trees; at the other, the Pacific Ocean provided a terminus. But visually the sea was not the real, or even symbolic, end of the project. As the fence marched into the surf the artists diminished the size of each successive panel, making the fence seem to slide beneath the waves—marking off the ocean floor all the way to China.

The Christos' earlier curtain spanning Rifle Gap in Colorado had a similar effect, creating a barrier where none should have existed (Fig. 194). A single two-lane road at the base of the curtain heightened the project's appeal by allowing motorists uninterrupted passage through a supposedly impermeable barrier.

Frank Lloyd Wright's Marin County Civic Center, tightly wedged between the California hills, also suggests an enormous barrier, but it too is pierced by openings. Giant arches at the base of the building, one of which serves as a porte cochere for the front entrance, allow vehicles free passage back and forth to a parking lot behind the courthouse (Fig. 195). The building, then, does not stop us; it simply makes us pause.

As a marker in the open landscape, the Yellowstone gate has great power

194. Above: Valley Curtain, *Rifle Gap, Colorado, Christo and Jeanne-Claude (1970–1972).*

195. Left: Marin County Civic Center, California, Frank Lloyd Wright, 1962.

to signify a change in circumstance. Yet, we could do better at delineating these often abstract transitions, like the borders between states. Most signs at the boundary are relatively small and nondescript. Hugging the side of the road, they give a state's name, the governor's name, sometimes the fines for speeding, and occasionally the state flower. The possibilities are greater. For example, the border between Kansas and Colorado cuts across the flat open land of the Great Plains. To the west, the Rocky Mountains will not appear on the horizon for several hours. If, in anticipation, Colorado were to mark its border with man-made Rocky Mountains rising out of the wheat fields, Americans would recognize these shapes as more than strange incongruities in an open landscape (Fig. 196). We would know that the ersatz mountains were a symbol of changed conditions ahead—they would be a gate marking the promise of real snowcapped mountains soon to come. (The designer's skill would, of course, be tested on the other side of the mountains by how he or she portrayed Kansas to motorists traveling in the opposite direction.)

In a similar vein, tunnels and rest stops once gave interest to the Pennsylvania Turnpike, marking a traveler's progress across the state. Often the rest stops came in pairs with rusticated stone gas stations and restaurants typically sitting directly opposite each other. The paired buildings provided modest milestones on the trip, offering an opportunity to pause for those who wanted to, and a benchmark on the journey for those who did not. Unfortunately, many of the rest stops are now gone, and recently much of the symbolism of the remaining stations has been obliterated by large canopies covering the gas pumps. The canopies do not sit opposite each other, diluting the sense of pause.

The Angola Travel Plaza's very different configuration on the New York State Thruway southwest of Buffalo also acts as a trip marker (Fig. 197). An enclosed bridge spans the highway connecting the facility's single restaurant in the median to parking lots on both sides of the road. Large windows on the bridge allow patrons to watch the traffic passing below. By contrast, rest stops on the Delaware and Maryland Turnpikes are far less dramatic. While these stops are also located in the median, they are set away from the road, accessible only from the high-speed left-hand lanes of the highway. Because the rest stops

196. Proposed markers at the border of Kansas and Colorado.

neither frame the highway nor span it, they are less memorable markers on the journey.

Newer highways have necessitated newer ways of attracting the motorist's attention. Since limited-access roads first appeared, highway rights-of-way in America have widened. Broader shoulders, more lanes, and generous recovery areas along the road have all pushed commercial signs and billboards farther from passing cars. Greater traffic and increased speeds have also reduced the time a motorist has to absorb each message. Consequently, vendors alongside the highway and at rest stops within the right-of-way have adjusted their marketing techniques by using bigger signs.

The Connecticut Turnpike, which has several paired rest stops like those on the Pennsylvania Turnpike, offers examples of this leap in scale. Although the single-story buildings in the rest stops occasionally sit directly across from one another, the advertising signs along the highway and the much larger canopies over the gas pumps do not. Rather than being paired, these tall placards are pushed some distance apart to attract motorists approaching from opposite directions.

In the alternative, smaller traffic-flow signs could be used to direct motorists into the rest stop, relieving the larger signs of this task and allowing them instead to stand in pairs. This would create a symbolic pause, a reminder of the real pause offered by the rest stop itself. The McDonald's Corporation, for example, currently has the food franchise on the Connecticut Turnpike. Pairs of golden arches on either side of the road would be especially apt symbols for hungry travelers. They would also better mark where we are on an interstate highway with few interesting features.

197. Angola Travel Plaza, New York State Thruway, southwest of Buffalo; view looking east.

198. Above: Beach Road, Vineyard Haven, Martha's Vineyard.

199. Above right: Turrets, New Milford, Connecticut.

If paired signs or paired buildings create valid pauses by signifying a transition from one condition to another; it matters not whether the pairing is intentional. For example, on Martha's Vineyard a complex of warehouse buildings tight to the road and paired with a high wall and gas storage tank on the opposite side mark the beginning of a commercial strip in the town of Vineyard Haven (Fig. 198). At the foot of a bridge leading onto the main street of New Milford, Connecticut, two Norman turrets with different bulk and height act as effective gates to the downtown area (Fig. 199). Their similar style and shape are clear indications that the two structures share a common purpose, but because the turrets are at different heights and slightly offset from one another, they retain an appropriately independent character.

Edward Hopper similarly implied a subtle pause at the edge of town in his watercolor *High Road* (Fig. 200). From a vantage point just off the pavement on the right-hand side of the composition, Hopper directs our eye to an open landscape, even though we might more properly be focused on the road, which is about to descend a steep hill. Hopper makes us believe there might be more buildings to the right just beyond the picture frame. This possibility allows us the briefest of pauses to look at the view. There would be no reason to slow down unless we thought we were about to enter a town, that is, if the buildings on the right-hand side of the road were really there.

Occasionally corner buildings on a New York City block act as subtle gates or pauses, delineating an informal boundary between neighborhoods. On many of Manhattan's residential blocks, for instance, the row houses in the middle of the block typically sit back from the street to show off their opulent front doors. By contrast, the taller corner buildings press against the sidewalk. Because these buildings are closer to the street they seem to narrow its width at either end of the block. Squeezing together they create a pause, a gate of sorts, which suggests a community—or at least implies that those residing in the middle of the block have a slightly different view of the world from those on the avenues. The demar-

200. High Road,
Edward Hopper, 1931.
Watercolor on paper,
20 x 28 in. (50.8 x
71.1 cm). Collection of
Whitney Museum of
American Art.
Josephine N. Hopper
Bequest. 70.1163.

201. First building in
from the corner,
Twelfth Street, New
York City. The stair
turret is shaped to
resolve the differing
setbacks of the corner
building to the left
and the side-street
building to the right.

202. Gap created by an alley behind an apartment building on Queens Boulevard, New York City.

cation is often heightened by the first building in from the corner, which by its idiosyncratic shape can accentuate the transition from a busy avenue to the side street (Fig. 201).

Paired holes, like paired buildings, can mark an appropriate pause. For example, behind Queens Boulevard in New York City spaces between the larger buildings lining the boulevard and smaller residences on the side streets often create a pause. Six- and seven-story apartment houses push up to the sidewalk on the boulevard, leaving a swath of back yards, parking spaces, and sometimes even alleys behind them. As one turns the corner these open areas mark a transition from the more heavily trafficked thoroughfare to the quieter side streets (Fig. 202). The same transition occurs between the shops on Main Street and the houses on the intersecting side streets of many small towns. Service areas behind the stores create an appropriate pause between a commercial district and an abutting residential neighborhood. The transition can be reinforced by the size of this gap between stores and residences, which is often bigger than the gaps between the houses themselves.

Valid pauses, composed of several buildings by different architects in different styles, sometimes emerge only over time, their creation depending on a shared sense of pattern and context. Unfortunately, during the past several decades the ability of many architects to think in these terms has diminished. A dramatic recent example of this narrowed focus occurred in 1980 when a group of Chicago architects organized a reprise of one of the most discussed and debated American architectural competitions of this century, the Chicago Tribune Tower Competition of 1922. The winning entry in the original competition, by Howells and Hood, was chosen from among submissions by such noted architects as Eliel Saarinen, Eric Mendelsohn, Adolf Loos, and Walter Gropius. In the reprise, architects were asked to submit their own theoretical projects for the site. The submissions were later mounted in an exhibit called *Late Entries to the Chicago Tribune Tower Competition.* As was noted in a catalog accompanying the exhibition, however, "not one entrant went beyond . . . to consider the Tribune Tower as urbanism."[6] No one focused on the totality of the Michigan Avenue streetscape. Contestants ignored the vacant lot next to the Tribune Tower where there was an opportunity to create a natural pause at the edge of the Chicago River (Fig. 203). A new building, at the end of the bridge and opposite the Wrigley Building, would have made such a gate, while leaving Howells and Hood's quite handsome office building alone.

Occasionally a gate may suggest a pause where none is warranted. Sometimes this pause is for private gain at the expense of community, as in Atlantic City where architects used a symbolic gate to great effect at the Taj Mahal casino. Many of the casinos in Atlantic City front the boardwalk. Strollers and jitneys trundle back and forth between the casinos on one side and the beach on the other. At each casino, broad, low entries beckon passersby inside to the gambling halls. The Taj Mahal sits near one end of this parade of casinos. From the boardwalk the first view of the Taj Mahal is actually of an

203. Michigan Avenue Bridge, Chicago; the Wrigley Building by Graham Anderson, Probst and White, 1919–1921, left; the Chicago Tribune Tower by Howells and Hood, 1925, right. Note the parking lot in the right foreground. Photograph, 1950.

204. Pedestrian bridge over the boardwalk, Taj Mahal casino, Atlantic City, New Jersey.

enclosed pedestrian bridge spanning the boardwalk from the casino to the beach—the only structure of its kind on the boardwalk (Fig. 204). From a distance the bridge looks like a gate, suggesting subliminally that beyond it the boardwalk's character will somehow change—from lavish casinos and their promise of riches to something presumably of less value. The doors to the Taj Mahal are directly under the bridge, heightening the architectural suggestion that one need not, and should not, go beyond this porte cochere. If a Taj Mahal competitor—say, the Resorts Casino next door—built its own bridge, the Taj Mahal would be screened from view by this second gate, one casino closer to the boardwalk's center. If then, in a rush of competitive investment, all casinos constructed their own bridges spanning the boardwalk, no casino would any longer hold a competitive architectural advantage.

Another example of an invalid pause is the one created when companion buildings are erected on either side of a public road with their front doors facing each other. This is uncommon in America, but when it does occur, the arrangement suggests a conflict. We do not want to impede our trip, but we must slow down in anticipation of whatever or whoever may be moving back and forth across the street between front doors.

A farmhouse and dairy barn sited directly opposite each other on a Vermont lane create such an adventitious ambiguity (Fig. 205). In this rural setting close proximity indicates common ownership; we slow as we approach, watching for children and stray animals while wondering whether there may be spilled milk on the pavement.

The Beaux-Arts apartments in Manhattan, a complex of two buildings bisected by East Forty-fourth Street, also suggests such severed use. The two buildings are nearly identical, indicating common ownership and therefore an implied link (Fig. 206). Unlike the other buildings on the street, both facades step

205. Farmhouse and barn, Vermont.

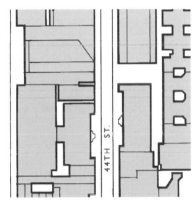

206. Beaux-Arts Apartments, New York City, Raymond Hood and Kenneth Murchison, 1931; site plan, left; view from Forty-fourth Street, below.

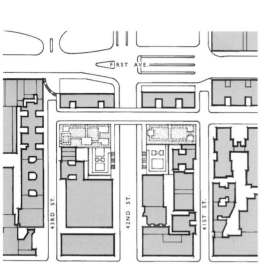

207. Tudor City, New York City, Fred F. French Company, 1928; site plan, above; view looking east, right.

back slightly from the sidewalk; a pair of American flags and identical canopies accentuate the buildings' affiliation. One can imagine a single tenants' group at these identically styled apartments faced with the problem of forever asking half their members to cross the street to attend the next meeting. Meanwhile out on the street we slow down, not wanting to hit the people crossing back and forth in the middle of the block. Large housing projects of identical buildings bisected by public streets often project the same mixed signals. In America if buildings are related and stylistically similar it does not seem appropriate for the public to pass easily between them unless the buildings mark a transition.

Tudor City, a large apartment complex of very similar buildings on both sides of East Forty-second Street in Manhattan, avoids this conundrum, which in great measure is why this complex has such appeal. Tudor City is grouped around two parks on either side of Forty-second Street. The two open areas are one level above grade, joined by a bridge spanning the street (Fig. 207). The bridge, for both vehicles and pedestrians, ties the two halves of the project together while simultaneously creating a gatelike transition at a fortuitously appropriate spot below on Forty-second Street—in front of the United Nations, which was built after Tudor City and lies beyond the end of the street on the other side of First Avenue.

If we have reached a destination, like the United Nations, we want to stop. When we cannot determine whether we have reached a goal or are still en route, however, the path becomes ambiguous. The Piazza Vittorio Veneto, a large rectangular piazza in Turin, which at one time was bisected in its longer dimension by trolley tracks, is a grand example of such unintended ambiguity (Fig. 208). Although the historian Paul Zucker considered the square "probably the most perfect classicistic square on Italian soil,"[7] an American can better imagine the plaza as the mise-en-scène for an Italian comedy. In the movie a large crowd would have gathered to hear speakers orating from a bandstand in the middle of the square. Meanwhile, a trolley car has inched forward through the crowd to within a handbreadth of the bandstand. Leaning from the window, the motorman screams at the speakers to get out of the way, and the speakers rage at the motorman to back the trolley up; everybody is yelling, nobody budges. The square sends conflicting messages, giving equal weight to moving and pausing. It thereby demonstrates the phenomenon of unintended ambiguity: the center has been usurped by a travel way, which says continue, but simultaneously the architecture around the square says stop and stay awhile.

In Manhattan the relationship of Stuyvesant Square Park to Second Avenue is equally ambiguous, implying a pause where none can exist. The park has no

208. Piazza Vittorio Veneto, Turin, Italy.

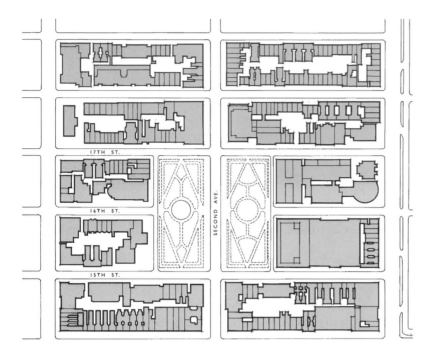

209. Above:
Stuyvesant Square
Park, New York City;
plan.

210. Right: The
Boston Common and
Public Gardens; aerial
view, ca. 1950. Note
Charles Street passing
between the two parks,
which are different
shapes. The Common
is on a hill; the Public
Garden in the fore-
ground is flat.

real center: it is not a single entity (Fig. 209). Second Avenue bisects it, creating two plots of identical size. Although the parks share the same name, each is a separate facility, suggesting that park users have ceded their place in the center to motorists, who cannot stop in traffic to enjoy being there. Either the park should be half as big, or somewhere else with a real center, or the avenue should be interrupted. By contrast, Bostonians use historic circumstance and different nomenclature to avoid the mixed message of an unintended pause on Charles Street as it passes between the two most important open spaces in the city. Although the greensward appears at first to be a single entity, each side has a different character and configuration. On one side of Charles Street is the Boston Common and on the other the Boston Public Gardens (Fig. 210).

The market square lying athwart Duke of Gloucester Street in the center of Williamsburg, Virginia, is unintentionally ambiguous because it too is bisected by a road. The earliest known map of Williamsburg, dating from 1782, more than three-quarters of a century after the town was founded, already shows a road running through the center.[8] The road and the square would both have been grass at that time, however, so the square would have been perceived as one large open space rather than two plots bisected by a street (Fig. 211). We do not know whether planner Francis Nicholson originally intended this configuration, but today the street is paved—which, of course, is historically inaccurate—clearly dividing the square into two separate areas. Because both plots are the same size, neither one dominates, and the street through the middle obviates the center. Williamsburg would benefit today if one square were turned to private lots or the two squares were combined into a single entity with traffic diverted around it.

The Metropolitan Museum creates an unintentional pause of a different

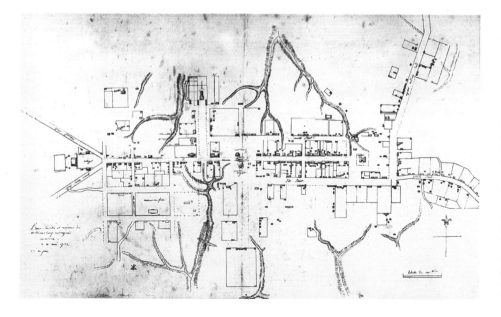

211. Williamsburg, Virginia; plan of 1782. Note the powder magazine and courthouse in the Market Square, slightly offset from each other. Note also the allée from the Governor's Palace ending at Duke of Gloucester Street. Today the houses terminating the view are gone and the allée extends to the woods beyond.

sort on Fifth Avenue. As essential as the museum is to New York City's cultural life, Central Park, bordering the building on three sides, is more important in the city's hierarchy of public places. As we drive along Fifth Avenue we want to take in the grand sweep of the park—we want to keep going. The museum, however, is sited near the street, squeezed against the buildings that line the other side of Fifth Avenue (Fig. 212). By slowing us down, by making us pause, and in effect cutting Central Park into two separate pieces, the museum draws undue attention to itself (see Fig. 64). The resulting pause is, by analogy, like that in

212. Metropolitan Museum, New York City.

213. Roadside billboards.

214. The Arsenal, Central Park, New York City, Martin E. Thompson, 1848; view from Fifth Avenue.

front of the single billboard on an open desert road facing many billboards across the way (Fig. 213). Both billboard and museum subordinate the surrounding open space, assuming greater prominence than they warrant. Frederick Law Olmsted had grave reservations about putting the Metropolitan Museum in the park in the first place. However, Calvert Vaux and Jacob Wrey Mould's original museum building was set much farther from the street, preserving the park's continuity along Fifth Avenue. Later additions by Richard Morris Hunt and McKim, Mead and White, however, have pushed the front door to Fifth Avenue.

By contrast, the effect on Central Park of the city's former Arsenal, some twenty blocks farther south, is very different. The building, which actually predates the park by several years, is small enough and set back far enough from Fifth Avenue to be nearly enveloped by trees (Fig. 214). We see both the Arsenal, resplendent in its verdant surroundings, and a continuous park on Fifth Avenue. Architecture critic Paul Goldberger regarded the Arsenal as "one of the few buildings that seems to have a right to be in Central Park."[9]

Other unintended pauses weaken the wall around Central Park as well. One example is the venerable Museum of Natural History, which sits opposite the park on Central Park West. Only the center portion and front steps of the museum press close to the sidewalk; the rest of the building is surrounded by greensward (Fig. 215). Consequently, the museum appears as an event in a hole-in-the-wall.

Unfortunately, the museum sits opposite the bigger hole of Central Park, creating a double hole, as it were. If, instead, the entire museum had been aligned close to the street, like the other buildings on Central Park West, with the bulk of its lawn placed behind the building, the arrangement would have generated a

215. Museum of Natural History, Central Park West, New York City; aerial view looking west.

216. Fifth Avenue;
view looking northeast
at Seventy-ninth
Street, right; site plan,
far right.

more satisfying complexity, even though the building remained freestanding, as befits its importance. The museum would still have have caught our attention, but simultaneously it would have continued to be part of the frame of buildings that define the park, rather than creating a pause or break where none was intended.

There are several other unintended pauses on the park's perimeter, one of the more gratuitous of which is at the corner of Fifth Avenue and Seventy-ninth Street. Both facades of a large apartment house step away from the intersection for no discernible architectural reason, weakening the corner and diminishing the sense of enclosure around the park (Fig. 216).

With its penchant for freestanding self-aggrandizing structures, Modern architecture has created many unintentional and ambiguous pauses. One Liberty Plaza, by Skidmore, Owings and Merrill, which replaced Ernest Flagg's elegant Singer Tower on Broadway in lower Manhattan, creates such a pause, one made more ironic because it detracts from another earlier building by the same architectural firm across the street. One Liberty Plaza, a large office tower together with a park in the next block, sits on one side of Broadway (Fig. 217). The park, which slopes downhill away from the street, was integral to the project because under the existing zoning laws additional open space was necessary for such a big building.

217. *Below: One Liberty Plaza, Broadway, New York City, Skidmore, Owings and Merrill, 1974; the building is to the right, adjacent to the park. The World Trade Center is in the background.*

218. *Above: Plaza in front of 140 Broadway, New York City, Skidmore, Owings and Merrill, 1967.*

219. *Left: Lower Broadway; site plan, 1995.*

Seven years before this fifty-four-story tower was built, Skidmore, Owings and Merrill designed another tower, originally known as the Marine Midland Building, located on its own plaza directly across the street from what would later become the park (Fig. 218). The building itself is an irregularly shaped slender black Modernist tower with a large red cube by Isamu Noguchi dominating the small plaza in front. Plaza and sculpture together created interest in what was at the time an unbroken wall of buildings on both sides of the street. As one traveled down Broadway, the cube, tilted up on one corner, seemed to rotate. The plaza, with the cube as an accent, created a perfectly framed hole-in-the-wall.

With the addition of One Liberty Plaza, however, Broadway now has an unintended pause created by the two holes opposite each other (Fig. 219). The pause does not mark a boundary or transition; there is no change in the street's character: north and south of the holes the street remains a commercial thoroughfare. The call for our attention by the park on one side of the street vitiates the focus of Noguchi's sculpture on the other. The park also pulls our eye downhill, away from Broadway toward the cacophony of the World Trade Center a block away.

Unintended pauses can detract from the best of streetscapes. One example is on Chapel Street, an important commercial artery in New Haven, bordering the Yale University campus. On the university side of the street four stylistically different buildings in a row—the Gothic Revival Street Hall, designed by Peter B. Wright; a neo-Romanesque art gallery by Egerton Swartwout; a Minimalist Modern addition to the gallery by Louis Kahn; and the Brutalist Modern Art and Architecture Building by Paul Rudolph—comprise one of the more exquisite architectural sequences in America (Fig. 220). The first two buildings, Street Hall and the art gallery, on opposite sides of High Street, are joined by an enclosed bridge over the street, which also functions as a symbolic gate to the university. Next to the gallery is Kahn's gallery addition, the linchpin of the composition. The front door–back door symbolism of Kahn's addition is particularly American. Kahn adorned the Chapel Street facade of what was otherwise a glass curtain-walled building with a decorative brick screen. Replete with string courses at every floor, the wall, like a colonial house with clapboards on the front only, is a traditional American front, proof that symbolic intent matters more than style. The newer addition and the older gallery are the same height and have setbacks of nearly identical size, an arrangement reminiscent of Frank Gehry's later composition of buildings in Venice, California (see Fig. 127).

In New Haven each building edges slightly closer to the street, squeezing our focus toward the corner of York and Chapel, creating a distortion in perspective much like the one Michelangelo created at the Campidoglio in Rome (see Fig. 144). The regular rhythm of solids and voids carries our eye past the buildings to a long low wall stretching to the intersection. Rudolph's ferociously expressionistic conclusion to the composition is on the far corner of York (see

220. Chapel Street, New Haven, Connecticut, 1964; elevation looking north, above; site plan, below (drawings by Paul Rudolph, 1962). Note in the plan the nearly solid wall of nondescript buildings on Chapel Street opposite the campus.

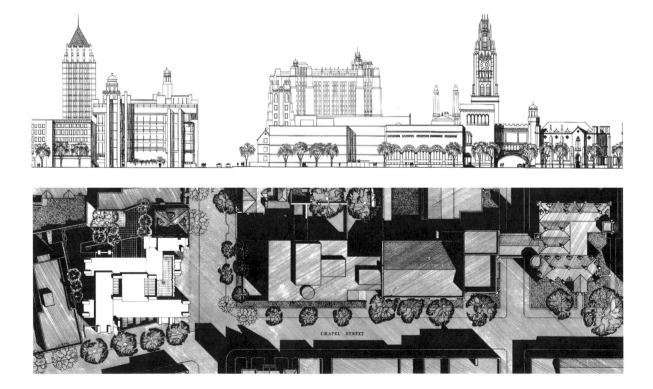

221. *Courtyard of the Center for British Art, 1974; view of the Art Gallery across the street.*

Fig. 65). Chapel Street bends slightly in front of Rudolph's building to suggest that the riff is over, that the sequence has come to an end, a sequence Vincent Scully called "a continuing dialogue between the generations . . . an environment developing across time."[10]

This entire ensemble also depended on a long line of silent partners on the far side of Chapel Street, a stand of anonymous buildings pressed to the sidewalk that provided a backdrop to the more sophisticated architectural play across the street. Most of these buildings were later demolished, however, when Yale selected Kahn to design a new Center for British Art. Kahn included a small sunken plaza along Chapel Street at the north side of the building as part of the center. Although the museum building itself abuts the sidewalk, the plaza makes a hole in the wall nearly directly across the street from the recessed front entrance to Kahn's earlier gallery addition (Fig. 221). The two holes together suggest a pause in the middle of the block. Although the pause is brief, it is disruptive; Kahn's second design unintentionally devalues his earlier composition.

Some pauses are massively inappropriate. Grand Army Plaza on Fifth Avenue, an esteemed New York City landmark designed by Olmsted and Vaux as part of Central Park, is an unwitting partner to one of the most egregiously unsuitable pauses in America. The plaza, at the southwest corner of Fifty-ninth Street, is actually an extension of the park, which ends across the street—a graceful reminder that the Fifth Avenue of mansions and expensive living is giving way to the Fifth Avenue of expensive stores (Fig. 222). Even as taller hotels and apartment buildings began to replace the mansions on Fifth Avenue the newer structures still extended to the sidewalk. The Savoy Plaza by McKim, Mead and

White, for example, which for four decades stood directly across the street from Grand Army Plaza, framed the plaza with a continuous two-story base that also tied together the separate wings of the building above (Fig. 223). In the opening scene of Elia Kazan's movie *Gentleman's Agreement,* Gregory Peck alights from a limousine against the backdrop of the plaza's fountain to enter the hotel. Seen from this vantage point, Grand Army Plaza behind Peck is still a hole in the wall and an elegant transition.

A year after the completion of the Savoy Plaza a new Bergdorf Goodman Building built out to the sidewalk filled the block immediately south of the plaza. The Bergdorf Goodman Building remains; however, the Savoy Plaza was torn down to make way for a new General Motors Building. The white marble-clad tower designed by Edward Durrell Stone with Emery Roth and Sons now occupies the entire block between Fifth and Madison Avenues (Fig. 224). The tower stands back from the sidewalk. Between the building and Fifth Avenue, Stone inserted a large sunken plaza like the one at Rockefeller Center—supposedly as a counterpoint to Grand Army Plaza directly across the street.

Before the General Motors Building was built, the transition at Fifty-ninth Street was obvious and smooth. Central Park was behind us, and Grand Army

222. Fifth Avenue looking south; photograph ca. 1923. Collection of the New-York Historical Society.

223. Savoy Plaza Hotel, east side of Fifth Avenue between 58th and 59th Streets, New York City, McKim, Mead and White, 1927; and the Bergdorf Goodman building, west side of Fifth Avenue between 57th and 58th Streets, Buchman and Kahn, 1928; view from Central Park looking southeast, 1931.

224. *Aerial view of the southeast corner of Central Park showing the General Motors Building, Edward Durell Stone and Emory Roth and Sons, 1968. Collection of The New-York Historical Society.*

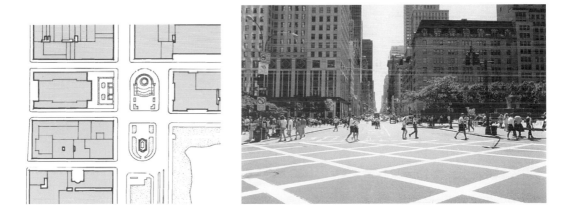

Plaza acted as a wedge, pushing us toward the shopping ahead. Now as we travel down Fifth Avenue, we are confronted by two plazas forming a large shapeless maw (Fig. 225). The holes do not mark the edge of Central Park—we have passed that boundary already. The pause on Fifth Avenue occurs one block too late and is without purpose. Just as valid pauses enhance the journey, so an unintended one, as at the General Motors Building, makes the trip more tedious. This two-hole mistake forcibly suggests the need to have the broader context in mind if we are to create pauses in the journey.

225. *Fifth Avenue at Fifty-ninth Street; site plan, above left; view looking south, above.*

Chapter **6**

What to put in the middle, . . . becomes a touchy issue.

SPIRO KOSTOF
The City Shaped

At the Crossroads

MARKING THE JOURNEY BY CELEBRATING THE SPECIAL PLACES ALONG THE WAY
gives meaning to the trip. However, this has always been a difficult chore in a
land devoted to unimpeded movement. The task is especially difficult at
America's open intersections.

We have used a simple crossroads as an organizing device throughout our
history. The first Puritan colony, built in Plymouth, Massachusetts, in 1621,
for example, was designed about a single intersection. That original settlement
has long since been buried under the present-day town; however, a reconstruction of the village is open to tourists nearby. Records on which the reconstruction is based show "that the elements used . . . were few in number and
elementary in nature."[1] In reality the plan was little more than the crossing of
two dirt paths. Miles Standish and his fellow settlers marked off lots and built
their homes along one path leading up from the beach to a fort atop a small
hill. Cabin front doors faced this street, which became the focus of the settlement. Halfway up Plymouth's Main Street, at right angles to it, the settlers laid
out a second path leading to the fields on either side. To decide who would live
where, the settlers drew lots, an act that in itself was a powerful symbol of
democracy. The term "building lot" derives from this exercise.[2] A small gun
emplacement sits at the crossroads of the two reconstructed streets, not as a
monument but because the intersection offers enfilade in four directions. The
settlers also surrounded the village with a wooden stockade.

171

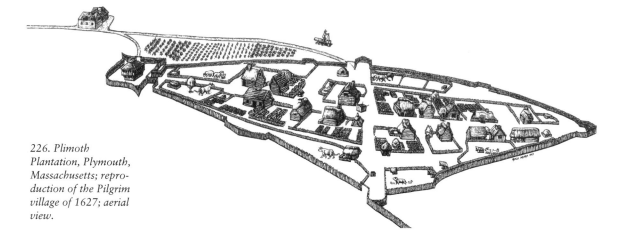

226. Plimoth Plantation, Plymouth, Massachusetts; reproduction of the Pilgrim village of 1627; aerial view.

When viewed from above, the composition of paths and palisade creates a pattern like the stretched paper and crossed sticks of a child's kite, the most prominent feature of the settlement being the intersection in the middle (Fig. 226). This design must have had symbolic resonance because in choosing it the settlers rejected other, more secure arrangements, like wrapping the palisade tightly around the base of the hill, as in a fortified Italian town.[3] Had the neighboring Wampanoag Indians mounted an attack on Plymouth, rather than fighting from house to house through the settlement to reach the fort, the Indians could easily have attacked and burned the fort directly by scaling the back of the hill.

Many early American municipalities, like Burlington, New Jersey, planned in 1677, also featured an open intersection as the center of town (Fig. 227). So prevalent is the concept that "Four Corners" has become an almost mythical small-town name. From these early plats, and with the passage of the Land Ordinance Act of 1785, our embrace of long straight roads and open intersections became an American norm. The Land Ordinance Act mandated that the unsettled portions of the country be cut into an enormous gridiron of one-mile-square sections, each containing 640 acres. These squares were often subdivided into quarter sections and then into even smaller parcels (see Fig. 9). The parcels, in turn, were frequently connected by roads laid out along the grid lines between sections.*

In one audacious stroke the Continental Congress cut up an entire country, most of which the legislators had never seen. Their original plat is still clearly visible on the land. From the air one can mark one's exact heading over much of the continent by looking at the deviation of the plane's path from the grid of farms below.

*Like the stripes of the American flag, roads running in an east-west direction can extend around the globe. Those running in a north-south direction, however, converge at the poles. To compensate for these merging lines and keep each section square, surveyors in the West would occasionally "lose" a section of land, thus putting a jog in the north-south roads. In Montana the lost sections are the apocryphal underpinning of a teenager's education in geography. Those who embark on a joyride in an east-west direction do fine. Those who choose roads running north-south, however, may learn too late the difference between latitude and longitude—as the road ends abruptly at some farmer's field.

The Land Ordinance Act also influenced the boundaries between states. These borders often coincide with section lines, thus many are straight lines hundreds of miles long, and several western states are no more than simple rectangles. From the Great Lakes to the Pacific Ocean the border with Canada is also a straight line, a political boundary drawn by surveyors rather than armies—an event impossible to imagine in Europe.

In America the most dramatic crossroads of all—also called Four Corners—is the place where the borders of Colorado, New Mexico, Arizona, and Utah meet. The juncture is an abstraction: only a small plaque set in the ground marks the exact spot where the states come together. Nothing surrounds the marker but parking lots and tents from which local Native Americans sell jewelry and sand paintings (Fig. 228).

To judge from the steady stream of tourist traffic to this remote crossing, however, the spot has symbolic value. The intersection reminds us that in America separate jurisdictions meet without conflict at abstract points on the earth. Each quadrant at Four Corners belongs to a different state, yet in the immensity of the land the states become one. The intersection is a symbol equally as powerful as that of the kivas dug into the earth nearby nearly a thousand years earlier by the Anasazi Indians.

227. Burlington, New Jersey; plan, 1797.

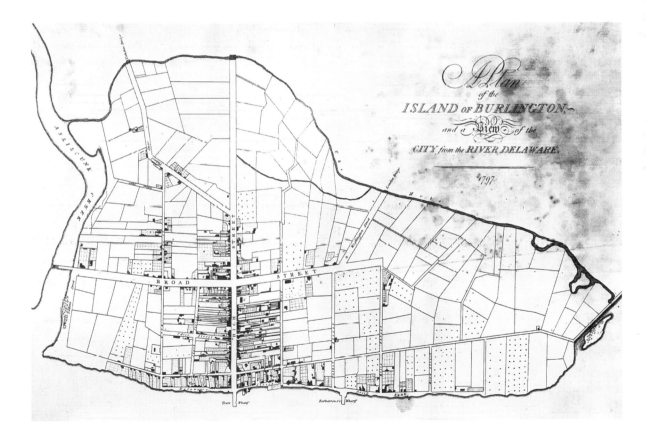

Although Four Corners is a jurisdictional boundary rather than an intersection of two roads, the small size of the marker in the middle is emblematic of another American trait—that of not wanting to impede movement through the center. The proclivity for organizing the landscape into gridded patterns, coupled with our desire for unimpeded movement, renders most intersections simply as coordinates on the journey rather than places to go. Americans navigate much of the country by heading in one direction, then turning at right angles and traveling in another. In America the phrase "turning the corner" is an expression of progress. People asking for directions often hear "Head out of town for a couple of miles, then take your first right—you can't miss it." Even on the freeway we steer by road coordinates rather than destinations: "Take I-80 to the New Jersey Turnpike southbound; from there it's about twenty minutes to exit 15W, where you take a left on Northfield Avenue." Our love of motion reduces most intersections to little more than places to check or change direction.

The contrast between how Americans think of their crossroads and how the French, for example, think of theirs can be seen by how we each identify the streets leading to them. In France the name of a road may change at every important building, junction, or landmark worth the pause. Rue Saint-Honoré in Paris becomes Rue du Fauborg Saint-Honoré, then becomes Avenue des Ternes, and so on.[4] In America a road, regardless of what it passes, usually keeps the same name as long as it heads in the same direction. Sunset Boulevard runs from downtown Los Angeles to the ocean, Broadway starts at the southern tip of Manhattan and ends in upstate New York, and Route 1 runs the length of the eastern seaboard from the Canadian border to Key West, Florida.

228. Navajo sand painting, 1989.

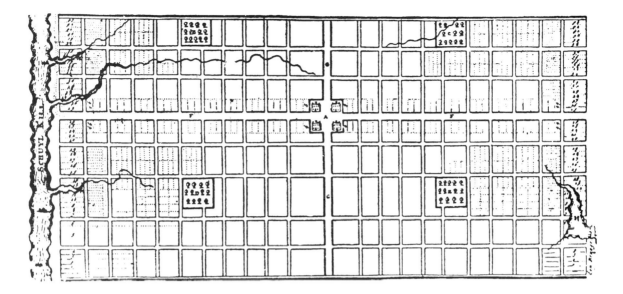

Our propensity for keeping the center open seems not to have held in Philadelphia, the best-known city in America organized about an intersection. A monumental City Hall sits squarely at the crossroads of the city's two most important streets, Broad and Market. In 1682 William Penn designated this crossing as the site for Philadelphia's civic buildings (Fig. 229). The design of City Hall nearly two centuries later by John McArthur, Jr., and Thomas U. Walter (Fig. 230) has fostered the impression that Penn wanted to mark the center of the intersection with some important monument. Consequently, Penn's plan is often cited as a rare example of enlightened planning within a grid.

Penn, however, actually left the center open. The site was intended to be bisected in both directions by streets, creating an intersection at the center with buildings grouped about it, as was typical of several other eastern Pennsylvania towns, like Eaton and Lancaster, planned in the same period. Rather than a shining example of paths leading to an important goal at the center of the city, the original plan for Philadelphia, like the plan for Plymouth, presages the primacy of movement over place—and a desire to keep the center open.*

In America concerns about unimpeded traffic flow are frequently manifestations of deeper values. We have always been ambivalent about celebrating intersections by placing monuments in the middle of them, regardless of how appropriate the symbolism or how easy the diversion around the monument might be. The open road and the open intersection are synonymous with freedom. One doesn't want to be stopped or turned aside, even slightly, by a statue of a king or some other notable blocking the path.

229. Philadelphia; plan by William Penn, 1682.

*Note also Penn's famous squares, the four eight-acre parks that have become the signature of his plan. These parks were only partially bordered by streets. Had they been built as planned, the parks would have had an awkward and ambiguous front door–back door relationship with the abutting properties.

230. Above: City Hall, Philadelphia, John MacArthur, Thomas U. Walter, 1874–1880; photograph ca. 1908, view toward south.

231. Above right: City Hall; view toward southeast, photograph 1994.

Even the architects for the Philadelphia City Hall showed some ambivalence about placing a symbol in the center. Although the complex sits in the middle of the intersection, and the City Hall tower is aligned with Broad Street in the north-south direction, it is sited well to the north of the east-west axis of Market Street (Fig. 231).

The most prominent example of our ambivalence about marking the center is the Washington Monument by Robert Mills, which was initially to have been placed at the intersection of L'Enfant's two grand allées leading from the Capitol and the White House. L'Enfant had wanted to ennoble this crossing with an equestrian statue of George Washington. For a new republic based on equality, however, such a statue would have been an awkward symbol indeed. Daniel Boorstin observed that "American democracy is embarrassed in the charismatic presence. We fear the man on horseback."[5] Deciding which way to face the statue would also have created a major predicament. If our first president looked toward the Capitol, he would have diminished the importance of the White House and thus the executive branch. On the other hand, had Washington been turned at right angles to look back toward his own residence, his heading would have been construed as an act of self-aggrandizement. In debating the point, but ignoring the symbolic dilemma, critics Hegemann and Peets thought horse and rider would probably have faced the Capitol because it was the longer axis.[6]

They suggested a comparison between this intersection and the crossing of the axes of the Madeleine and the Tuileries at the Place de la Concorde in Paris, where during L'Enfant's time a 50-foot-high equestrian statue of Louis XV stood facing the longer axis of the Tuileries.

Peets later sketched plans for the Mall showing Washington and his horse facing south, broadside to the Capitol and turned away from the White House. This, too, would have been an unfortunate choice.[7] The bulk of America's uncharted frontier lay to the west. More important, from the White House every president's gaze would be directed the length of the South Lawn to the horse's backside (Fig. 232).

After half a century of indecision over an appropriate symbol, a large obelisk designed by Robert Mills seemed to offer a solution. Nevertheless, the memorial was still not placed in the middle of the intersection. Supposedly, poor soil conditions led the government to move the monument away from the actual center, to higher ground to the east, leaving it completely off axis with the White House, and slightly off axis with the Capitol (Fig. 233). In retrospect, the engineering arguments that led to this change appear specious. Architects had known for several centuries how to build in swampy terrain. The entire city of Venice, for example, is built on piles. For one project alone, the seventeenth-century church of Santa Maria della Salute, the architect Baldassare Longhena specified 1,156,627 piles be driven beneath the building.[8] A comparable expenditure to support our national monument, a memorial that was to sit in the middle of the intersection leading from the two most important buildings in our capital city, would not have been an unreasonable expense.

Why, then, did we move the obelisk to one side? It would seem that placing the memorial at the symbolic termination of two grand axes was simply less compelling than putting it on higher ground. Rejecting a grand monument on axis—even one to the father of our country—was a choice entirely in keeping with American values.

Some early American city plats, like a 1796 plan of Cleveland, Ohio (Fig. 234), were able to gloss over the issue of whether the center was open or blocked. Although the central square in Cleveland indicates a place to stop, the long straight streets simultaneously suggest that traffic can gather enough momentum to pass straight through the center. As in the plan for Williamsburg, the only boundary lines in Cleveland were around the various private lots. Because the automobile had not yet forced planners to distinguish public rights-of-way from public places, Cleveland's center green and streets were treated as one. Wagons might have occasionally traversed the green, but the market stalls and grazing livestock would have made uninterrupted passage difficult.

More frequently, our desire for unimpeded movement led us simply to leave the center open, as in Columbus, Ohio. Although it's the state capital, planners did not consider the center of Columbus a

232. Equestrian statue of George Washington; view from the White House.

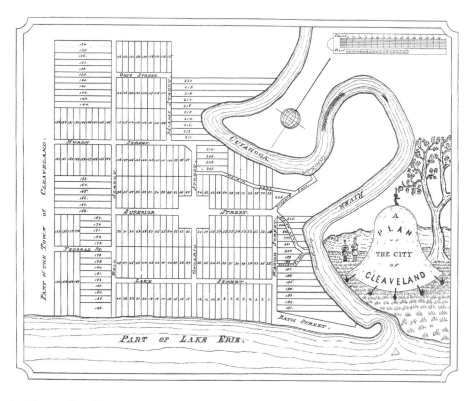

233. Opposite: Washington Monument, Robert Mills, 1848–1885; view from above 16th Street, looking south past the White House to the Jefferson Memorial. Note the off-axis location of the Washington Monument.

234. Left: Cleveland, Ohio; plan, 1796.

suitable site for the capitol building. Instead, the city, platted in 1812, marked its center with an intersection of two streets. Broad Street, lined with grand residences and the city's art gallery, was once old U.S. Route 40 heading west across the country. High Street, at right angles, is the city's principal north-south commercial street. "Broad and High" means the center of downtown. The city is nearly at the geographic center of the state. Thus, while the intersection would seem to have been the symbolically perfect spot for the capitol, the building was relegated to one of the intersection's four corners (see Fig. 160). The state's most important edifice was less important than the uninterrupted stream of traffic passing by on Broad Street, heading across the continent (Fig. 235).

An 1874 map of Jefferson, Ohio, a town that was originally laid out at the beginning of the nineteenth century, illustrates the dilemma of trying to create a sense of place and movement simultaneously (Fig. 236). The central square in Jefferson is like Cleveland's, but the smaller peripheral squares in the plan have a very different character. The dotted lines through them indicate public rights-of-way and show an ambiguity on the mapmaker's part, as if he hoped the squares would remain intact—although he knew they were too plentiful to be used as market areas, that they were too small for grazing livestock, and that the unimpeded passage of wagons through the middle would eventually turn them into conventional intersections.

Despite the appeal of an open center, planners have often argued that a coherent architectural composition could never be derived from an open crossroad. Intersections without statues, buildings, or obelisks to mark them remain abstractions. Peets, for example, thought good plans had to bring about "a concrete experience, and not merely [be] an intellectual conception built up out of a spectator's knowledge of American history and government. . . . The composition must be sensible to the senses and not merely knowable to the mind. Here you stand, and there you look, and that you see—and you like it with the help of no diagram."[9]

Peets's bias emanated from his admiration for the Renaissance and Baroque monuments of Europe, erected at a time when designers made much of important crossroads and squares, marking them with grandeur. Beginning with the Renaissance, European architects invested considerable thought in the quest for the ideal. As they came to realize that the buildings surrounding a plaza were interrelated with the space within a plaza, they also came to believe that the relative proportions between the two could be perfected. As the height of the buildings changed, so did the quality of the space it enclosed.

Designers still viewed streets leading to plazas, however, largely as a means of showing off individual buildings along the way. But the promulgation of Pope Sixtus V's plan for Rome in 1585, featuring long vistas terminating at important buildings and monuments, brought Baroque architects to the realization that streets were part of an artistic whole. Streets could be grand voids formed by the buildings facing them, with both street and buildings sublimated to a goal at the end.

235. Ohio State House, Columbus; view from Broad Street. Abraham Lincoln's funeral cortege is passing in the foreground, heading east.

Americans, by contrast, have wanted grand buildings, but without their domination, and they have desired a path defined, but without a goal as its termination. The focus of the American experience was not buildings or monu-

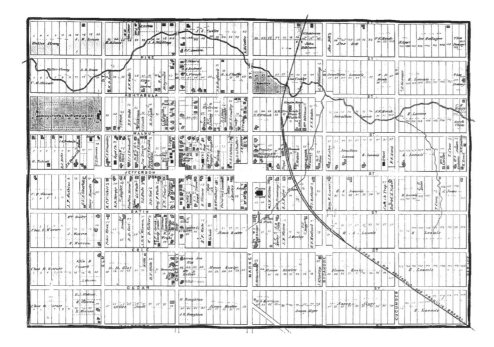

236. Jefferson, Ohio; plan, 1874.

ments at the end of the road but the road itself, with Americans in motion on it. Buildings, like any adventure along the way, were part of the lore to be recounted over a campfire each night—before getting on the trail again.

In Europe, whether the goal was a town square or a monument, its purpose was to create a center, a place to stop. By terminating or rerouting streets to create these focal points, architects and planners could assert the supremacy of place over journey, of goal over path, of that which was fixed and eternal over that which was moving and transitory. The central square of Vitry-le-François, for example (Fig. 237), sits athwart the town's two principal streets. The discontinuous streets and the surrounding L-shaped blocks clearly mark the square as the town's center. Squares like this, common throughout Europe, were often used as symbols of regal authority. In Paris the Place Vendôme once sported an enormous statue of Louis XIV (Fig. 238), which was torn down during the French Revolution, and the obelisk at the center of the Place de la Concorde was once the site of the equestrian statue of Louis XV, which Hegemann and Peets thought was the perfect prototype for Washington, D.C.

Notwithstanding the sense of permanence and the opportunity for symbolic expression that these squares offered, by the seventeenth century some European architects had begun to realize that "the great distinctive element in [what was then] modern civic form [would be] the dominance of the street over the building."[10] Peets thought that both Christopher Wren and John Evelyn, who submitted plans for the reconstruction of London after the center of the city burned in 1666, understood this, because each showed long straight streets in their plans. Apart from the precedent that Sixtus V had set in Rome, Peets

VITRY·LE·FRANÇOIS

237. Above: Vitry-le-
François, France,
1634; aerial view.

238. Right: Place
Vendôme, Paris, begun
1680; aerial view,
ca. 1790.

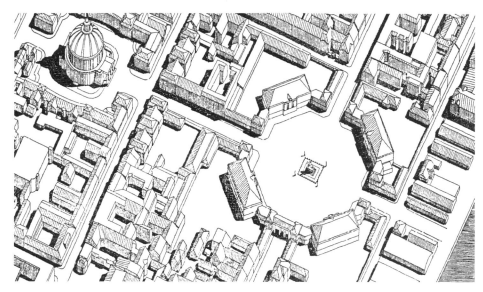

239. Amalienborg Plaza, Copenhagen, Nicolai Eigtved, 1749; aerial view; drawing by Steen Eiler Rasmussen, 1948.

believed these designers realized that the hackney coach, a newly invented light two-wheeled vehicle capable of considerable speed when hitched to a fast horse, would soon bring a demand for longer and straighter thoroughfares.

The emerging dominance of streets over buildings—of the dynamic over the static—created an aesthetic tension that on occasion came to be expressed architecturally. For example, the eighteenth-century Amalienborg Plaza, designed by the Danish architect Nicolai Eigtved at the intersection of Amalien and Frederiks Streets in Copenhagen (Fig. 239), and Laura Place, designed by Thomas Baldwin at the end of the Poultney Bridge in Bath, are turned at forty-five degrees to the surrounding streets. Whether or not these squares were planned to facilitate traffic, they did speed the flow of horse-drawn vehicles by lessening the acuity and the number of turns.

By the end of the nineteenth century, still before the automobile had made its impact, the dilemma of creating a sense of place without interrupting traffic had become for many planners, including Sitte, the central unresolved conflict in modern civic design. Hegemann and Peets studied the problem extensively without arriving at a satisfactory solution. In the end their preferred scheme was quite similar to the one Penn had proposed for Philadelphia over two centuries earlier—essentially allowing two streets to cut a single central square into four smaller ones.[11] They cited the Marché du Quartier Saint-Louis and the Marché Notre-Dame at Versailles as prototypes for this approach (Fig. 240). That these two squares at Versailles were actually intersections in the middle of two small local shopping areas mattered little to Hegemann and Peets, who still thought the squares were paradigms for marking the center of twentieth-century cities.

By adding pylons in the street aligned with the adjoining building facades, Hegemann and Peets produced their own variation on the theme, and hailed the concept as the perfect prototype for a modern civic center. The resulting square still had an open center, however, allowing traffic to flow past the pylons and through the middle. The solution, like the one for the little squares in Jefferson, Ohio, was an ambiguous hybrid, neither a square nor an intersection (Fig. 241). Moreover, because the streets would have cut one big square into four small ones, the symbolism unintentionally connoted an absurdity—a city where it had been decreed that every large civic function would either be repeated four times or broken up into four identical events to be staged simultaneously. (Penn's plan for Philadelphia would have created a similar dilemma. Four city halls would have made no sense, and a single grand city hall on one corner would have unbalanced the composition.)

In America the debate over whether to favor unimpeded movement over a sense of place has always mattered less because few intersections designed to facilitate traffic have at the same time been celebrated as points of interest. Occasionally traffic rotaries have given character to a certain place, although they were seldom built for purposes of civic enhancement. The rotary at the base of the Bourne Bridge over the Cape Cod Canal in Massachusetts, for example, has only in the last decade been planted with hedges that spell out the name "Cape Cod."[12]

240. Marché du Quartier Saint-Louis and Marché Notre-Dame, Versailles; drawing by Hegemann and Peets.

MARCHÉ DU QUARTIER ST. LOUIS, VERSAILLES

THE MARKET HOUSES ARE MODERN

MARCHÉ NOTRE DAME·VERSAILLES

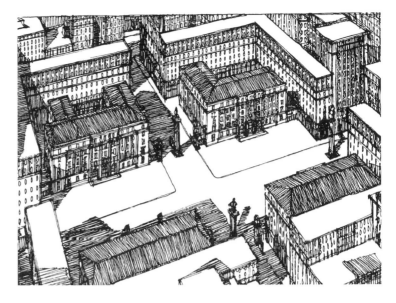

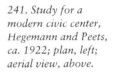

PROTECTIVE BELT OF OFFICE BUILDINGS
DESIGNED IN HARMONY WITH THE GROUP AND
WITH CORNICE LINE TWO OR THREE STORIES HIGHER.
THE OBJECTS ON THE CENTER LINES OF THE
STREETS ARE HIGH ORNAMENTAL COLUMNS OR POLES.

241. Study for a modern civic center, Hegemann and Peets, ca. 1922; plan, left; aerial view, above.

Despite our cultural propensity for the open road, American architects and planners have often sought to strew the path with monuments, and they have frequently turned, as Peets did, to European precedents as a justification. The historical obeisance to Europe on this issue was never more evident than in the recommendations of the Senate Park Commission appointed in 1901 to beautify Washington, D.C. Among its members were some of America's leading designers and foremost advocates of what was then called the City Beautiful movement.

Architects Charles McKim and Daniel Burnham, in particular, believed the only sources of civic beauty were the classicism of ancient Greece and Rome as expressed through Renaissance and Baroque cityscapes. America would never achieve architectural greatness or make its mark as a mature civilization unless its artists and architects first studied and internalized the great monuments and cities of Europe. To demonstrate the point, upon receiving their appointment to improve Washington, McKim, Burnham, and others immediately embarked for Europe to look at precedents. The irony of the trip, as one critic put it, was that from looking at "all these legacies of aristocrats and nobles . . . all these seemingly tireless survivals of departed or decayed societies, they hoped to fashion on the banks of the Potomac . . . a city honoring men who had revolted against a tyrant."[13]

Oblivious to this contradiction, the Senate Park Commission suggested, as the centerpiece of its report, that L'Enfant's two open-ended allées be terminated (Fig. 242). Each of L'Enfant's axes then extended to the Potomac River, which

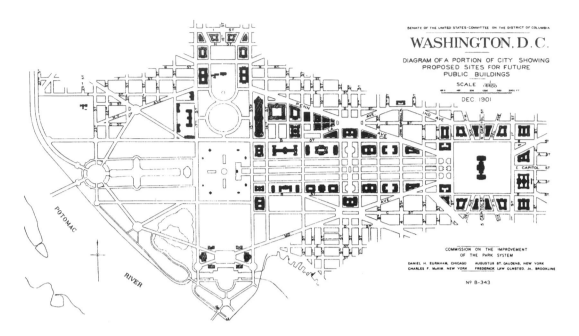

242. Above: Washington, D.C., plan of Senate Park Commission of 1902. Note the extension of Maryland Avenue, but without the Supreme Court as a terminus. Note also the closing of L'Enfant's open axes.

243. Above: Lincoln Memorial, Washington, D.C., Henry Bacon, 1922.

244. Right: Jefferson Memorial, Washington, D.C., John Russell Pope, 1944. Photograph by Paul D. Spreiregen.

flows diagonally across the city. The commission recommended lengthening the allées by placing landfill in the river, then plugging the open vistas with sculptural features and memorials.

L'Enfant's long, open axes had seemingly led to nothing, but soon they would lead to something. Today the Mall from the Capitol ends at the Lincoln Memorial (Fig. 243). The axis from the White House, which was originally to end at a fountain, is now the site of the Jefferson Memorial (Fig. 244).

As McKim and his Senate Park Commission colleagues began work on the plan for Washington, McKim's firm had just finished a conceptually similar project at the University of Virginia. There, what Scully has called "the dogged probity of American classical desires"[14] led to the closing of one of this country's more spectacular open allées. The centerpiece of Thomas Jefferson's design for the University of Virginia is the grand lawn that once stretched from the central rotunda of his library to the wooded hills beyond the campus. In 1898 McKim, Mead and White closed the open end of Jefferson's allée with a complex of academic buildings (Fig. 245).

The open-ended central court of Louis Kahn's magnificent Salk Institute, completed in 1965 at La Jolla, California, has also been closed at one end, a decision that, when it was announced, triggered an outpouring of opposition.[15] The court, running between two rows of study rooms, originally allowed one to look the length of the complex to the Pacific Ocean (Fig. 246). New laboratories at the inboard end of the court now block the view. That American cultural values underpinned the passion of the opposition to this change can be seen by perusing *Zodiac 17,* a biannual Italian architecture magazine, which in 1967 gave extensive coverage to the Salk Institute. The mind set of the Italian editors was such

245. Academic Building, University of Virginia, Charlottesville, McKim, Mead and White, 1898.

246. Salk Institute, La Jolla, California, Louis I. Kahn, 1956–1965; view through the courtyard toward the Pacific Ocean.

that not one of the twenty-nine photographs of the finished project shows the open court and view toward the ocean.

In contrast to the classical notion that all important paths must end at a goal, Oglethorpe's plan for Savannah gives equal weight to the goal and to the more American desire for unimpeded movement. A pattern of through streets alternating with streets interrupted by small squares gives subtle recognition to both proclivities (see Fig. 117). The multitude of squares in Savannah is also in tune with American pluralist values, creating many centers rather than one while the through streets in between give one the choice of avoiding the squares altogether.

Typically, architects have left the design of open roads and unfettered movement to traffic engineers while still believing, ironically, that engineers are less in tune culturally than they. As Peets put it, engineers simply "ask the buildings to stand aside while the streets rush madly by."[16] Streets hurtling through unmarked intersections seemingly reinforce critic Norberg-Schulz's observation that "while the Baroque network really joins different foci, the modern network of motorways is mere infrastructure, never leading to any goal but passing by everything."[17] Unfortunately, the view that a path to an explicit goal is worthy of architectural concern, whereas a path without an apparent goal is not, has led to an unrealistic nostalgia among some architects and critics for a preindustrial pedestrian-dominated world. Since the automobile's invention, this view has left the design of much of America's built landscape, except for single buildings, outside the realm of artistic endeavor.

Indianapolis is an excellent example of how designers can spend considerable effort on creating a sense of place while leaving movement to the engineers. An enormous Soldiers and Sailors Monument emphatically marks the center of Indianapolis. Although a symbol like this at the center is a relatively uncommon phenomenon in American cities, the original layout of Indianapolis seems far less an anomaly when one learns the designer was Alexander Ralston, a former assistant to Pierre L'Enfant.

Even Ralston's efforts at symbolism ran afoul of intractable American values. He originally intended the center of the city as a site for the governor's mansion (Fig. 247). When a house was duly erected, however, the incumbent governor refused to move in. His wife vociferously complained she had no back yard. "'Live in that house?' she exclaimed. 'No, indeed! . . . Every woman in town would take account of our washing when we hang it out on Monday morning.'"[18] Succeeding governors had similar views. The Indiana legislature subsequently voted down plans to convert the residence into a statehouse before the monument was finally approved.

247. Indianapolis; plan by Alexander Ralston, 1821.

But when the time came in Indianapolis to designate one street as U.S. Route 40, the primary east-west traffic artery through the city, the decision was left to the engineers. Because the road was to go through Indianapolis, not to it, the engineers picked a street just south of the monument. This road, still a major conduit even after creation of the interstate highway system, was never encumbered by the folderol of high design and is not part of the city's imagery.

To leave decisions like these to the engineers, however, is to foreclose possibilities. Kevin Lynch brilliantly elucidated that in a complex world of many choices there are limited opportunities for civic design, if only paths leading to specific goals are worth designing. Lynch believed that any meaningful modern plan must accommodate sequences that can be "broken in upon at many points. A carefully constructed sequence, leading from the introduction, first statement, and development to climax and conclusion, may fail utterly if the driver enters it directly at the climax point. Therefore, it may be necessary to look for sequences which are interruptible as well as reversible, that is, sequences which still have sufficient imageability even when broken in upon at various points, much like a magazine serial. This might lead us from the classic start-climax-finish form to others which are more like the essentially endless, and yet continuous and variegated, patterns of jazz."[19]

Put simply, the architectural problem is to give meaning to the pathways, and especially the important open intersections, traveled by millions of Americans who, for example, might leave their driveway in the morning to drop their children at school, then take their clothes to the dry cleaner, and finally go to work. After work they might go to the market, back to the cleaners, then to

248. Nighthawks, *1942, Edward Hopper, American, 1882–1967. Oil on canvas, 84.1 x 152.4 cm, Friends of American Art Collection, 1942.51. Photograph © 1944, The Art Institute of Chicago.*

the playground to pick up a child from Little League practice before finally returning home.

Because the American intersection is seldom a place to stop, except for a traffic light, and monuments in the center can be a symbolically dissonant obstruction, the only features left to give meaning to an important intersection are the buildings and signs surrounding it. Consequently, corner buildings have particular iconic value in America—"standing on the corner watching all the girls go by" and "hanging out at the corner drugstore" are American idioms. Street corners appear upon occasion as themes in American art. Edward Hopper returned to the street corner many times in his work. One of his best-known paintings, *Nighthawks* (Fig. 248), has become a popular staple in the art-poster market—in America a sure sign of symbolic resonance with the general public.

Corner sites can shape and organize buildings, occasionally making even the simplest structure more interesting, as with a modest-sized house on Martha's Vineyard where two different-sized rooms flank the front door (Fig. 249). The larger room, to the left of the front door, has one window facing the street, but the smaller room, toward the corner, has two. These two windows push the front door off-center, creating, in conjunction with the corner, a more complex and architecturally satisfying facade. Similarly, a corner store in Cape May has display windows of equal size on either side of the front door. The prospect of shoppers passing by on both streets, however, has pulled the entire ground floor facade toward the corner, creating an asymmetrical tension with the building's upper floors (Fig. 250).

Perhaps the most memorable corner edifice in America is Daniel Burnham's Flatiron Building in New York City. Set on a narrow triangular corner lot at the intersection of Fifth Avenue and Broadway, the thin office slab fills the site and more (Fig. 251). The window bays swell out toward the sidewalk, and the sur-

249. Above left: House, Martha's Vineyard, 1840.

250. Above: House, Cape May, New Jersey.

rounding streets push back, constricting the tower, squeezing it upward toward a high cornice. The tension between the Flatiron Building and the intersection is a potent symbol of two often conflicting American beliefs—our great faith in the ability of the private sector to prevail and flourish, even on an impossibly narrow site; and our simultaneous conviction that the open road can wear away any obstacle, be it a church, a statue of the king, or in the case of the Flatiron Building, a monument to capitalism.

The best historical examples of an open intersection defined by the buildings around it come from ancient Rome. The imperial Romans typically divided each new city into four quadrants. Two principal streets crossed at right angles in the center of the city, defining the quadrants' boundaries. The primary street, known as the *cardo* and representing the axis of the world, ran in a north-south direction. The secondary street, or the *decumanus*, ran east and west, following the path of the sun. The intersection in the middle remained open, an abstract but effective reminder that Rome was the one true center of the imperium, even though that center might be hundreds of miles distant.

The finest existing expression of such an open intersection is the tetrapylon in the provincial city of Palmyra, built in the early third century A.D. (Fig. 252). Because it is identical on all four corners and open in the center, the monument celebrates the traffic through its middle rather than itself. Open intersections still had resonance for the Romans as late as the fourth century, when one served as the organizing idea for Diocletian's palace, built on the Adriatic coast in Split (Fig. 253).

251. Opposite: Flatiron Building, New York City, Daniel H. Burnham and Company, 1902; photograph by Rudy Burckhardt, 1948.

252. Below left: Tetrapylon, Palmyra, Syria, third century A.D.

253. Below: Diocletian's palace, Split (Spalato), A.D. 300–306; plan. The principal entrance is from the broad porch facing the Adriatic. The gates on the other three sides of the palace were subordinate entrances.

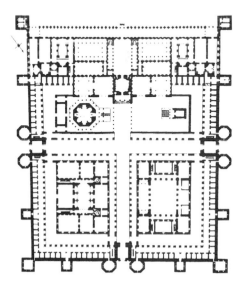

254. Four fountains at the intersection of Strada Felice and Strada Pia, Rome.

In Rome the open intersection of the old Strada Felice and Strada Pia occurs at the highest point of the Quirinal Hill. This crossroads, however, had no particular meaning until the sixteenth century when it was upgraded by Pope Sixtus V as part of his plan. From the intersection one can proceed in all directions to other monuments and points of interest. Despite the crossroad's importance, however, Sixtus left it open. Instead of putting a monument in the center of the intersection, he reshaped high garden walls on the four corners, cutting them back forty-five degrees from the corner, and placed fountains at the base of the cuts (Fig. 254).

At the *quattro canti*, as the intersection is called, figures representing Diana, Juno, and the rivers Tiber and Arno, hover above each fountain's basin, giving each a separate identity; yet the reclining pose and similar scale of the figures brings the four fountains together into a single composition. Built between 1588 and 1593, the fountains were later incorporated into the buildings then filling this rural part of Rome. One fountain became the corner of a palazzo designed by Domenico Fontana, a contemporary of Sixtus, whose five-year papal reign ended in 1590. More than half a century later Francesco Borromini incorporated the fountain across the street into the facade of the Church of San Carlo alle Quattro Fontana. The third corner had been filled by the time Giambattista Nolli produced his famous map of Rome in 1748 (Fig. 255), but it was not until more than a century later that a building finally filled the fourth corner. The

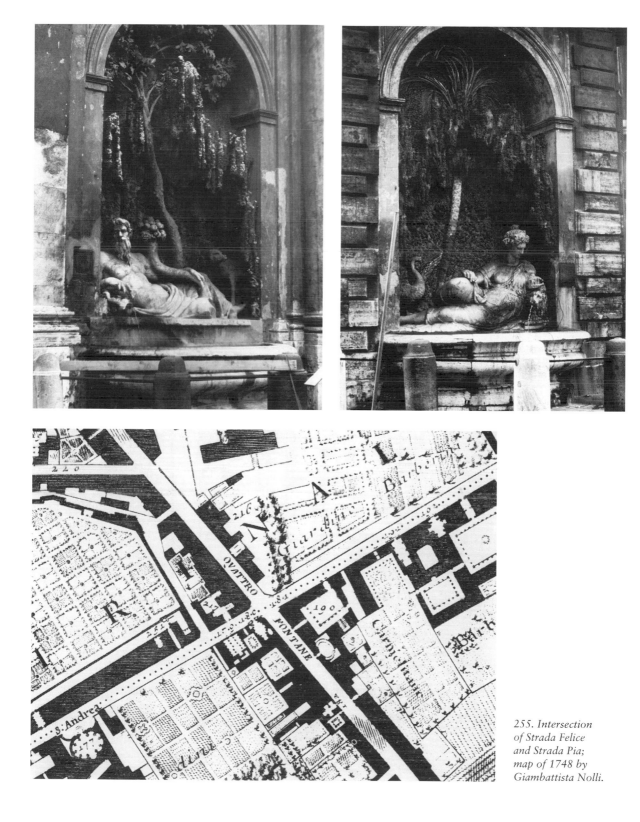

255. Intersection
of Strada Felice
and Strada Pia;
map of 1748 by
Giambattista Nolli.

fountains in front of the buildings have endured over time partly because the influence of the church dissuaded those who might have had other plans, but also because the strength of the architectural idea led the abutters to accommodate their interests to Sixtus's vision.

Paul Zucker wrote that the *quattro canti* were "well in tune with Baroque concepts because of the long vistas." He thought the crossing created the "character of a miniature octagonal square."[20] So strong was Zucker's belief that all paths really led to (or from) a goal that he was able, despite the open intersection, to imagine a terminus to the vistas where none existed. Zucker's reaction showed that despite Sixtus's decision to eschew a square and leave the intersection open, he had still created a sense of place at the top of the Quirinal Hill—without blocking traffic. A similar arrangement of four fountains marks the open intersection at the crossing of the Via Toledo and the Via Maqueda in the center of Palermo (Fig. 256). The fountains were laid out by Viceroy Marques de Vellena in 1609 and modeled after the four fountains in Rome.

The opportunity to mark the corners of an important intersection occurs less often in a capitalist democracy, if only because the properties on four corners almost always have different owners with different interests. In urban areas, particularly, only when some larger public purpose is served do we have an opportunity to shape an important intersection. One such rare occasion presented itself in 1984 when plans were announced for the upgrading of the area around Times Square in New York City. The most important building in Times Square, the old Times Tower, sits on a small island at one end, its original facade now badly mutilated. The exterior of the building was to be redone as part of the redevelopment project. That decision occasioned, in turn, an architectural competition to make suggestions for the Times Tower site.

The Times Tower, however, is only one component of Times Square, an area of Manhattan that actually has two identities. Times Square is a metaphor

256. Quattro canti, *intersection of Via Maqueda and Via Toledo, Palermo, Italy; aerial view.*

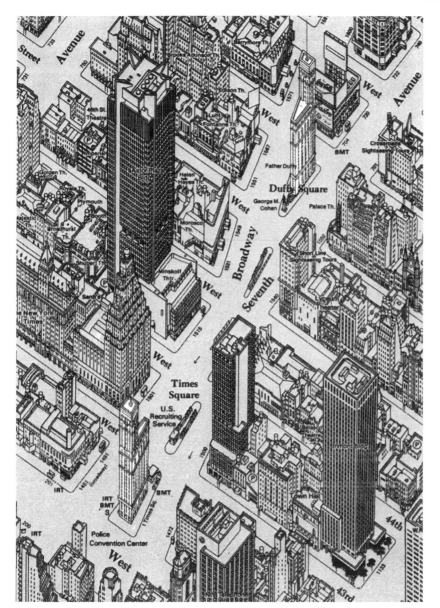

*257. Times Square,
Craig Whitaker,
Demetri Sarantitis,
Ting-i Kang, 1984;
axonometric.*

for the hustle and glitter of New York, and therefore a place with symbolic importance. But it is not a specific place or even a square, as the name implies. Times Square, despite its fame, is only a long narrow bow tie of asphalt at the intersection of Broadway and Seventh Avenue. Therefore, two colleagues and I suggested, in a submission to the competition, that rather than focusing solely on the existing building, the jury should request that a second tower be built on the other small plot of land at the opposite end of Times Square (Fig. 257). The second structure would be the mirror image of the first—that is, the second structure would be identical to the remodeled original building. As a consequence,

258. Regent Street;
view looking south.
Piccadilly Circus, built
between 1815 and
1820, with identical
buildings on all four
corners, is in the
foreground.

both buildings would be subordinated to the intersection, celebrating the spot in the middle where thousands of Americans gather at midnight on New Year's Eve, but where on all other days of the year people and cars pass without stopping.

Corner buildings need not be as dramatic as those in Times Square as long as they are similar in bulk and character. John Nash, for example, in his Regent Street plan of 1812 for London, marked the four corners of two important intersections with simple concave building facades. None of the corner facades at Oxford Circus and Piccadilly Circus, as the intersections are called, were particularly memorable, but taken together they read as a single composition—the pleasure in each being simply the recognition that four separate parties had been bound together by a single architectural idea (Fig. 258).

Repetition of separate ordinary elements is a common theme in American art. The repeated squares in a Robert Rauschenberg painting, an Andy Warhol multiple, a quilt, and a Norman Ives print mark them as American (Figs. 259 to 262). Ives's print, in particular, illustrates the recurring tension in American culture between being number one and being equal.

Because ordinary objects grouped together can become high art, they suggest, in turn, that in the open landscape almost any structure, repeated four times around an intersection, can take on an architectural character. This is certainly true at the corner of Fourth and Fremont Streets in downtown Las Vegas (Fig. 263). Casinos sit on all four corners. Each has a canopy over the sidewalk, and three of the four casinos bulge out toward the corner in a riot of signs and moving lights. None of the facades is architecturally distinctive. Taken together, however, their similar character clearly marks Fourth and Fremont as the

259. Top left: Self-portrait of Robert Rauschenberg with White Painting, 1951. © 1996 United Press Inc./Licensed by VAGA, New York, NY.

260. Top right: Portrait of Joseph Beuys State II, Andy Warhol, 1980–1983. Screenprint on Lenox Museum Board, 40 x 32 in. © 1995 The Andy Warhol Foundation for the Visual Arts, Inc./ARS, New York.

261. Above left: Sunburst, crib quilt, Lehigh County, Pennsylvania, ca. 1885.

262. Above right: Screenprint; Number 1, 1967, Norman Ives.

*263. Intersection of
Fourth and Fremont
Streets, Las Vegas,
Nevada; view looking
north, 1995.*

center of gambling in downtown Las Vegas, and an alternative to the more
famous Strip.

These relatively mundane buildings also suggest, ironically, that civic
improvement—certainly around an open intersection—may be easier in a suburban landscape than in older downtown areas. The combination of ordinary
buildings, low densities, and relatively smaller capital investment makes suburban areas more susceptible simply because there is less to preserve or reconfig-
ure, just as low densities and plain garden walls on the Quirinal Hill gave Sixtus
the same latitude in Rome.

A desire for suburban civic improvement has a fortuitous consonance with
how a typical suburban real estate market functions around an important intersection. Northwest Houston, Texas, an area that has experienced extraordinarily
rapid growth over the past twenty years, clearly demonstrates this congruence.
Northwest Houston was once predominantly agricultural, with large tracts of
land interlaced by occasional two-lane farm-to-market roads. Residential development, beginning in the 1970s, put considerable pressure on the existing
road network. Within a decade, roads were being widened to four, six, and even
eight lanes.

Many of the new subdivisions along these thoroughfares were set well back
from the road, separating themselves by high fences and strips of empty land
from traffic noise and potentially noxious uses on the abutting unzoned property

(Fig. 264). The strips of land also provided a cheap hedge against future growth. Some of them could be sold for highway right-of-way, if and when demand grew for more roadway lanes. The rest of the land, called a commercial reserve, could be cut into small parcels and sold for offices and strip malls at a higher price than the residential land behind it.[21]

At major intersections owners frequently subdivided further, extracting additional value by carving out a second, smaller lot from a larger corner parcel. These smaller lots right at the corner are especially attractive to small high-volume businesses, giving credence to the old saw that the best place to put a gas station is on a corner with three other gas stations. The selling price of such a lot is often twice the price of the L-shaped parcel wrapped around it, which, in turn, is considerably more valuable than land even one hundred yards away, making the difference in price from lot to lot orderly and predictable.

At the intersections themselves each time the traffic lights change, hundreds of motorists surge forward. The crossroads are abstractions, and yet in one important sense they are really places, confluences so large they become reference points. The thought of commemorative squares or monuments marking them, however, takes on a surreal quality, evoking the image of motorists overrunning or dodging obstacles in the middle each time the light turns green. Louis Kahn's dictum that "center city was a place to go—not to go through,"[22] posits the obverse of what is happening at these gigantic crossroads.

264. Commercial reserves, Houston, Texas.

265. Four gas stations.

The value of the corner parcels, however, and the need to pull customers out of the passing stream of traffic creates ample opportunities to mark these intersections using only a planner's conventional tools of height and setback regulations, as well as some simple rules about the placement and character of the signs. While one gas station with a tall sign is entirely forgettable, four gas stations of similar size with similar signs, one on each corner, are memorable (Fig. 265). Their redundancy alone marks the intersection as special. Robert Venturi showed that one duck along the road can be unforgettable, but that we are more likely to recall the duck itself than where we saw it (Fig. 266). If we see four ducks on four corners, however, we will remember not only the ducks but where

266. Duck, Long Island, New York.

we saw them. Like the four figures above the Roman fountains or the numerals in an Ives print, each duck, or each gas station, can be slightly different without undermining the symbolic intent.

We need not confine ourselves to marking only simple crossroads. Highway interchanges, where one major freeway crosses another, are special sites in America. Some interchanges we remember simply because they mark a change of course, like the juncture in Maryland of I-95 and the Beltway around Washington, D.C. Other interchanges, like the meeting of the Harbor, Pasadena, and Santa Monica Freeways in Los Angeles, take on almost totemic qualities because of the enormous tangle of roads.

These interchanges are places, even though actually stopping at them is an invitation to mayhem. We do not yet mark them, largely for the same reasons that we do not yet see unimpeded movement as an aesthetic opportunity. We do, however, have the tools to ennoble these interchanges. Most tall signs announcing gas stations or fast-food restaurants are consigned to private property beyond the right-of-way. The signs strain to be seen from the highway. Conversely, searching out these signs is a distraction that requires drivers to divert their attention from the road. If some signs were placed within the tangle of ramps, organized so as not to compete with highway directional and safety signage, these commercial placards could heighten the drama of the interchange, creating, as it were, a very American version of the towers at San Gimignano (Figs. 267, 268). Each intersection would still be a place to pass by, but it would also be a place worth remembering.

267. Below left: San Gimignano, Italy.

268. Below: Interchange study.

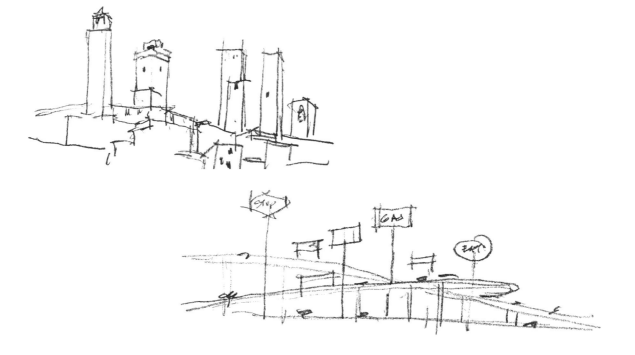

Chapter **7**

To travel hopefully is a better thing than to arrive.

ROBERT LOUIS STEVENSON
"El Dorado," *Virginibus Puerisque*

Around the Bend

JUST AS WE AMERICANS DO NOT WANT THE PATH BLOCKED BY SYMBOLS OF AUTHORity, we have frequently tried to minimize or undercut the power and influence these symbols represent. We have often arranged our important buildings, and the roads leading to them, to leave a choice: to let the viewer approach the building, engage it—and then move on.

Elbert Peets suggested that for Americans "domes, monuments, and malls are not the deep and stirring personal experience that they have the power to be."[1] Quite the opposite, they were often deep and stirring symbols of the wrong kind. Moholy-Nagy noted that "Washington's spatial monumentality is incongruous to American urbanism." Her observation was true not, as she asserted, because monumentality is "outside the ability of American city builders"[2] but rather because it connotes the wrong values: it conflicts with our even deeper desire for equality.

By contrast, when Louis XIV gazed from his bedroom at Versailles toward the three grand avenues ending in the courtyard below him, or when a Frenchman approaching the palace looked back, the message could not have been clearer or more explicit (Fig. 269). Straight as pokers, the converging avenues suggested only one possibility—Louis's supremacy. Versailles was at the center of the universe, all matters of state came only to the king. All roads met at his palace, then literally burst forth into the dazzling axes of Le Nôtre's gardens behind it (see Fig. 12). Around the king's personage only did the world turn.

269. Versailles; aerial view.

For American colonists such explicit symbolism was repugnant if only because the king's supremacy was the principal issue fomenting the American Revolution. Rather than submit to King George III, Americans chose to confront him. Confrontation has become a national legacy; it is central, literally as well as symbolically, to the right to speak out and the right to bear arms, both of which are embedded in the Constitution as amendments.

In America good triumphs over evil only through confrontation. An entire genre of Hollywood films celebrates the good guys standing up to the bad. Whether it's Jimmy Stewart in *Mr. Smith Goes to Washington* or Gary Cooper as the architect Howard Roark in *The Fountainhead*, the message is the same—to combat evil an American needs to confront it. *High Noon,* featuring Gary Cooper marching down a dusty street alone to face the desperadoes, is an American classic (Fig. 270).

270. Gary Cooper on Main Street in High Noon. *Note the bend in the road.*

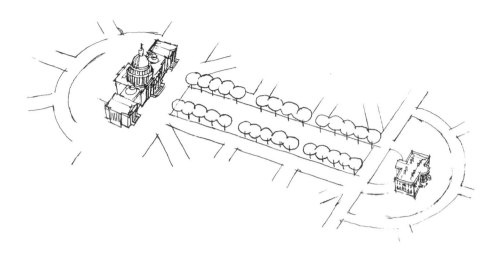

271. *The White House on axis with the U.S. Capitol, Washington, D.C.; an alternative study.*

In a confrontation when one side wins, the other must lose—and that too can be unacceptable in an egalitarian culture. In a nation with so many opportunities for conflict—church against state, ethnic group against ethnic group, rich against poor—we often seek to avoid direct confrontation and the possibility of a loser. Although, for example, the framers of the Constitution designed a governing mechanism with separate but equal branches each having its own powers, the separate branches were intended not to engender confrontation but to ensure checks and balances that would forestall civil strife. So too our civic design has often sought to minimize direct confrontation—and the possibility that someone will be seen as the loser.

These ideals were reflected in Pierre L'Enfant's plan for Washington, D.C. By creating two grand axes from the White House and the Capitol, L'Enfant eschewed several options that were clearly more confrontational. One of several alternatives the expatriate Frenchman might have chosen was a single allée, putting the president at one end and Congress at the other, with streets radiating out from both buildings (Fig. 271). Such an alternative, however, with two buildings directly facing each other, would have been symbolically confrontational.

Consciously or unconsciously, L'Enfant avoided any hint of confrontation by orienting the two buildings to stand at right angles to each other.* The open

*Many have pondered why there were only two axes when we have three branches of government—why the Supreme Court was to be left at the head of its own square off to one side. When L'Enfant made his plan, the case of *Marbury* v. *Madison,* establishing the judicial branch as an active and fully equal third partner, was still twelve years in the future, so L'Enfant's design, celebrating only two branches of government, was consistent with the times.

Architect Paul Rudolph suggested in 1963 that the Supreme Court be relocated from its present home behind the Capitol to a new site at the end of Maryland Avenue, which intersects the Capitol on the south side of the Mall at roughly the same angle as Pennsylvania Avenue does on the north side. This solution would have effected a gigantic triangle, symbolically more in keeping with three equal branches of government. ("A View of Washington as a Capital—Or What Is Civic Design?" *Architectural Forum* 118 [January 1963]:64).

272. The Capitol; view from the Mall.

axes extending from each edifice met at a giant intersection, which as we saw earlier, L'Enfant intended to be marked and celebrated by some large symbolic feature. Nevertheless, when one stands at L'Enfant's intersection and looks at the White House, or particularly back up the Mall toward the Capitol on its own hill (Fig. 272), the sensation is uncomfortably similar to the feeling one has when facing the palace at Versailles. Although from this intersection we are facing the back door of both the White House and the Capitol, not the front entrance, as at Versailles, the symbolism of long axes leading directly to the seat of power is similar. Consequently, we have found a way to ameliorate the submission to authority—or the confrontation with it—that these views imply. We have adopted the diagonal swath of Pennsylvania Avenue as the connecting link between the two seats of power.

Pennsylvania Avenue was, to be sure, a principal feature of L'Enfant's design. L'Enfant intended it to be a grand boulevard lined with large homes, government buildings, a playhouse, and a market exchange. Even though Pennsylvania Avenue was an important street, however, it was clearly subordinate to the much larger green axes of the South Lawn and the Mall, and little different in character from many of the city's other wide diagonal streets.

Peets has written extensively about L'Enfant's treatment of Pennsylvania Avenue. From his twentieth-century perspective, Peets thought L'Enfant had wanted the street to have the same overarching symbolic stature we now give it. Consequently, he chided the Frenchman, thinking L'Enfant had desired the avenue to be directly on axis with the White House, but had miscalculated either the location of the building or the angle of the street. Peets demonstrated that if the avenue were to be extended west through the White House grounds, it would not have directly intersected the White House but would have passed south of the original building, nicking only the later West Wing addition (Fig. 273).[3]

Even if L'Enfant had realigned Pennsylvania Avenue, or otherwise repositioned the White House to end the long diagonal from the Capitol, this would not have solved the problem satisfactorily for Peets: the president's residence could never have provided the symbolic climax L'Enfant supposedly intended for it because the White House is so small and the distance between it and the Capitol so great.

Peets's gloss leaves us with only one possible conclusion: L'Enfant, like many Americans since, saw Pennsylvania Avenue as a clear and preeminent link between the Capitol and the White House. However, this conclusion is not sustained by the evidence we have of L'Enfant's real intentions. L'Enfant did not design the avenue to be an unobstructed connection between the two buildings. His aims are evident from the three plazas he wanted to place between the two buildings (Fig. 274). L'Enfant surely knew these plazas would have interrupted

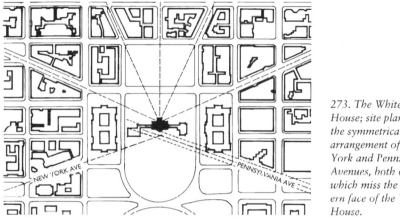
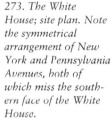

273. *The White House; site plan. Note the symmetrical arrangement of New York and Pennsylvania Avenues, both of which miss the southern face of the White House.*

274. *Washington, D.C.; detail of plan, Pierre Charles L'Enfant, 1791. Note the three squares on Pennsylvania Avenue between the Capitol and the White House.*

any direct link, breaking the street into several discrete sections. From L'Enfant's perspective, in fact, the plazas, like the Capitol and the White House grounds, were just pauses and stops along a much longer route. Pennsylvania Avenue does not begin and end between the Capitol and the White House, but traces a line extending from the Eastern Branch of the Potomac River across the entire city to Georgetown.

Nevertheless, we Americans ascribe great significance—transcendent value, in fact—to the stretch of Pennsylvania Avenue between the Capitol and the White House. This importance, in large measure, comes from the view the avenue provides of the Capitol, a view that has become a staple of postcard and calendar art (Fig. 275). We can look up at the Capitol, but we are not forced to face the building directly. The Capitol is at a slight angle to us; we can engage it, but we are not stopped by it. This view is very different than the one from the Mall—and the one a Frenchman has when approaching Versailles from the Avenue de Paris. The United States Capitol is an important symbol to us, but it is not the end of the journey. After perusing the facade, our eye moves on, and we can move on also—we're free to get back on the road again.

In an eerie presentiment of L'Enfant's design, a similar relationship between buildings and streets exists in Annapolis, Maryland. Planned at the end of the seventeenth century by Francis Nicholson, Annapolis is the only other important American city to be organized around a plan of radiating streets (Fig. 276). The focal points of the plan are two large circles that Nicholson reserved

275. Pennsylvania Avenue, Washington, D.C. Lyndon B. Johnson's 1965 inaugural parade en route to the Capitol.

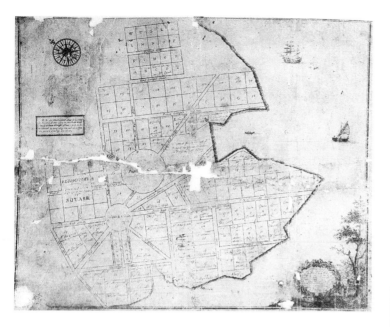

276. *Above: Annapolis, Maryland; plat of the city and port as it appeared in 1718, by James Stoddert, 1743.*

277. *Right: Statehouse, Annapolis; view from one of the radial streets.*

for the town's two most important buildings, the statehouse and the church. The larger Public Circle was to contain the capitol.[4] Yet despite the seeming obviousness of aligning the intersecting streets directly on axis with the statehouse, they are offset slightly in pinwheel fashion around the circle. Later, to compensate for the offset streets, and to face directly the principal road leading into town, the capitol was located eccentrically at one side of the circle rather than in the middle. This location further softens the building's authoritarian sway over all the other streets ending at the circle (Fig. 277).

The smaller Church Circle, located atop a hill above the harbor, is the site of Saint Ann's Episcopal Church. Several streets terminate at this circle as well. Among them, Main Street, leading up from the harbor, is clearly the most important. Nevertheless, church fathers rejected the obvious and architecturally satisfying choice of facing their front door squarely down Main Street, turning it instead away at an angle (Fig. 278). Had the front door of the church ended the axis of Main Street, it would have been, in a country that separated church from state, an even more inappropriate symbol than that of a dominating statehouse. The spire of Saint Ann's remains on axis with Main Street, but it too is at an angle. Rather than terminating the street, the spire acts as a Maypole, something to grab on to as we continue around the circle. Laid out almost eighty years before the American Revolution, Annapolis offers evidence that Americans were already uncomfortable with a plan in which paths led directly to a symbol of power.

In America even when we find a goal at the end of the road it is often, like Dorothy's Emerald City in *The Wizard of Oz,* a chimera. The town of Williamsburg, Virginia, exemplifies this phenomenon. Also planned by Nicholson several years after Annapolis, Williamsburg came into being as the British capital of the Virginia colony, and served briefly after the American Revolution as the state capital. Two of the town's most important buildings, the colonial statehouse and an administration building for the College of William and Mary, sit at either end of Duke of Gloucester Street, which runs for approximately three-quarters of a mile between them (see Fig. 211). Because of this arrangement Williamsburg has frequently been cited as an exception to the American propensity for paths without goals and roads without ends—proof, supposedly, that we can produce civic architecture when we really want to.

The symbolic link between Duke of Gloucester Street and these two buildings is tenuous at best, however. The capitol is not actually on axis with the street, but is sited in seemingly haphazard fashion slightly north of it. The build-

278. Saint Ann's Church, Annapolis; view from Main Street.

279. Left: Capitol,
Williamsburg, Virginia,
1706–1720, burned
1781, reconstructed
1930–1934; view of the
front entrance. Duke of
Gloucester Street is
beyond the photograph
to the left.

ing itself is H-shaped, composed of two separate chambers connected by an enclosed gallery above an entry portico (Fig. 279). This shape would seem a natural terminus, ideally suited to receive the thrust of the street's long axis. The building goes to great lengths to avoid this role, however, turned as it is ninety degrees from the street and set well back from it. The front door faces an adjoining lane instead, leaving only a side entrance from the chambers to face the street (Fig. 280). Architectural historian Carl R. Lounsbury has argued persuasively that the architects supervising the reconstruction of the Capitol in the 1930s erroneously located this side entrance. An adherence to Beaux-Arts principles of axial symmetry and a knowledge of Georgian architecture led the architects to place the door in the middle of the facade, rather than one bay farther south as dictated by the archaeological evidence.[5] The change suggested by Lounsbury, pushing the door to the right, would, nonetheless, still have left it off axis with Duke of Gloucester Street.

280. Above: Capitol,
Williamsburg; view
from Duke of
Gloucester Street. Note
the location of the side
door with respect to
the axis of the street.

281. Right: Administration building, College of William and Mary, Williamsburg, ca. 1696; view of the back door from the end of Duke of Gloucester Street.

282. Below: Administration building; front entrance; view from the William and Mary campus.

The administration building at the other end of Duke of Gloucester Street provides an even more ambiguous ending. This structure is located nearly three hundred feet from the street's terminus and at a slight angle with its axis (Fig. 281). Its front door is on the opposite side of the building and is the conclusion of a grand allée inside the William and Mary campus (Fig. 282), leaving the back door to face Duke of Gloucester Street. Thus, Williamsburg's salient feature, a main street stretching between two goals, actually runs from a building off axis with the street and showing only its side door at one end, to the back door of a building set well back from the road, at the other. Louis XIV would certainly never have tolerated such a composition.

Perhaps the feature at Williamsburg most resonant with American values is the 200-foot-wide lawn marching from the Governor's Palace across Duke of Gloucester Street and off into the forest on the other side (Fig. 283). Like the view from the courtyard of Kahn's Salk Institute (see Fig. 246), the view from the Governor's Palace is open and seemingly unbounded. Several early maps of Williamsburg show buildings opposite the lawn on the far side of the street that would have partially blocked this open allée. Their subsequent disappearance seems appropriately American as well (see Fig. 211).

The buildings at Williamsburg are not isolated examples of ambiguous endings. The Ferry Building, for instance, at the head of Market Street in San Francisco, is turned at a slight angle to approaching traffic, aligned instead with the shoreline (Fig. 284). Near the building, Market Street is also closed to vehicular traffic, further undercutting the tower's confrontational power. We sometimes vitiate the authoritative potential of a building by moving it off axis, as happened with the courthouse in Litchfield, Connecticut. The building sits at the head of North Main Street, a long, straight lane flanked by some of Litchfield's more splendid residences. The courthouse tower would have been tall enough to terminate the axis of the street, but it is sited to one side instead (Fig. 285).

283. Open lawn, Williamsburg; view from the Governor's Palace, 1994.

284. Above: Ferry
Building, San
Francisco; photograph
ca. 1922, aerial view.

285. Right:
Courthouse, Litchfield,
Connecticut; view
from North Main
Street.

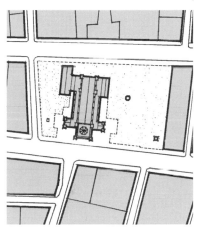

286. Trinity Church, New York City, Richard Upjohn, 1846; view from Wall Street, ca. 1900, left; site plan, above.

Trinity Church in New York City by Richard Upjohn projects a similar but more subtle deflection of conflict (Fig. 286). Opening onto Broadway at the head of Wall Street, the front of the church has become a favorite postcard view. Its articulated Gothic Revival facade, juxtaposed against blander modern buildings, creates an architectural tension, as does the scale of the spire, once the tallest structure in Manhattan but now dwarfed by the surrounding office towers. The entire tableau is heightened by the location of the church: not precisely on axis with Wall Street as it appears, but slightly north of the intersection.

Only part of the church would be in view if Wall Street were straight. However, the old protective walls that originally gave Wall Street its name left behind an irregular right-of-way. Wall Street splays open at its terminus with Broadway. Consequently, the buildings on the south side of Wall Street seem to stand back to reveal the church. As we approach, we have a choice. We can bend right and engage the church's front door, which is at a slight angle to us, or turn

*287. Above: State
Capitol, Carson City,
Nevada.*

*288. Right: State
House, Boston, Charles
Bulfinch, 1795–1798;
view from Park Street.*

left down Broadway and avoid the front door entirely. Trinity Church changes
the confrontation between avarice and virtue from one that is inevitable to one
that is only likely—an apt symbol for Wall Street.

Even when a building is supposed to have authoritarian presence, its confrontational potential is often undercut by other features that vitiate that
authority. Often an American state capitol building will be sited in a parklike
setting, which makes the structure seem less dominant and more publicly accessible. The neoclassical facades and strong axial frontality of a number of these
buildings transmit one message while semicircular or angled driveways transmit
another.

The Nevada state capitol is actually masked from the road by a stand of
trees (Fig. 287). The Massachusetts State House by Charles Bulfinch has a more
subtle relationship with the public. The structure sits amid other buildings at
one corner of the Boston Common, a site that in itself diminishes the imperious

289. Left: Television cameras on the White House lawn, 1995.

290. Below: McDonald's drive-in window, Miami.

sway the edifice would otherwise have had over the park and the city (Fig. 288). Although the proximity of the State House to the street heightens our interest, and steps from the sidewalk lead directly to the front door, the angle of the building with respect to Park Street still allows us to engage, then continue on around the corner onto Beacon Street.

The ability to engage at an angle and then move on is implicit in the view of the White House often presented to Americans by television network news. Correspondents habitually place their cameras west of the building on the North Lawn. In this setup the White House is behind the reporter and at a slight angle (Fig. 289). The curved drive eases the approach and renders the White House less imposing, as does the green lawn between building and the street. We look along the drive into the portico where the president greets his guests: if it is after dark the porte cochere will be brightly lit. The camera angle suggests that as a free people we too should be able to drive right up to the president's house, give him

IN THIS TEMPLE
AS IN THE HEARTS OF THE PEOPLE
FOR WHOM HE SAVED THE UNION
THE MEMORY OF ABRAHAM LINCOLN
IS ENSHRINED FOREVER

291. Abraham Lincoln in the Lincoln Memorial; statue by Daniel Chester French, 1922.

a piece of our mind, and then move on. "He's not home? Well, be sure to tell him I was here. I'll catch him next time I'm in town."

Our imagined stop at the White House front door is similar to the pause many Americans make at the drive-in window of a neighborhood bank or a McDonald's restaurant (Fig. 290). We approach the attendant at right angles, and the encounter is brief: we get money or hamburgers and then move on. In a heterogeneous society, engagements like these minimize stress, allowing us lives of relatively less friction.

Even when an angled approach is impossible, we often seek to lessen the confrontation by choosing other views by which to remember a monument. The Lincoln Memorial, designed by Henry Bacon, sits at the opposite end of the Mall from the Capitol. The site, as we have seen, was chosen by the Senate Park Commission to close the Mall and balance the Capitol at the other end. The memorial's focus is Daniel Chester French's statue of Lincoln, one of America's best-known pieces of sculpture. Lincoln sits in his chair, dead center in the middle bay of Bacon's neoclassical peristyle, looking back toward the Capitol. Despite this impressive location, the statue is frequently remembered and more often photographed at an angle rather than head-on as the Senate Park Commission might have expected (Fig. 291).[6] We have also made it impossible to approach the Lincoln Memorial directly on axis from the Capitol by placing a nearly 2,000-foot-long Reflecting Pool in front of the building. (The Capitol also has a large pool in front of it at the base of Capitol Hill.) Finally, many people do not regard the more dramatic calendar-art view of the Lincoln Memorial to be from the Mall at the front of the building, but behind it at an angle from either Rock Creek Parkway or Memorial Bridge (see Fig. 184).

Similarly, we have blurred the connection between the Jefferson Memorial and the White House by "indenting" the Potomac River, creating the Tidal Basin, which separates the two buildings. As a result, the Jefferson Memorial is seen as an idyllic temple surrounded by cherry trees on its own island, rather than the conclusion of a grand axis stretching from the White House (see Figs. 233 and 244).

Edward Hall reported on an experiment in a hospital ward that demonstrates our penchant for reducing confrontation. Although the hospital in question was actually in Saskatchewan, Canada, the experiment itself has considerable resonance in America.[7] Doctors and staff had recently installed tables and chairs in the patients' recreation room. They wanted to know whether any particular arrangement of furniture was more or less conducive to encouraging patient interaction. Each table was rectangular and seated six people, two on each long side and one at either end. All the furniture was movable. By watching the patients over a period of time, doctors discovered that when two of them stopped to converse they almost invariably pulled up chairs to a corner of the table, and sat down at right angles to each other (Fig. 292). Patients normally looked past each other as they chatted, turning at forty-five degrees to face each other directly only when they wished. The spatial arrangement was nearly identical to the one L'Enfant had created for the Capitol and the White House.

Innumerable American homeowners mitigate the confrontation their house may suggest to visitors approaching the front door (Fig. 293). While the house

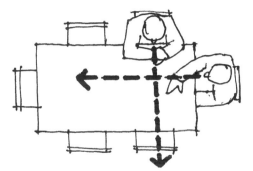

292. Typical two-patient seating arrangement, Saskatchewan hospital.

*293. Below: Curved front walk,
Columbus, Ohio.*

294. Right: Home, Sweet
Home, *Mary Englebreit, 1991,
ink and colored pencil on
paper. © ME Ink.*

*295. Vanna Venturi House, Chestnut Hill,
Pennsylvania, Robert Venturi, 1961–1964; site
plan, above left; front facade, above.*

296. Oak Alley Plantation, on the Mississippi River, Vacherie, Louisiana, ca. 1830.

typically sits square to the street, the front walk will frequently wiggle, bend, and meander. The pattern is common enough to be an American icon (Fig. 294). Similarly, Robert Venturi angled the driveway of the seminal house he designed for his mother in Chestnut Hill, Pennsylvania. The house sits on a small flag lot, connected only by the driveway to the street (Fig. 295). In this instance the tiny residence would have been overmatched by a long drive at right angles—the house would have lost the confrontation.

Perhaps the only building types in America for which strong axial frontality seems completely natural are the antebellum plantations in the South, which were often placed at the end of a lane, like Oak Alley in Louisiana (Fig. 296), and southern courthouses, like the one in Warrenton, Virginia (Fig. 297). The approaches to these buildings—straight ahead to the front door—seem appropriate to a culture of hierarchy and subjugation.

Many Americans want to move toward a goal, achieve it, and then keep on going to another adventure. Because New York City's Grand Central Terminal, directly on axis with Park Avenue, appears at first to be a simple goal at the end of a

297. Courthouse, Warrenton, Virginia, William H. Baldwin, 1853–1854.

298. Above: Grand
Central Terminal,
New York City, Reed
and Stem, Warren
and Wetmore, 1913;
viaducts completed,
1919; photograph
ca. 1939.

299. Above right:
New York Central
Building, New York
City, Warren and
Wetmore, 1929;
photograph 1936.
Collection of The
New-York Historical
Society. The Pan Am
Building (now Met
Life), 1963, today
looms between the
New York Central
Buiding and Grand
Central Terminal.
Despite its inappropri-
ate bulk, the Pan Am
Building does not
interrupt vehicular
traffic through the
complex.

path, the terminal should be an exception to this norm. Even here, however, an
elaborate network of roads carries us around the building one full level above the
actual front door (Fig. 298). For those who do enter Grand Central the building
is an apt American symbol, its primary purpose being to get us on a train for yet
another journey. To the north of the terminal, the New York Central Building
(now the Helmsley Building) has holes cut in its base to let the traffic keep on
going. Both buildings let us pass (Fig. 299).

We remember sharply buildings that draw us toward them, then let us continue on. A Mormon temple sitting on a promontory above the Beltway outside
Washington, D.C., has that power (Fig. 300). Motorists on the Beltway coming
toward the temple from the east approach it head-on, then swoop down and
away just before reaching the hill. When seen from nearby streets, the temple is
not a particularly memorable edifice. Yet from the Beltway, it is a landmark.
Since the temple opened in 1974, it has been a frequent reference point for
Washingtonians giving directions to visitors arriving by car.

A utilitarian silo at the bend of a rural upstate New York lane stays in our
memory simply because it suggests there is more to come—more adventures
around the bend (Fig. 301). The silo's lack of any architectural features reminds
us that a building's placement is as important as any of its other qualities. In this
regard, a small house on Martha's Vineyard would have seemed undersized and
overwhelmed had it been placed at right angles to the approaching street. Turned
to align with the tangent of the curve, the house keeps us moving around the
bend. In so doing it exudes a certain grandeur despite its modest size (Fig. 302).

Our ability to glance off and keep on moving explains in part the special

300. *Mormon temple, Washington, D.C.; view from the Beltway.*

301. *Farmhouse and silo, Salem, New York.*

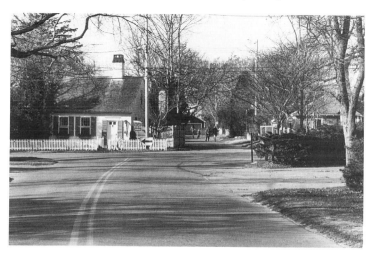

302. *House, Martha's Vineyard.*

appeal to many Americans of the Spanish Steps in Rome (Fig. 303). The facade of the Church of Santa Trinità dei Monti, skewed with respect to the steps below, seems more congruent with American values than the monuments and long Baroque axes of Pope Sixtus V. Certainly the frequency with which church and steps are used as a location shot in American movies suggests a strong attachment to the composition. Taking advantage of the site's popularity, the American Express Company, a quintessential U.S. enterprise serving travelers abroad, has its Rome office nearby.

Engaging a building, then passing it by, is only half the experience. Unless a particular street is one-way, the return trip is usually along the same route. Therefore, as Kevin Lynch noted, "the series of elements must have sequential form taken in either order." He added that "it is as if a movie or a recording had to be played backward as well as forward."[8]

Even though in America one direction is almost always as important as the other, we still find few examples that exploit the return trip. James Renwick Jr.'s Grace Church on Broadway in New York City exemplifies the phenomenon (Fig. 304). Broadway, from its beginning in lower Manhattan, is a long, straight stretch of road until it reaches the church. In front of the Grace Church the street bends, starting its diagonal path across the Manhattan grid. As one approaches the church from lower Manhattan, the body of the building is at an angle beyond the bend, but its spire is directly on axis with Broadway. The symbolism is complex: the spire acts as a goal, while the facade of the church deflects us onward to something not yet in view—an appropriate symbol in a robust city growing uptown.

Unfortunately for Renwick's efforts, vehicular traffic on Broadway is now

303. Spanish Steps, Rome, Specchi and de Sanctis, 1721, with the Church of Santa Trinità dei Monti behind them; plan, below; view from the Piazza di Spagna, below right.

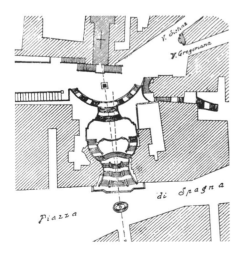

one-way in the opposite direction. As one approaches the building by car heading toward lower Manhattan, church and spire have no presence at all (Fig. 305). The best view of the edifice is through the rearview mirror after passing the bend. Had a second, equally striking building been built next to the church on the downtown side of the bend, travelers would have had a similar experience in either direction. Each building might well be very different, and though each would dominate in one direction, neither could dominate in both. As Robert Venturi noted, when we move past "a complex composition . . . at one moment one meaning can be perceived as dominant; at another moment a different meaning seems paramount."[9] Grouped together the two buildings on Broadway would have celebrated the passing traveler rather than themselves.

Coming or going, bends in the road mark a change in direction—and thus in many ways a new beginning. Charles Moore thought bends were intrinsically

304. Above left: Grace Church, New York City, James Renwick Jr., 1846; view from Broadway looking north.

305. Above: View from Broadway looking south. Grace Church is at left.

306. The grids of San
Francisco, above right;
Denver, far right; and
Dallas, below right.

307. Below:
Downtown Houston.

interesting features, calling them "the fold in the system, the place where the pattern stutters."[10] As examples he cited the downtown business districts of Denver, Dallas, and San Francisco where bends formed by the collision of different grid systems create energy and possibilities (Fig. 306). Similarly, the entire downtown of Houston, Texas, is cocked at an angle with the surrounding streets. Each approach road presents an opportunity as it turns toward downtown (Fig. 307). The bends are hinges, seen and understood in both directions over long distances. Individual architects, of course, take advantage of sites like these to express the tension between two different axes, or simply to catch the eye of the passing motorist, as has happened on the Strip in Las Vegas where the biggest and most exuberant signs are located at the one bend in the roadway (Fig. 308).

Hinges like these should be treated as special places in this country's zoning ordinances, but currently they are not. Signs, special facades, and increased bulk are some of the obvious tools for making these hinges special. Allowing an even bigger and more ebullient sign and building at the bend on Canal Street, in the heart of New York City's Chinatown (Fig. 309), for example, would give focus to an entire neighborhood.

308. Above left: Treasure Island sign at the bend in the road on the Las Vegas Strip.

309. Above: Canal Street, New York City; view looking west.

310. Duck at the bend in the road.

To avoid the pitfalls of spot zoning, a legal construct that holds a municipality cannot treat a single small area or individual building, like the one on Canal Street, differently than its neighbors, perhaps one would first have to create a class of "hinges" throughout a city and treat each by the same rules. One might even encourage hinges whose base responds to one set of criteria and whose top responds to another, much as Grace Church does. Put simply, we could, as it were, encourage the duck to turn its head (Fig. 310).

Yet in trying to match buildings to the bend, one must take cognizance of the American penchant for simple solutions, and often, simple building shapes. Sitte, for one, believed that building parcels left by tightly curved city streets offered great opportunities. "What architect is afraid of an irregularly shaped building lot?" he mused.[11] Thomas Jefferson knew the American psyche better. He feared that a practical-minded people of strong egalitarian bent would not fill the irregular lots created in Washington by L'Enfant's diagonal streets. His concerns were borne out by the many maladroitly shaped spaces and remaindered parcels that still exist in the nation's capital some two hundred years after the city was founded. His fear has also been vindicated by the poor fit of building to street on other diagonal avenues in America, such as the Benjamin Franklin Parkway in Philadelphia (Fig. 311),* or lower Seventh Avenue in New York City, which was hacked through Greenwich Village early in this century, leaving to this day a number of awkwardly shaped and clumsily filled building lots (Fig. 312).

When buildings do not align with the street, uncertainty ensues; the building seeming to have one agenda, and the street another. Such was the problem with Philip Johnson's master plan for a new residential community on Roosevelt Island, in New York's East River. Johnson decided that the community's Main Street should be a series of tangents connected by tight curves rather than run-

---

*Jacques Greber, the designer of the Benjamin Franklin Parkway, was, like L'Enfant, a Frenchman. Greber too brought the memory of the great diagonals of Paris to his work in America.

311. Above: Fairmount Parkway, Philadelphia, Jacques Greber, 1917; view from City Hall tower, ca. 1920.

312. Left: Small parcels on Seventh Avenue, Greenwich Village, New York City. The irregular shape of the lots and exposed side walls of the adjacent building are typical of new roads cut through existing neighborhoods.

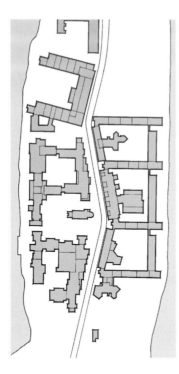

*313. Above:
Roosevelt Island,
New York City, Philip
Johnson, 1969; site
plan.*

*314. Above right:
Main Street,
Roosevelt Island.
Note the haphazard
relationship of the
steps in the fore-
ground to the
sidewalk.*

ning in a straight line the length of the island (Fig. 313).[12] By bending the street, Johnson could avoid having open views at either end, creating a more intimate and contained streetscape. The narrowness of the island, however, combined with the size of the U-shaped buildings pressing in on both sides makes Main Street seem more like a street found in a medieval town. Some of the architects who later designed the actual apartment houses responded by stepping the buildings back from the street. Some building facades and entrances do not align with the sidewalk, leaving an inchoate streetscape of irregular spaces between buildings and between the buildings and the street (Fig. 314).*

On Riverside Drive in New York City Frederick Law Olmsted dealt with the problem of fitting buildings to the street by making the radii of the curves large enough that the buildings since constructed seem to fit the gentle curves, bending in concert with them (Fig. 315). In reality some of the facades do not follow the curve of the street but, like the small house on Martha's Vineyard, are at a tangent to it.

The curves and bends of American highways, particularly the beltways ringing many large cities, create similar opportunities for architectural interest.

---

*Johnson's plan dramatizes a dilemma which Sitte himself understood, but could not solve. Although Sitte wanted tightly curved streets he knew that if "sundry curves, twisted streets and irregularities [are] included artificially in the plan" the result is "an affected artlessness, a purposeful unintentionalness." He wondered whether "the accidents of history over the course of centuries [could] be invented and constructed ex novo in the plan. Could one, then, truly and sincerely enjoy such a fabricated ingenuousness, such a studied naturalness? Certainly not," he concluded (*City Planning*, 111).

315. Riverside Drive,
New York City,
Frederick Law
Olmsted, 1886;
aerial view.

Products of the interstate highway program begun in the 1950s, the nearly continuously curving geometry of these roads offers many locations where buildings and signs can be seen over longer distances. Authors Christopher Tunnard and Boris Pushkarev saw the untapped synergy between high-speed roads like these and the buildings flanking them. As one example, they described the appeal of a hospital complex sited on a hill near West Haven overlooking the Connecticut Turnpike (Fig. 316).[13] The buildings are not distinguished, but their location along the highway, like that of the Mormon temple on the Washington Beltway, draws us toward them. For the most part, however, just as we have not yet grasped ways of using paired signs as gates and transitions so we have not yet encouraged appropriately scaled signs and buildings at strategic locations to draw us toward them and then let us pass.[14]

In this regard John Nash's plan for London's Regent Street is worth studying for the interrelationship of street and building. Of particular interest is Nash's use of colonnades and convex and concave building facades lining the street to hold the tight curves and keep the eye moving (Fig. 317). Where possible, he located the more interesting buildings at the head of the street or on the outside of the curve, where they could be seen over longer distances. He also recognized that the viewer's interest depended on the character of the buildings on the inside of the curve. By forcing these good soldiers to hug the street, he framed views as they changed, preventing each new vista from opening too rapidly. The interrelationship of one side of the road to the other was key to making the trip along Regent Street seem continuous.

The tight curves and bends, a solution that was not Nash's first choice, were needed so as to avoid various existing buildings. Consequently, Regent Street is a rather tortuous route, reflecting, if nothing else, the artistic difficulties of working in a democratic culture that puts high value on the rights of private property owners. By contrast, Haussmann, working for Napoleon III in Paris, and the architects working for Sixtus V in Rome, would certainly have demolished more buildings and straightened the street. To an expansive people like Americans, even in the early nineteenth century the tightness of Nash's curves

316. Veterans Hospital, West Haven, Connecticut, photograph ca. 1962.

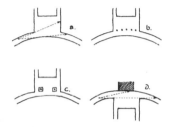

317. *Left: Regent Street, London.*

318. *Below left: Bruges (Sitte). Sitte considered Place Stevin on the outside of the curve (III on the plan) a fortuitous exception to the rule that all holes should be on the inside of the curve.*

319. *Above: Diagram by Le Corbusier showing various schemes for displaying a building of importance. Scheme a, with a hole on the outside of the curve, is the least attractive. The hole can be mitigated by trees, as in Scheme b, or by monuments, as in Scheme c. The superior answer for Le Corbusier is Scheme d, a hole on the inside of the curve.*

would have seemed claustrophobic. Today, for reasons of traffic safety, they would be illegal.

Both Camillo Sitte and Le Corbusier gave considerable thought to the problem of interdependency. Both believed it wrong, for example, to create an opening in a wall of buildings on the outside of a curve where a missing building would be more apparent. Sitte regarded the hole on the outside of the curve at Place Stevin in Bruges as "the rare exception because one tried in general not to interrupt the concave face of the street since it displays buildings to good advantage" (Fig. 318).[15] Le Corbusier came to the same conclusion, producing a series of sketches in his notebooks[16] to suggest ways of ameliorating what he thought were the disruptive effects of openings on the outside of a curve (Fig. 319).*

In an American landscape dotted with small freestanding structures, the issue of where to place an opening along a curve is reversed. It is on the inside of a curve that a gap, a hole, or a missing building will short-circuit the trip. When these gaps occur, we believe we should be able to save time by cutting across the

*Le Corbusier, after initially endorsing many of Sitte's ideas, later rejected them bitterly. He particularly criticized Sitte's fondness for the picturesque curves of Italian hill towns, attacking him for "a philosophy of disorder and mere aesthetics." He called Sitte's roads *"les chemins des anes."* Straight roads, by contrast, were *"les chemins des hommes,"* the difference being that *"L'homme marche droit parce qu'il a un but."* (Quoted in Reyner Banham, *Theory and Design in the First Machine Age* [New York: Praeger, 1960], 248). That Le Corbusier thought men traveled in a straight line because they had a purpose, while donkeys did not, prompted Banham to suggest that Le Corbusier had made an unfair comparison—"that both men and donkeys would travel in a straight line if there were some end in view" (*First Machine Age*, 248). The truth is that both men and asses will also travel around a bend if they are convinced of the necessity of doing so.

open landscape. For example, when Roosevelt Island officials decided to retain a preexisting chapel designed by Frederick Withers in the middle of the island, reconciling this building with Main Street presented an awkward problem. Johnson chose to bend the street around the back of the chapel, giving importance to its rear facade (see Fig. 313). Even though the building is on the inside of the curve, there is still enough room between it and the sidewalk on Main Street to create a plaza of sorts in between. Many pedestrians leave the sidewalk when they reach the chapel and cut straight across the plaza (Fig. 320). This shortens the trip, but it also short-circuits the effect of the curve, heightening its ersatz quality.

Art and architecture sometimes have antithetical imperatives with regard to the curved road. For example, Edward Hopper used short-circuiting to great pictorial effect in his painting *Gas* (Fig. 321). To bring our eye to the center of the painting, to pull us into the light, Hopper put the station on the inside of a gentle curve. We have left the road and are about to stop between the fuel pumps and the station's open door. The brightly lit pumps bracket the warm light flooding from the building. Beyond is a dark forest and the resumption of an uncertain journey.

What works brilliantly for Hopper as an artistic construct becomes unintentionally ambiguous and confusing in the real landscape, however. A Martha's Vineyard gas station on the inside of the curve is a case in point (Fig. 322). As we come around the bend, an illicit possibility suggests itself: we can take a shortcut through the station. If no cars are lined up for gas, we can sneak through to rejoin the road on the far side. The time saved must be weighed only against the consequences of hitting a gas pump. That we even consider the possibility indicates the station's location has short-circuited the trip.

To hold a curve effectively in the open American landscape, buildings need not be pressed hard against the bend, as they were on Nash's Regent Street. Hopper shows us in another painting that a curve can be held with just a small freestanding building and several trees at a modest distance from the road (Fig. 323). The painting's title, *Solitude*, is derived in part from the absence of people, but the title also has resonance because we know how difficult it is to stop and

321. *Left: Gas,
Edward Hopper,
1940. Oil on canvas,
26¼ x 40¼ in. (66.7 x
102.2 cm). The
Museum of Modern
Art, New York. Mrs.
Simon Guggenheim
Fund. © 1996 The
Museum of Modern
Art.*

322. *Below: Gas
station, Martha's
Vineyard.*

323. *Left:* Study for Solitude
#56, *Edward Hopper, 1944,
drawing for painting Solitude.
Conte on paper, 15¹/₁₆ x 22⅛
in. (38.3 x 56.2 cm).
Collection of the Whitney
Museum of American Art.
Josephine N. Hopper Bequest.
70.855. Hopper deleted the
house on the left in the final
painting.*

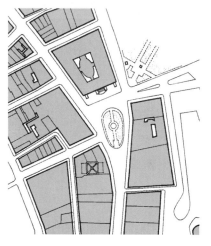

324. Above: United States Customs House, Broadway, New York City, Cass Gilbert, 1907. The trees soften the building's authoritarian presence. Battery Park is in the background on the right.

325. Right: Plan of lower Broadway.

linger on the inside of a curve. Our eye is pulled around the bend, beyond the tiny house on the right, leaving us little time for the people living there.

One particular combination of three buildings at the foot of Broadway in lower Manhattan propels us around the bend as adroitly as any group of buildings in America. The appeal of each building is enhanced by the presence of the other two—a mutual interdependence that is rare in America, and therefore worth noting. The most important of the three is the United States Customs House by Cass Gilbert (Fig. 324). This irregularly shaped Beaux-Arts confection, fronted by a small plaza called Bowling Green, seems to terminate the street. Vehicular traffic moves one-way toward the building; at the plaza the street

326. *Standard Oil Building, Broadway, New York City, Carrère and Hastings, 1922.*

splits into two separate roadways signaling that Broadway has come to an end (Fig. 325).

Equally important to the composition is Carrère and Hastings's Standard Oil Building on the inside of the curve of Broadway (Fig. 326). The building is crowned by a large tower. Rather than being congruent with the base below, the tower, "a giant incense burner from which, in the cold of winter, wisps of white smoke and steam wave in the wind,"[17] is turned to align with the skyscrapers farther north. The lower portion of this Italianate palazzo pushes robustly outward, its convex shape faithfully holding the curve, slowly unveiling the facade of the Customs House.

327. Proposed obelisk for Battery Park. From this distance the Customs House is not yet in view. One Broadway stands in front of the obelisk. Regional Plan Association, 1931.

The Customs House is not on axis with the long, straight stretch of Broadway extending north from Bowling Green, but is slightly around the bend at the end of the street. One first sees the building at the far end of Bowling Green plaza, its front door and grand stairs flanked by Daniel Chester French's statuary. From several blocks north, the view down Broadway is open toward Battery Park. The only suggestion of something yet to come is the last building before the park on the east side of the street; sitting at a slight angle to its neighbors, the building, called One Broadway, subtly suggests a conclusion not yet in view.

The importance of One Broadway can be seen vividly in the rendering of an unbuilt obelisk proposed in the 1920s to be sited in Battery Park on axis with Broadway (Fig. 327). The enormous monument asserts that it is the terminus of the street. However, One Broadway, despite its diminutive size, quietly contradicts that claim.

Because it is small, One Broadway acts as a transition in scale to the even smaller Customs House beyond.[18] Without this mediation, and had the Customs House been located directly on axis with Broadway, it would have seemed hopelessly undersized, its details, even its overscale windows, lost over the great distances involved. From farther up Broadway, the Customs House would have disappeared entirely, blocked from view by the rolling topography of the street.

Although the entire tableau at first seems simply a path leading to a goal, in fact, it is not. As we proceed down Broadway toward its conclusion, we realize there is a choice: we can bend slightly and end our trip at the Customs House or we can enter Battery Park, pass through it, and continue out across the waters of the harbor to the horizon beyond.

Chapter **8**

The Endless

On the road again, just can't wait to get on the road again . . .

WILLIE NELSON
"On the Road Again"

Procession

PATH AND GOAL HAVE ALWAYS SEEMED TO GO TOGETHER—AN AISLE LEADING TO the altar, a street meandering toward the town plaza, or the grand avenue heading straight to the statue of the king—creating a pattern that Kevin Lynch has called "the classical introduction-development-climax-conclusion sequence." Through history this pattern has organized the architecture of everything from Christian churches to Mayan temples and the paths through the Forbidden City in Beijing. Consequently, some architects, as we have seen, still view the world in these terms because it is difficult to accommodate fully to an American architecture that arranges buildings more to ennoble the trip than as the symbolic resolution of the journey. In fact, designers have largely ignored the architectural possibilities of those pathways that, as Lynch put it, "avoid final conclusions."[1] Yet we must focus on the journey itself if we are to produce an American architecture that closely matches our cultural values.

A journey without a beginning or end—with no apparent goal—may seem pointless and without resolution. Yet some of America's most memorable places celebrate the trip rather than its culmination. The opportunity to move back and forth without interruption and without conclusion creates much of the appeal of Robert H. H. Hugman's plan for Riverwalk in San Antonio, Texas. In 1929 Hugman, then a young architect, convinced city fathers that a pending proposal for covering a flood-control ditch running through the center of the city was shortsighted.[2] He argued, instead, that the half-mile-long trench

243

should be left open, and landscaped walkways and other amenities constructed along both sides.

Riverwalk has since become a priceless asset in San Antonio (Fig. 328). Stores and eateries line both sides of the watercourse, and the walkways are filled with people. From street-level bridges, tourists first glimpse a tiny green Nile, one full level below grade, magically snaking its way behind the dust-colored buildings. Only after they have descended the stairs and started tentatively along the river's edge does Riverwalk's full scope become evident. The walkways are continuous—Hugman has blazed a trail. The paths work their way around bridge piers, pass by cafés selling nachos and margaritas, and keep on going. For as long as Riverwalk continues, the public enjoys uninterrupted rights-of-way.

Start and finish have no symbolic importance at Riverwalk: in some locations large blank walls unceremoniously mark the termination of Hugman's efforts, in other areas the walkways simply cease. These ends matter little, however, because many Americans already believe the climax of the trip has no special meaning. Inasmuch as life is an unending journey, the end, as it were, is simply a place to turn around and start back in the opposite direction.

Crucial to the success of Riverwalk is the grade change behind the buildings, which allowed Hugman to avoid the front door–back door problems that bedevil so many efforts to create pathways through the middle of the block. Typically, the paths would have faced unattractive rear yards and back doors on both sides. Because the walkways are one level below the street, however, they are framed by the basements of the abutting buildings. Many buildings lease these basement spaces to commercial establishments, which, in turn, face their front doors toward the walkway.

The Vietnam Veterans Memorial on the Mall in Washington, D.C., by Maya Lin, has a very different impact from Riverwalk, but the sequence one fol-

328. Riverwalk, San Antonio, Texas, Robert H. H. Hugman, begun 1929.

lows when visiting the memorial is quite similar (Fig. 329). At the memorial, we follow a long V-shaped path fronting a wall of black marble panels on which are inscribed the names of those Americans who died in Vietnam. The path descends into the ground at a shallow angle, then rises again so that the marble wall takes on the shape of two long tapers meeting at the low point of the path. The most intense moment along the journey is in the middle, at this low point. The marble wall, covered with names, rises well above head height—and the number of dead becomes overwhelming. Then one ascends again, and the number of names on each panel diminishes until we reach the Mall, where the vista before us is filled only with lawn and trees. The end of the journey has no special meaning; we remember most our feelings at the bottom of the path.

Even in our more formal ceremonies that entail journeys, we often de-emphasize the beginning and end of the trip. For a president's State of the Union address, television takes no note of his departure from the White House, or his return home afterward. It covers only his address. By contrast, when the queen of England leaves Buckingham Palace on official business she does so with great ceremony. News photographers and television cameras sometimes chronicle the moment the gates swing open and her carriage clatters forth, and they also mark her arrival at Westminster Abbey or Saint Paul's Cathedral.

In America because it is the journey itself that matters, and because the trip is etched into memory by the events along the way—the buildings passed; the bends, holes, and pauses—then in an architectural sense, the distances separating these events become equally important. These spaces create rhythms, expressing patterns that Lynch believed would become increasingly important in the modern world. Lynch thought the patterns "might be called melodic in analogy to music," believing that "the events and characteristics along the path—landmarks, space changes, dynamic sensations—might be organized as a melodic line, perceived and imaged as a form which is experienced over a substantial time interval."[3]

329 Vietnam Veterans Memorial, Washington, D.C., Maya Lin, 1983.

330. Burma-Shave signs.

Particularly when one is in motion, the spaces between disparate elements bring each element into focus as part of a larger sequential experience. The Odell family, owners of a shaving cream company in southern Minnesota, discovered this in an elementary way when in 1925 they stumbled onto one of the most famous advertising campaigns in American history. Wanting to put their product before the motoring public, the family erected advertising placards spaced at regular intervals along the highway (Fig. 330). To animate the signs they added rhyming jingles, and almost immediately thereafter Burma-Shave became a household word.

The six signs in each sequence were spaced so that motorists traveling thirty-five miles an hour passed a sign every three seconds, keeping Burma-Shave in a traveler's consciousness for a full eighteen seconds.[4] The Odells also came to understand the interrelationship between speed and spacing. They realized that if motorists sped up, they would miss the message, as evidenced by their 1955 jingle: "Slow down, Pa / Sakes alive / Ma missed signs / four / and five / Burma-Shave."

When the campaign finally ended four decades after it had begun, over three thousand jingles had been placed along roadsides nationwide. Millions of Americans knew the verses; many could even recite them backwards. Mumford, writing about cities some thirty-five years after the Burma-Shave campaign began, said that "in walking, the eye courts variety, but above this gait, movement demands repetition of the units that are to be seen: it is only so that the individual part, as it flashes by, can be recovered and pieced together."[5] He could have added that—as the Odells had demonstrated—cadence and spacing count as well. To the motoring public the Burma-Shave signs connoted motion, much like running a stick along the stiles of a banister.*

*Highway officials have long seen the value of recurring signs. Exit and interchange information are frequently repeated on the open highway. In Virginia, highway officials recently tried using rhyming jingles. Evenly spaced signs along the median of Interstate 66 just outside Washington, D.C., evocative of the Burma-Shave campaign, extoled in rhyme the advantages of carpooling.

The Burma-Shave signs, however, were all on one side of the highway; a richer rhythm is one that brings both sides of the road together. Something on the left followed by something on the right, like the caroms in a pinball machine, creates an alternating rhythm and a counterpoint to the cadence of America's frequently repeated block patterns and regularly spaced buildings. We shift our attention from one side of the road to the other as each separate event glides by.

Sometimes a sequence of buildings creates this rhythm; occasionally holes between buildings produce the pattern. In the past, street trees often set the beat. In the nineteenth century, confident of their new status in the world, Americans burst forth with a desire to beautify the country. Improvement societies and neighborhood associations sprang up across the land. One of their frequent projects was planting trees along the street, and often the trees were elms. Henry James saw the simple power of the elms on the streets of Litchfield, Connecticut: "having spoken of [the streets] as 'elm-shaded' you have said so much about them that little else remains. . . . The great verdurous vista, the high canopy of meeting branches, has the air of consciously playing the trick and carrying off the picture. See with how little we do it; count over the elements and judge how few they are." Scully also wrote of Litchfield's splendor as an "elm forest marching in dark pillars and arching and interlocking over all."[6] Across America the elms were frequently planted in a simple alternating rhythm—one on the traveler's left, followed by one on the right.

Even on Hillhouse Avenue in New Haven where the elm trees were paired rather than staggered (Fig. 331), the regular spacing of the trees stood in coun-

331. Hillhouse Avenue, New Haven, Connecticut; plan of the street in 1879, left; photograph ca. 1885, right.

*332. Commonwealth
Avenue, Back Bay, Boston.*

terpoint to the irregularly spaced buildings behind them.* An alternating rhythm
seems natural enough that on Commonwealth Avenue, in Boston's Back Bay, a
double row of paired trees originally planted in the median has changed character at several locations in almost unnoticed ways. Although the trees are still
aligned with the two roadways, replacement trees have often been irregularly
spaced, creating more of an alternating rhythm (Fig. 332).

An alternating rhythm is so autochthonous as to seem immutable to
Americans, and its connotations are very different from the slower rhythm of
paired poplars marching down a French lane, or the double row of trees on the
Champs-Élysées or the paired columns of the monastic church at Vèzelay. It is an
American rhythm: it's the rhythm of swing and rock and roll. It's also the rhythm
of the Strip in Las Vegas, echoed in crude fashion by many of the large casino
signs, which offset each other. Their frequently alternating rhythm helps us
answer the question posed by Venturi, Scott Brown, and Izenour: how is it that
"in spite of 'noise' from competing signs we do in fact find what we want."[7]
Even though diagrams in their treatise showed the Flamingo and Caesar's Palace

---

*Elm trees do best when planted no closer than 45 feet apart. On a 30- to 36-foot-wide carriageway
of a suburban street, trees planted 45 feet apart on the diagonal will, at maturity, canopy over the
road, their branches just touching. This staggered spacing also allows trees to leap across intersections without interrupting the spacing. Sometimes, on wider streets, double interlocking rows of trees
flanked the sidewalks, creating side aisles on either side of the carriageway.

On Hillhouse Avenue, the paired trees, together with a residence that stood at the head of the street—
a goal at the end of the road—gave the street a distinctly ecclesiastical feeling. (The elm trees are now
gone, lost to disease, and a house at the head of the street has since been demolished, opening the view.)

333. *Las Vegas Strip;*
photograph 1968,
above; 1990, below.
The larger Mirage sign
in the lower photo is at
a bend in the Strip.

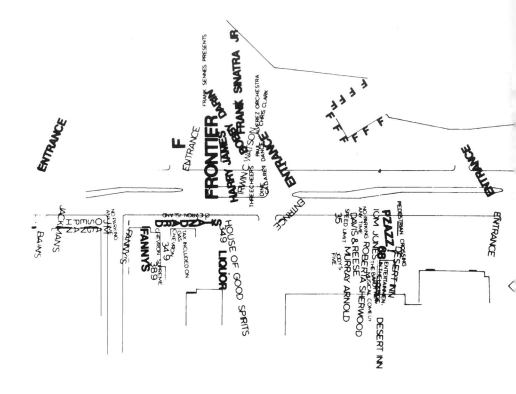

334. Las Vegas Strip; partial sign plan, 1968 (Venturi, Scott Brown and Izenour).

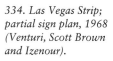

standing directly across the Strip from each other, their signs were not directly opposite but were pushed as far from one another as curb cuts and property boundaries would allow (Fig. 333). Each casino wants its own few seconds of a motorist's undivided attention. Each sign requires some open space around it to set it off, to let it pitch to the passing parade.

Though the casino owners are in competition, they know, like a gaggle of salesmen who simultaneously arrive on the front porch, that a homeowner is unlikely to buy from any one of them if he sees them together; far better to show up one at a time. A close reading of the sign maps in *Learning from Las Vegas* bears this out (Fig. 334), as does a trip up and down the Strip today. None of the Strip's larger signs is directly opposite another. The signs, in a rough approximation of the elm trees, create a sometimes abused, but very real, order amid the apparent riot of different messages. They more or less pull the road together into the continuous experience Americans think it should be.

The same alternating rhythm is even more pronounced in front of the famous Marlboro sign on Sunset Boulevard in West Hollywood (Fig. 335). Sunset Boulevard, as it passes west through Hollywood, is a long straight stretch of road until it reaches the base of the Hollywood Hills. There the road bends to the driver's left and begins a curving descent to lower elevations. The Marlboro man is right where he should be—at the head of the bend—much bigger than the nearby buildings, and in full view of approaching motorists.

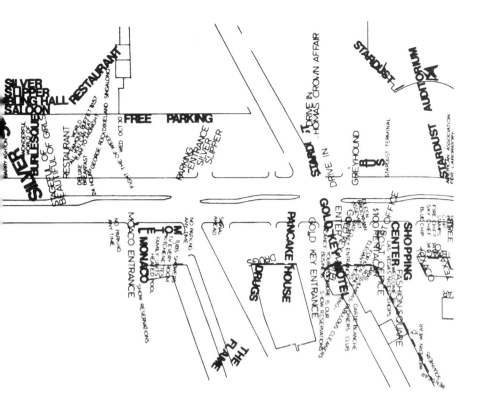

335. Marlboro sign, Sunset Boulevard, West Hollywood; view looking west. Note the erotic poses on the two large figures preceding the Marlboro man.

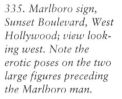

*336. Breezewood,
Pennsylvania.*

The sign's appeal is further heightened by two other large signs featuring human figures, which amid the commercial clutter loom into view on either side of the road before one reaches the bend. The two signs are simple rectangles but nearly as large as the Marlboro billboard. The spacing between all three is the same, and they read in sequence: right, left, and back again to the right and the Marlboro man, who concludes the trilogy. As motorists pass, they swoop down and to the left in much the same way motorists pass the Mormon Tabernacle on the Beltway in Washington. The Marlboro man, however, has a more complex appeal because of the two equally spaced signs that precede him.

Commercial strips, like the one on Sunset Boulevard, have been bugbears for American architects and planners because the cacophony of competing interests seems beyond ordering, and certainly beyond ennobling. Many books and exhibits in the past twenty-five years have recorded and celebrated American commercial strips, particularly their often exotically shaped buildings and signs. Yet many designers continue to believe that any attempt to alleviate the riotous discord that accompanies this vigor will have the opposite of its intended effect. Better to marvel at the strip from afar, because serious design, in lessening the dissonance, or "the endless inconsistencies of roadtown,"[8] as Venturi called it, would dampen the strip's vitality, and thus its reason for being.*

---

*Despite Venturi, Scott Brown and Izenour having brought commercial strips into serious architectural discourse through their book *Learning from Las Vegas*, the programmatic demands and actual dimensions of a typical strip remain largely unstudied. Passing motorists do not have time to delectate over signs, for example, however, little is known about how to get motorists' attention without compromising their safety. And although every national food franchiser has strong ideas about his own particular lot requirements, building size, signage, and seating layout, there is little in the general architectural literature about these dimensions, as there is, by contrast, for other generic building types, like schools and office buildings.

Notwithstanding the dilemma, the rhythm of the signs in Las Vegas and on Sunset Boulevard show us ways to think about the issue. The purpose of all commercial strips is simple: businesses lined up along the road are trying to sell something, and motorists traversing the road—assuming they have a choice of routes—want to buy something. Every architectural decision made on a commercial strip is intended to enhance this potential transaction.

Breezewood, Pennsylvania, a town at the confluence of the Pennsylvania Turnpike and Interstate 70, coming from Washington, D.C., is one of the purest examples in America of the synergy between motorist and merchant. The town, in fact, is all commercial strip. It has no mayor, no police department, no residences; it's just one long street whose only purpose is to sell to passing travelers (Fig. 336).

As on most commercial strips, there is a hierarchy in Breezewood amid the plethora of signs, and a rationale to their placement. The bigger signs announcing gas, food, lodging, and places to shop are pushed up toward the road. Many times these signs have a single logo at the top. Occasionally additional messages are tacked below, most frequently quoting rates and prices or listing the names of individual proprietors. Most of the messages are set high enough above the road so as not to block the view of the buildings and parking areas. Usually the signs are positioned so that motorists are directed to turn off the road before they reach the sign, as one does in front of the McDonald's signs on the Connecticut Turnpike.

Bigger placards are occasionally augmented by very low Enter and Exit signs that crouch along the edge of the road, channeling vehicles to and from the highway. In Breezewood there is one last general category of signs: exceptionally tall placards with a logo at the top, which are set well away from the road. Like the tall signs positioned at some distance from a highway, the signs in Breezewood announce a place of business that is not directly on the strip but on another road or lane nearby.

Each class of message in Breezewood could be assigned airspace vertically above the road and each sign given its own location along the roadway, spaced like commercial airliners in flight. This arrangement would allow every purveyor, as it does each salesman lined up just off the front porch waiting to ring the bell, a better chance to close a deal with passing motorists. Like differently styled front doors, each sign can be unique, and all merchants would be able to hawk their wares more efficiently, but those passing by would have a bit more rhythm to their journey.*

The stores behind the signs also group themselves into different classes or building types. Even without the exuberant signage that inevitably covers these buildings, Americans know the difference between an eatery and a gas station

---

*Property boundaries obviously determine where an owner can and cannot put his sign. The owner of a narrow lot might find it advantageous to place his sign on neighboring property in order to give motorists time to slow down, but that seldom occurs. This, in turn, suggests that, just as we now often require minimum distances between curb cuts for reasons of safety, we might use the same rationale to space out signs, while keeping an economic and aesthetic end in mind.

337. Above: Super sign,
Houston, Texas.

338. Right: Porta Pia,
Rome, Michelangelo,
1561.

just by a building's layout and fenestration. This suggests that, just as three differently styled churches ennoble the New Haven Green through their similar bulk and spacing, so too would McDonald's, Wendy's, and Burger King lend some approximation of that aesthetic tension to a commercial strip by being equally spaced from each other and from the road.

Purposefully placed placards would enhance many of America's large interstate highways, particularly those leading in and out of major cities. Interstate 10 in Texas, for example, is the principal connecting link between downtown Houston and Houston Intercontinental Airport. For first-time visitors heading into the city from the airport, the highway, with the skyline of downtown Houston in the distance, gives a strong first impression of the city. Interstate 10 is already dotted with gigantic billboards just outside the right-of-way (Fig. 337). The scale of these large signs, particularly when seen against a backdrop of small buildings and a flat landscape, gives testament to advertisers' interest in this particular stream of traffic. Together the buildings and signs create an American equivalent to what Venturi called the "superadjacencies" of scale at places like the Porta Pia in Rome (Fig. 338).[9]

Most of the billboard messages along Interstate 10 are regional or national in nature. They advertise such things as airlines, whiskey, and underwear—products that the motorist need not leave the highway at the next exit to buy. For marketing purposes, therefore, the exact placement of these signs is seldom critical. Consequently, one would be relatively free to locate these signs where the spacing between them would have the most dramatic impact. If the signs were much larger still, as befits the enormity of the highway, and if they were placed at regular distances from each other and offset with signs on the other side of the road, they would create rhythms not unlike those of an elm-shaded street, but at a very different scale (Fig. 339).

Just like signs and trees, buildings and holes have created alternating rhythms on some of America's more famous streets. On Fifth Avenue in New

339. The road to downtown.

340. Far left: Plan of Fifth Avenue from Sixty-second to Thirty-ninth Street, New York City.

341. Left: Saint Patrick's Cathedral, New York City, James Renwick Jr., 1858–1888.

342. Below: International Building, Rockefeller Center, New York City; view from Fifth Avenue.

York, for example, if one were able to step backward in time, as in Jack Finney's novel *Time and Again*—back far enough so that the General Motors Building had not yet been built, and the Savoy Plaza Hotel still stood across from Grand Army Plaza—we could see clearly the sequence of holes on Fifth Avenue that created a rhythm unique to that street (Fig. 340).

As we headed down Fifth Avenue, starting somewhere south of the Metropolitan Museum, the great wall of expensive apartment buildings would press up against the street on our left, their windows straining to look out over the trees into Central Park on our right. Ahead, also on the right, Grand Army Plaza would soon come into view, a block-sized hole signaling the upcoming stores and offices.

Seven blocks past the plaza we would pass a second hole on the left—actually an event in a hole—formed by James Renwick Jr.'s Saint Patrick's Cathedral (Fig. 341). The front of the edifice presses forward to the street. Directly opposite, the front door of the International Building at Rockefeller Center sits back from the sidewalk to receive the thrust of the church (Fig. 342). One block farther south we glimpse the long allée leading into the heart of Rockefeller Center (Fig. 343). The narrow width of the opening makes the walkway seem less like a hole and more like an elegant entryway in the middle of the block. Finally, seven blocks south of Rockefeller Center, the New York Public Library by Carrère and Hastings creates a two-block-long hole on the west side of the avenue (Fig. 344).

343. Above left: Rockefeller Center; view from Fifth Avenue looking toward the skating rink.

344. Above: Public Library, New York City, Carrère and Hastings, 1898–1911; view from Fifth Avenue looking southeast.

The big events directly on Fifth Avenue—the Grand Army Plaza, Saint Patrick's, and the Public Library—create a three-hole sequence of right, left, right. Within this cadence a smaller four-hole sequence is created by the gaps on both sides of Saint Patrick's, the recessed front door of the International Building, and the opening to the allée of Rockefeller Plaza—left, right, left, and right again—two alternating rhythms that echo the pattern of the shoppers browsing here and browsing there. Although these sequences were never consciously planned, the spacing between the bigger holes is nearly equal—seven blocks from Grand Army Plaza to Saint Patrick's, and eight blocks from Saint Patrick's to the library—and the spaces around Saint Patrick's and Rockefeller Center are exactly equally spaced.

This portion of Fifth Avenue is the heart of the city's retail shopping district, yet it has no symbolic start or finish. The goals along it are all en route, not at either end. Most of Fifth Avenue is still either behind us or before us, from its beginnings at the Harlem River Drive over three miles to the north, to its terminus one and a half miles farther south at Washington Square Park. An excursion along Fifth Avenue seldom goes from one end to the other, just as few people ever drive the full length of Route 66 or walk the entire Appalachian Trail.

In similar fashion, but on a much smaller scale, Main Street in Vineyard Haven on Martha's Vineyard has no goal at its beginning or end. Despite a mélange of architectural styles, running from vaguely Queen Anne and Colonial Revival to mock Tudor, Modern Cape Cod, and California Strip Commercial, Main Street's three-block-long stretch of stores and eateries has a decided cohesiveness. The street has a very different character from either of the island's other two principal commercial centers. The predominantly white clapboard Greek Revival buildings in Edgartown and the Carpenter Gothic motif on many of the stores in Oak Bluffs make these shopping streets seem stylistically more of a piece than the eclectic assemblage in Vineyard Haven. Nevertheless, as William Styron wrote, although Main Street "will never win a contest for beauty or charm, . . . the ugly duckling gains its place in one's heart by way of an appeal that is not immediately demonstrable."[10] That appeal is partly a function of the rhythm of the holes along the street (Fig. 345).

Main Street in Vineyard Haven begins as one arm of a Y-intersection. At the corner, on the right as we start our journey, sits the town's hotel, a nondescript sum of many additions over many years (Fig. 346). The building's three-story height seems appropriate to the corner, however. As the tallest structure on the street, the hotel is a newel post subtly marking the beginning of the trip. Five buildings farther along, on the opposite side of the street, a small group of shops forms a "plazaette" (Fig. 347). Here too the architecture is undistinguished. An unpainted wood fence separating the plaza from the sidewalk is too high, and the fake mansard roofs and large panes of glass in the storefronts surrounding the plaza make the composition more stylistically appropriate to southern California than to New England. The open area, however, is one of the more popular gathering spots on the island, offering a respite in the midst of surrounding buildings all pushed out to the sidewalk.

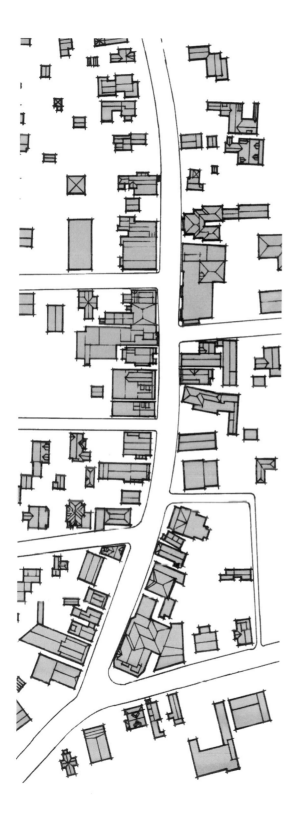

345. Left: Plan of Main Street, Vineyard Haven, Massachusetts. Note the number of freestanding buildings.

346. Top: Tisbury Inn at the head of Main Street.

347. Above: Hole on the left, Main Street.

348. Above: First hole on the right, Main Street.

349. Right: Second hole on the right, Main Street.

Beyond this first hole, Main Street begins to drop and bend to the left, appearing to sag and curve simultaneously. A sequence of three holes appears on the opposite side of the street from the plaza. Clustered together on the outside of the curve at the lowest part of the street, the holes seem to have slid downhill like beads on a string. The first hole is a concrete pad, the forecourt of a store that was once a stable (Fig. 348). The middle hole, a small patch of ground filled with an enormous linden tree, is the symbolic center of Vineyard Haven, a spot where islanders hold bake sales and pass out petitions (Fig. 349). Then a third hole, a small recess at the next corner with a single bench, functions as a popular waiting area (Fig. 350).* From there Main Street rises until it passes a gate, as it were, formed by two holes opposite each other. The two holes suggest a slight pause, marking the end of the commercial district and the beginning of a residential zone. The left-hand hole is formed by two larger freestanding buildings on either side of a small recessed house (Fig. 351). The right-hand hole is a gap between buildings that offers a view of the harbor (Fig. 352). One side of this gap is formed by a tiny stone bank, its style a mix of California bungalow and Bavarian hunting lodge, and the other side is lined with a white clapboard house.

---

*All three holes are on the outside of the curve, contrary to where Sitte and Le Corbusier thought holes in a street should be. On the inside of the bend, various merchants have struggled valiantly to give focus to a narrow vacant lot and the open space behind it. A series of seasonal businesses have come and gone, each trying to create an identity on the inside of a curve, where it is difficult to stop.

The change in style across the gap reinforces the message that the shopping district has ended.

The pattern on Main Street—a hotel on the right, followed by a hole on the left, then three holes on the right, and ending with a two-hole pause—is a variant of the more regularly alternating rhythm of Fifth Avenue. The sequence on Main Street, particularly the three-hole riff on the right, seems appropriate to a curved street, however, because the three holes are all on the outside of the curve, each one pulling us farther around the bend. And though traffic on Main Street is one-way in the direction just described, the sequence also functions equally well in the opposite direction. This street suggests that many smaller-scale shopping streets across America are susceptible to similar rhythms.

Regularly spaced holes and events on Broadway in lower Manhattan contribute to that street's special character. Broadway has considerable symbolic importance to New Yorkers because it is where they stage ticker-tape parades to welcome home heroes. Processions start in front of the U.S. Customs House (see Fig. 324) and head uptown to end at City Hall a half mile away. Before tracing the parade route, however, let us go back in time, as we did on Fifth Avenue, remove the United States Steel Building and the park just south of it, putting back the wall of buildings that was there before. Across the street we can leave Marine Midland as it is (Fig. 353).

Now we begin the procession, and pass by in sequence the separate holes

350. Top left: Third hole on the right, Main Street.

351. Above left: Half a gap on the left, Main Street.

352. Above: Half a gap on the right, Main Street.

353. Above: Plan of Broadway from the Customs House to City Hall.

354. Right: Broadway, New York City; view looking north. Trinity Church is partially hidden at left.

and architectural events that we noted in previous chapters. We start with the Customs House at our back. No television cameras will be positioned to catch the exact moment we step out from the building, but we can still start with a flourish if we wish, moving down the grand stair of the Customs House between the flanking statues, on to the backseat of the waiting convertible (see Fig. 324). As we get under way, we see One Broadway ahead and to our left, subtly pulling us up the slight hill. On the other side of the street the gentle curve of the Standard Oil Building smooths our way around the bend and into the darkened canyon of lower Broadway (see Fig. 326). Moving north, we pass the hole containing Trinity Church on our left. The church presents a different appearance to us from the postcard view that most people remember (Fig. 354). It sits in the middle of a grassy burial ground, its front door pushing forward, directing our eye across the street for a quick glimpse down the wedge-shaped opening of Wall Street.

Broadway is packed with people; ticker tape streams from the windows through the sunlight, the paper and light reinforcing the narrowness of the street. Next, a hole opens on the other side of the street at the Marine Midland Building plaza (see Fig. 218). A large bright red cube gives focus to the plaza, and people cluster around it waving flags. The wall closes again. Several blocks farther along, back again on the left, a third hole opens at the churchyard of Saint Paul's Chapel, by Thomas McBean (Fig. 355). Just one block past the chapel, back on the right, the long wedge of City Hall Park slides into view. (City Hall Park follows Saint Paul's Chapel too closely. The transition between the two events would have been smoother had they been separated by several more blocks or had the U.S. Post Office that once graced the south end of City Hall Park remained standing.)

Up ahead, the mayor is waiting on the steps of City Hall. We turn toward

355. *Broadway; view looking north. Saint Paul's Chapel, Thomas McBean, 1766, is at left.*

him from Broadway, not because he is at a natural terminus of the trip, but because barriers across the street keep us from going farther.

The left-right-left-right rhythm of the journey just completed, like the melodies on Fifth Avenue and Main Street, was a composite of many decisions. None of the streets was the product of a single grand vision, and none of our processions along these streets led to a grand conclusion.

By contrast, the stretch of Pennsylvania Avenue between the Capitol and the White House does have a real goal at either end, although the Capitol is at an angle, and the White House—as Elbert Peets so strongly lamented—is off axis with the street. These goals make Pennsylvania Avenue one of the few streets in America not needing holes and events along the way to give it purpose. Rather than being an end in itself, the street is subordinate to the institutions that terminate it. What has happened to Pennsylvania Avenue since L'Enfant first laid it out, however, is testament to the frequent disparity between our architecture and our cultural values.

Despite its status as America's first street, Pennsylvania Avenue's great diagonal swath is so poorly integrated with the underlying grid of streets that the avenue quickly developed a decidedly ragged, unkempt appearance. Although the odd buildings and small unbuildable lots that graced it were no different from those on other diagonal streets in L'Enfant's plan, Pennsylvania Avenue's prominence prompted the Senate Park Commission of 1901 to put special emphasis on its upgrading. The commission suggested that a new Federal Triangle of government offices be constructed east of the White House grounds and south of Pennsylvania Avenue. Although Henry Bacon, who later designed the buildings, gave them a consistent massing and style, their "vast walls of stone" give no real life to the avenue. The monotonous facades only further deadened America's grand parade route.[11] Peets, at the time, called the street "poor old Pennsylvania Avenue."[12]

In 1962 President John Kennedy appointed an advisory council to recommend further improvements, particularly to the north side of the street, which still featured a mélange of parking lots and irregular parcels. This second plan, prepared under the chairmanship of Nathaniel Owings of Skidmore, Owings and Merrill and published in 1964, specified a number of changes for "the Nation's ceremonial way,"[13] the most prominent of which were the addition of bigger buildings on the north side of Pennsylvania Avenue to balance the earlier efforts on the south. These additions were to form a new wall of buildings running the length of the avenue, but they were to be sited farther back than the small stores and lots they were replacing.

Instead of widening the avenue by moving its center line, thus keeping the sidewalks the same width on both sides, the council recommended widening only the sidewalks on the north side, leaving the curbs and sidewalks on the south side untouched. Both sides of Pennsylvania Avenue were to be planted with trees, but there were to be three rows on the north side and two rows on the south (Fig. 356). The rationale for this asymmetry—the reason why people on the north side of the avenue cheering the president's inaugural parade should

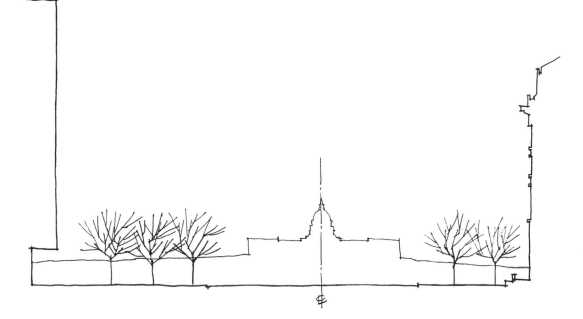

356. *Section through Pennsylvania Avenue between Tenth and Eleventh Streets.*

get three trees while those on the south side should get only two—was never explained. Regardless, the imbalance was a precursor of bigger problems yet to come.

Soon after the plan was adopted, a bombastic-looking new headquarters for the Federal Bureau of Investigation became the first building to adhere to the new setback line (Fig. 357). It has since been followed by other buildings, including an equally overbearing Canadian embassy three blocks farther east. The architectural character of these buildings was less problematical, however, than their relationship to the other buildings on the street.

Concurrent with the plan's adoption, America was beginning to embrace historic preservation. On the north side of Pennsylvania Avenue several buildings originally marked for demolition by the advisory council, including the Washington and Willard Hotels, now seemed eminently worth keeping.[14] The decision to save these hotels created an insoluble conflict because they had been built right to the property line, thirty feet closer to the avenue than the new setback line called for by the council. Historic preservation eventually won out, despite the jumble of differing setbacks. Now, nearly thirty years after the plan's promulgation, Pennsylvania Avenue has an even more chaotic look on its north side than it did before the council began to work toward shaping the avenue into a "unified whole."[15]

Paul Rudolph suggested at the time that Pennsylvania Avenue be redesigned with an alternating rhythm of gigantic buildings bridging the cross streets. The buildings were to form massive alcoves of space in a left-right-left pattern similar to that of Fifth Avenue and lower Broadway. The scale of this solution, however, would have drawn attention to itself rather than to the goal at

357. Pennsylvania
Avenue ca. 1972; view
looking northwest
toward the White
House. Note the
Federal Triangle of
office buildings (trape-
zoidal shaped) on the
south side of the
avenue and the F.B.I.
Building set back from
the street on the north
side in the middle of
the photograph.

358. Model of Western Plaza (now Freedom Plaza) showing pylons, Venturi and Rauch, 1977.

either end of the avenue, and would have been even more disruptive than the solution recommended by the advisory panel.[16]

A decade later, in 1974, the symbolic connection between the White House and the Capitol was obliterated altogether by the adoption of yet a third initiative known as the Pennsylvania Avenue Plan. Among that plan's recommendations was a suggestion that a new plaza be built in the middle of Pennsylvania Avenue between Thirteenth and Fourteenth Streets at the spot where L'Enfant had originally shown a plaza in his own plan.

L'Enfant, it should be remembered, did not give the unimpeded connection between Capitol and White House as much weight as did later generations of Americans. In obeisance to L'Enfant's original ideas (see Fig. 274) the new plaza was to lie athwart Pennsylvania Avenue, diverting traffic to one side (Fig. 358). This left two choices for planners of the inaugural parade: the parade could bend around

359. U.S. Treasury Building, Washington, D.C., Robert Mills and Thomas U. Walter, 1836–1839; view from Pennsylvania Avenue.

the plaza, or it could terminate several blocks short of the White House. Both options weakened the direct symbolic link between Congress and the president.*

Venturi, Rauch and Scott Brown were given the commission to design the western end of the new plaza. Their first scheme in 1979 gamely attempted to reestablish the link that was about to be interrupted. The architects proposed two large pylons in the plaza, offset from each other so as not to suggest a gate or an unintended pause. Approached from either end of Pennsylvania Avenue, the pylons would frame the view of the avenue beyond. The symbolism was confused, however, because the plaza itself proclaimed a pause while the pylons invited us to continue on through without stopping. Intensifying an already ambiguous situation, the pylons were later deleted from the design.[17]

Had the symbolic function of Pennsylvania Avenue been truly understood, had we all realized that architecture's only role there was to frame the trip and move it along, the original report of the advisory council would simply have opted for keeping the building line where it was, allowing everyone to focus on the parade. If opportunities later arose for filling in ragged spots along the avenue and realigning some of the cross streets, so much the better. Today the

*In trying to find some symbolic reason for a pause and a diversion at this location, one might argue, surreally, that when the president addresses Congress, he is first introduced at the door by the sergeant-at-arms. There might be congruity in a plaza sitting astride Pennsylvania Avenue dedicated to all the sergeants-at-arms who have momentarily come between the president and Congress.

One cannot resist pondering another surreal possibility—that a new president, during his inaugural parade, would arrive at the plaza, get out of the car, trudge straight through the plaza on foot, and then get back into his vehicle, which in the meantime had been brought around to the other side. This scenario highlights the inherent contradiction of using Pennsylvania Avenue to connect the Capitol and the White House and then littering it with obstacles.

best option is remedial—tearing out the plazas and adding new fronts to the recessed buildings. All the buildings on Pennsylvania Avenue, like those of us watching the parade, have only one function: to line up along the sidewalk and cheer.

The climax of the inaugural parade, as a new president approaches the White House from the Capitol, has presented its own problems, particularly for a culture that is ambivalent about endings. Elbert Peets's concern over the avenue's supposed misalignment was heightened by what he and other critics since have seen as the misplacement of the U.S. Treasury Building, designed by Robert Mills and Thomas U. Walter.[18] The building sits between Fifteenth and East Executive Avenue, across the street from the White House grounds. The south side of the Greek Revival Treasury Building faces what was once a large sunken piazza, now filled with earth and flowers (Fig. 359). If Pennsylvania Avenue were ever extended in a straight line, the flower beds and part of the building behind them would have to be demolished (see Fig. 273).*

A better solution would be to extend Pennsylvania Avenue but bend it when it reaches the Treasury to align with the building's facade. The Treasury, like Grace Church and One Broadway in New York, would deflect our eye around the bend to something not yet in view (Fig. 360). A new building in the block between 14th and 15th Streets on the south side of Pennsylvania Avenue would also help bring us to the intersection of Pennsylvania and East Executive Avenue. (The avenue, which has been closed to vehicular traffic and turned into an amorphous, ill-defined pedestrian mall, would also have to be reopened to cars.) From this intersection we could turn left or right on East Executive Avenue. But on inauguration day the president would continue across the street through a modestly scaled gate to his own back yard and from there to the front door of the White House to greet the inaugural day celebrants. The gate would be a suitable terminus to the parade, not because it signified a conclusion but because it marked a transition (Fig. 361). After passing through the gate, the president would take possession of a new house, and America would celebrate a new beginning. The president would have entered through a gate he knew was there but which he could not see until he reached the bend in the road—a symbol that would have been too small had it been visible the length of Pennsylvania Avenue. It would be like many American goals—more in the mind than in the eye.

Because so many American goals are delimited only by the imagination of the person who strives for them, most roads in America still remain unimpeded. The open road connotes an endless journey, and it also symbolizes unbounded

---

*Exasperated by the lengthy deliberations of a committee appointed to site the Treasury, America's first populist president, Andrew Jackson, supposedly walked out of the White House, planted his cane near what is now the northeast corner of the building, and said, "Right here is where I want the cornerstone." (The committee had wanted to keep the view down Pennsylvania Avenue open.) In light of America's long ambivalence toward symbols of authority, it would be interesting to know exactly what Old Hickory was thinking as he made his declaration. [*The WPA Guide to Washington, D.C.* (Washington: Government Printing office, 1937, under the title *Washington: City and Capital*; reprint, New York: Pantheon Books, 1983), 248–249.]

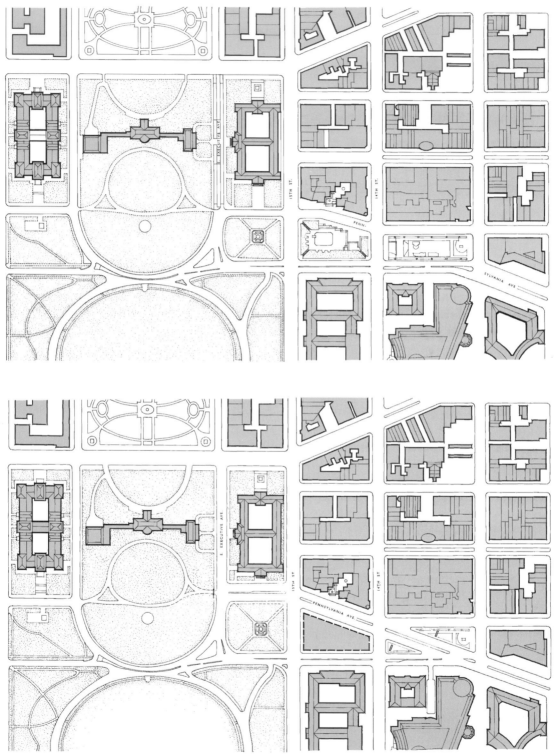

360. *Opposite, above: Existing terminus of Pennsylvania Avenue at the south lawn of the White House. Opposite, below: Proposed redesign, Craig Whitaker Architects, 1996. If the avenue was reconfigured, the two pylons from Venturi and Rauch's original scheme might be redeployed on the splintered remains of Freedom Plaza. The block west of the pylons would be an excellent building site.*

361. *Above left: Proposed White House postern at the terminus of Pennsylvania Avenue.*

opportunity. And in this regard there is no more apt icon for American travelers than the image Thomas Jefferson created in his campus plan for the University of Virginia (Fig. 362). For some, the broad central allée seems to end at the library, suggesting a path to the metaphorical city on the hill. As we move up the grass terrace to the library steps, we approach a goal. On both sides the professors' houses are each slightly different from one another. The narrowing spaces between the houses quicken our pace, and we end at the library door.

But in fact the great lawn leads to the library's back door. We are already in the back yard—our back yard—stretching across a continent. It is only when we realize this, when we turn around and move down the terrace toward the dark forest, that the tableau makes sense. At each level the Arcadian city drops farther behind, like the myth that it is. In front of us is an entire continent—and freedom. In America that freedom has always been expressed by the open road. It is only when we finally acknowledge the power of that road in American culture, and understand that architecture's best role is as one more grand event along it, that we will be able again to produce and arrange a myriad of buildings worthy of the dream.

362. *University of Virginia, Charlottesville, Thomas Jefferson, 1817–1825; view toward the library from the lawn.*

Afterword

Where Do

We Go From Here?

RENAISSANCE ARCHITECTS WERE FREQUENTLY PAINTERS AND SCULPTORS AS WELL AS designers of buildings: their creative talents touched everything from stage sets to the ramparts of fortified cities; they were the maestros of the built world. This was possible, so one learned, only because these artists were Renaissance men. Despite the obvious tautology, today such broad scope is all but impossible. Although today's architects may design tapestries, teapots, and furniture, few have the opportunity to intervene effectively at the scale of the whole landscape, despite a growing number who are concerned about its degradation. Those architects who do want to work at this scale must share the task with planners, landscape architects, urban designers, civil engineers, and traffic planners.

Nonetheless, as Vincent Scully wrote, "no history of architecture can deal any longer with individual buildings only, or with buildings in a vacuum. There is no difference between architecture and city planning; all must now—or, rather, again—be treated as one."[1]

In the quarter century since Scully sought to broaden the historian's perspective, the architect's scope has continued to narrow as has his intellectual focus and feeling of relevance.[2] At several leading universities the sense is conveyed that even thinking about architecture as the making and arranging of buildings and forms in which people conduct their daily lives has lost currency as a serious artistic endeavor. Some architects have even called for a complete retreat from relevance, advocating instead "a return to pure architecture, . . . in the best cases, sublime uselessness."[3] According to this view, the architect's mission lies elsewhere—in poetry or abstract design exercises. As one architectural theorist recently asserted, "I cannot build because I am an architect . . . nobody who builds nowadays can be called an architect."[4]

The roots of these feelings go back well beyond the pronouncements of the architect Howard Roark, Ayn Rand's principal character in *The Fountainhead*, who vows "not to be afraid of the world, not to take any notice of it." Indicted for blowing up a building after others have changed his design for it, he announces at trial, "we are approaching a world in which I cannot permit myself to live."[5] Roark knew that architects infrequently produce work that has resonance with a large popular audience. Much has been written about the nineteenth-century roots of this sensibility—the artist's belief in his role as an iconoclast and, in Europe especially, certain artists' contempt for the bourgeoisie.[6] This attitude firmly persists—even at the end of the twentieth century and in a largely middle-class culture like America's—and it will continue to have power until more architects again effect visions and designs congruent with America's underlying cultural values.

The idea that architects can grapple with the whole environment raises, to be sure, important institutional and political problems. Americans resist concentrating power in the hands of one person or one constituency. Patrons like Haussmann and Sixtus V are rare in America. Americans also divide government and professional responsibilities by function. In Europe, where aesthetic sensibilities are given greater weight, it has often seemed just good common sense to put many disciplines and talents simultaneously to work on a project, but in America this sort of coordination is more difficult.

American agencies that provide housing, for example, are entirely separate from those providing transportation and from those charged with caring for the environment. To take the simplest of examples: out on the commercial strip, the county highway engineer will decide how wide the lanes will be, and how frequently the driveways will occur. The local planning and zoning authority will decide what kinds of buildings can be built and how big the signs can be—where they go having already been decided in part by the actions of the traffic engineer. If the project is big enough, an environmental agency will decide what mitigation is needed. Finally an architect may design the buildings—unless they have already been designed by an engineer, a contractor, or a design team from the headquarters of the national chain occupying the lot. If there is considerable pressure to do so, a landscape architect may plant the median strip and the right-of-way, and an urban designer will locate the benches and trash baskets. Consequently, very few designers think of the aesthetic whole—because very few have more than partial responsibility for it. Thus, bringing the various strands together again presents a very large and difficult task. The alternative, however, is to continue to watch the abasement of the environment.

If, as a new beginning, we were to widen the range of problems studied in an architectural education, while simultaneously opening the door to broader participation in that educational process—that is, inviting back into the drafting room civil engineers, landscape architects, and historic preservationists as well as traffic planners and developers—we might start to bring these differing perspectives together again.

The search for common ground must emanate, however, from those who have an aesthetic agenda—despite Camillo Sitte's hope that if only "the traffic expert would just let the artist peer over his shoulder occasionally . . . one could establish a peaceful coexistence between the two."[7] The initiative must also come from those who care about improving the quality of the built American environment, but who at the same time embrace the cultural values underlying it.

Of course, the architect who takes the lead in this search risks his or her identity. As Reyner Banham once suggested of an earlier epoch, the architect will again have to "discard his whole cultural load, including the professional garments by which he is recognized as an architect."[8] The architect will have to acknowledge that motion is as powerful a symbol as place in this culture and that this value must have expression. He or she will also have to concede that cities may never hold the same shining value for Americans as they do for Europeans. Americans will always prefer living in less dense surroundings. Consequently, the architect will have to try harder to understand and accommodate these proclivities instead of ignoring them.

The architect must learn again that although we celebrate individual accomplishment, we also respond to buildings that balance this veneration with a sense of obligation to the larger community. For architects this will often entail sublimating a personal need for artistic expression—for producing one memorable note in the symphony—to the music as a whole. If more architects were to embrace the mission, they might again participate more fully in shaping the built environment—in mending the ravaged whole.

NOTES

FOREWORD

1. Fernand Braudel, *The Mediterranean and the Mediterranean World in the Age of Philip II*, 2 vols, trans. Sian Reynolds (New York: Harper & Row, 1972–1973).
2. Camillo Sitte, *City Planning According to Artistic Principles*, trans. George R. Collins and Christiane Craseman Collins, Columbia University Studies in Architecture and Archeology, no. 3 (London: Phaidon Press, 1965). Equally important to the understanding of Sitte's work is the companion volume: George R. Collins and Christiane Craseman Collins, *Camillo Sitte and the Birth of Modern City Planning*, Columbia University Studies in Art History and Archeology, no. 2 (London: Phaidon Press, 1965).
3. Collins and Collins, *Camillo Sitte*, 92.
4. Frances Trollope, *Domestic Manners of the Americans*, ed. Donald Smalley (London, 1832; reprint, New York: Knopf, 1949), cited in John Reps, *The Making of Urban America: A History of City Planning in the United States* (Princeton: Princeton University Press, 1965), 355.
5. Collins and Collins. *Camillo Sitte*, 34–44.
6. H. Allen Brooks, "Jeanneret and Sitte: Le Corbusier's Earliest Ideas on City Planning," in Helen Searing, ed., *In Search of Modern Architecture: A Tribute to Henry-Russell Hitchcock* (Cambridge: M.I.T. Press, 1982), 278–297.
7. Siegfried Giedion, *Space, Time and Architecture*, 5th ed. (Cambridge: Harvard University Press, 1967), 780.
8. Thomas Sharp, *The Anatomy of the Village* (Harmondsworth, Middlesex, England: Penguin Books, 1946).
9. Joan Didion, *The White Album* (New York: Simon & Schuster, 1974), 126–127.
10. Sybil Moholy-Nagy, *Matrix of Man* (New York: Praeger, 1968), 81.

I. AMERICAN DREAMS MAKE AMERICAN PATTERNS

1. Jefferson referred to Palladio's famous treatise, *Quattro Libre*, simply as "the Bible." Susan R. Stein, *The Worlds of Thomas Jefferson at Monticello* (New York: Abrams, 1993), 13.
2. Virginia McAlester and Lee McAlester, *A Field Guide to American Houses* (New York: Knopf, 1989).
3. Charles W. Moore, "You Have to Pay for the Public Life," *Perspecta 9–10: Yale Architectural Journal* (1965): 60.

4. Geoffrey Scott, *The Architecture of Humanism: A Study in the History of Taste* (New York: Norton, 1974), 19.

5. Vincent Scully, introduction to *Complexity and Contradiction in Architecture,* by Robert Venturi (New York: Museum of Modern Art, 1966), 14.

6. John Brinckerhoff Jackson, *Discovering the Vernacular Landscape* (New Haven: Yale University Press, 1984), 30.

7. Daniel J. Boorstin, *The Image: A Guide to Pseudo-Events in America* (1961; reprint, 25th Anniversary ed., New York: Atheneum, 1987), 188, 190.

8. Henry James, *The American Scene* (London: Chapman and Hall, 1907; reprint, Bloomington: Indiana University Press, 1968), 139–140.

9. Vincent Scully, *American Architecture and Urbanism* (New York: Praeger, 1969), 146.

10. Charles Jencks, *The Language of Post-Modern Architecture* (New York: Rizzoli, 1977), 39.

11. Elbert Peets, *On the Art of Designing Cities: The Selected Essays of Elbert Peets,* ed. Paul D. Spreiregen (Cambridge: M.I.T. Press, 1968), 223.

12. Werner Hegemann and Elbert Peets, *The American Vitruvius: An Architects' Handbook of Civic Art* (1922; reprint, New York: Benjamin Blom, 1972), 1.

13. Ibid., 1.

14. Christian Norberg-Schulz, *New World Architecture* (New York: Architectural League of New York, and Princeton Architectural Press, 1988), 8.

15. Jackson, *Vernacular Landscape,* 67.

16. Frances Halsband, introduction to Norberg-Schulz, *New World Architecture,* 5.

17. Jackson, *Vernacular Landscape,* 35.

18. Ibid., 67.

19. Transcribed by Kate B. Carter, *The Mormon Village,* Daughters of Utah Pioneers, Lesson for November 1954, cited in Reps, *Urban America,* 468.

20. Author unknown, "Architecture in the United States," *American Journal of Science and Arts* (New Haven): 103, quoted in Reps, *Urban America,* 290.

21. Reps, *Urban America,* 240–262.

22. Undated communication by L'Enfant entitled "Note relative to the ground lying on the eastern branch of the river Potomac and being intended to parallel the several positions proposed within the limits between the branch and Georgetown for the seat of the Federal City," Kite, *L'Enfant,* 47–48, quoted in Reps, *Urban America,* 248.

23. Hegemann and Peets, *Vitruvius,* 287.

24. Paul Zucker, *Town and Square: From the Agora to the Village Green* (New York: Columbia University Press, 1959; reprint, Cambridge: M.I.T. Press, 1970), 253.

25. Governor Hull's report, December 23, 1808, Michigan Pioneer and Historical Society, *Historical Collections,* Lansing, 1888, XII, 468, quoted in Reps, *Urban America,* 271.

26. Reps, *Urban America,* 488.

27. See the discussion of the history of the American suburb in Robert A. M. Stern and John Massengale, eds., *The Anglo-American Suburb* (London: Architectural Design; New York: St. Martin's Press, 1981).

28. Sitte, *City Planning,* 126, 120.

29. Lewis Mumford, *The City in History* (New York: Harcourt, Brace & World, 1961), 424.

30. Reps, *Urban America,* 314.

31. William A. Bell, *New Tracks in North America* (London:1869), I, 17–18, quoted in Reps, *Urban America,* 397.

32. Sitte, *City Planning,* 66; Charles Dickens, preface to *Pictures from Italy and*

American Notes (1885), quoted in Mireille T. Ayoub, "European Travelers," *Architectural Forum* (September 1973), 63.

33. Quoted in Reps, *Urban America,* 410.
34. Scully, *American Architecture,* 245.
35. John Summerson, *Georgian London* (London: Barrie & Jenkins, 1962), 65–83.
36. Jackson, *Vernacular Landscape,* 30.
37. Three excellent sources for the study of American multifamily housing are Robert A. M. Stern, "With Rhetoric: The New York Apartment House," *VIA* 4 (Philadelphia: Journal of the Graduate School of Fine Arts, University of Pennsylvania, 1980), 78–111; Gwendolyn Wright, *Building the American Dream* (Cambridge: M.I.T. Press, 1981); and Richard Plunz, *A History of Housing in New York City: Dwelling Type and Social Change in the American Metropolis* (New York: Columbia University Press, 1990).
38. Edward T. Hall, *The Hidden Dimension* (Garden City, N.Y.: Doubleday, Anchor Books, 1969), 144–48.
39. Howard Newby, *Country Life: A Social History of Rural England* (Totowa, N.J.: Barnes & Noble Books, 1987), 58–60.
40. Mumford, *City in History,* 503.
41. Christian Norberg-Schulz, *Existence, Space and Architecture* (New York: Praeger, 1971), 35.
42. Frederick Jackson Turner, *The Frontier in American History* (1920; reprint, Tucson: University of Arizona Press, 1986), 37.
43. Noel Grove, "Greenways," *Land and People* 6 (Fall 1994): 2–8.
44. Robert Lindsey, "Higher Gas Prices Put Crimp in California 'Cruising,'" *New York Times,* August 23, 1980.
45. James, *American Scene,* 8.
46. Sara Rimer, "Cruising Takes on New Image," *New York Times,* August 16, 1994.

2. FRONT DOOR, BACK DOOR

1. Nathaniel Hawthorne, *The Blithdale Romance* (1852; reprint, New York: Meridian Classic edition, 1981), 119.
2. Quoted in Joel Garreau, *Edge City: Life on the New Frontier* (New York: Doubleday, 1991; reprint, New York: Anchor Books, 1992), 234.
3. Boorstin, *Image,* 259.
4. Wright, *American Dream,* 15.
5. James Cannon, former area director, Bureau of Indian Affairs, telephone interviews by author, 1995.
6. Summerson, *Georgian London,* 65–66.
7. Mumford, *City in History,* 399. Richard Westmacott, *African-American Gardens in the Rural South* (Knoxville: University of Tennessee Press, 1992), 34, 127–75, demonstrates a similar tendency among rural African-Americans to treat the back yard more as a utility than as a private preserve. Decorations, plantings, picnic benches, and outdoor seating are usually in front of the house. The smokehouse, privy, and storage sheds are usually in back.
8. Kent C. Bloomer and Charles W. Moore, *Body, Memory, and Architecture* (New Haven: Yale University Press, 1977), 120–121.
9. Robert Venturi, Denise Scott Brown, and Steven Izenour, *Learning from Las Vegas* (Cambridge: M.I.T. Press, 1972), 116–119.
10. Robert A. M. Stern, *Pride of Place* (Boston: Houghton Mifflin; New York: American Heritage, 1986), 11–12.
11. As recently as 1993, Houstonians defeated a proposal to institute citywide zoning.

For a discussion of the consequences of this vote see Bruce C. Webb and William F. Stern, "Houston Style Planning: No Zoning but Many Zones," *Cité: Architecture and Design Review of Houston* 32 (Fall 1994–Winter 1995): 14–15.

12. Christopher Tunnard and Henry Hope Reed, *American Skyline* (New York: Houghton Mifflin, 1953; reprint, New York: Mentor Books, 1956), 44.
13. Scully, *American Architecture,* 110.
14. Gwendolyn Brooks, *Blacks* (Chicago: Third World Press, 1991).
15. Garreau, *Edge City,* 206.
16. Sitte, *City Planning,* 182.
17. Mr. and Mrs. Troup Mathews, homeowners, interviews by author, 1994.
18. Venturi, *Complexity,* 88.
19. Clarence S. Stein, "Toward New Towns for America," *Town Planning Review* 20 (October 1949): 233–234.
20. Ibid., 245.
21. Robert A. M. Stern, *Pride of Place* (Boston: Houghton Mifflin; New York: American Heritage, 1986), 146.
22. Lewis Mumford, *From the Ground Up* (New York: Harcourt Brace, 1956), 5, quoted in Stern and Massengale, *Anglo-American Suburb,* 48.
23. Voorhees, Walker, Smith and Haines, "Explanation of Commercial Bulk Regulations," *Zoning New York City; A Proposal for a Zoning Resolution for the City of New York*, submitted to the City Planning Commission August 1958, 128.
24. Jeff Wilkinson, "The Story of Porches," *Old-House Journal* 18 (July–August 1990): 30–37.

3. FROM HOUSE TO ROAD

1. Jane Jacobs, *The Death and Life of Great American Cities* (New York: Random House, 1961), 182–186.
2. Ibid., 184.
3. Giedion, *Space, Time,* 849.
4. William H. Jordy, *The Impact of European Modernism in the Mid-Twentieth Century,* vol. 5 of *American Buildings and Their Architects* (New York: Oxford University Press, 1972), 22.
5. Steven Izenour and David Dashiell III, "Relearning from Las Vegas," *Architecture* 79 (October 1990): 46–51.
6. Robert Venturi and Denise Scott Brown, "The Significance of A&P Parking Lots or Learning from Las Vegas," *Architectural Forum* 128 (March 1968): 41.
7. Hunter Thompson, *Fear and Loathing in Las Vegas: A Savage Journey to the Heart of the American Dream* (New York: Random House, 1976).
8. Ironically, it is the traffic engineer's craft which today offers more promise of creating slow-street neighborhoods. Architects and planners, when faced with the task of slowing or restricting traffic, are more likely to suggest physical changes like speed bumps and street closings. Sitte, for example, in his diagrams for a modern city arranged whole neighborhoods to create turbine-shaped plazas that would impede vehicular through movement. Traffic engineers, on the other hand, think in terms of "friction," which increases travel time on a given route, making it more likely that a motorist will pick an alternative. Two-way streets, narrow travel lanes, small turning radii at intersections, on-street parking, traffic lights, and stop signs increase friction and thereby slow speeds. Most slow-street neighborhoods have some or all of these features.
9. The most famous auto-free street in America would likely have been the proposed closing of much of Madison Avenue in New York City. Put forward by Mayor John

Lindsay in 1973, the plan was scrapped in the face of vigorous opposition by affected merchants. Without alleys the merchants would have had to take off-peak deliveries, and their customers, many of whom might normally have arrived by taxi, would have had to walk. For a defense of this proposal see Jaquelin Robertson, "Rediscovering the Street," *Architectural Forum* 140 (November 1973): 24–31. See also Spiro Kostof, *The City Assembled: The Elements of Urban Form through History* (Boston: Little, Brown, Bullfinch Press, 1992), 240; and "Buffalo Rethinks Street Traffic Ban," *New York Times*, February 22, 1994.

10. Elaine Pofeldt, "River Access No Open-and-Shut Case at Condos," *Jersey Journal,* June 2, 1994; Keith Sharon, "A Troubled Path," *Jersey Journal,* July 15, 1991; Zachary Gaulkin, "Edgewater Condo Fences Off Public Walkway along the River," *Jersey Journal,* July 5, 1991; Anthony DePalma, "About New Jersey," *New York Times,* June 23, 1991.

11. Kevin Lynch, *The Image of the City* (1960; reprint, Cambridge, Mass.: M.I.T. Press, 1964), 66.

12. Craig Whitaker, *A Plan for the Hoboken Waterfront* (Hoboken, N.J.: Coalition for a Better Waterfront, 1993).

13. Craig Whitaker, "Rouse-ing Up the Waterfront," *Architectural Record* 174 (April 1986): 66–71.

14. F. Scott Fitzgerald, *The Great Gatsby* (New York: Scribner's, 1925), 42.

15. Scully, *American Architecture,* 111.

16. Moore, "You Have to Pay for the Public Life,": 57–97.

17. Randy Bright, *Disneyland: The Inside Story* (Tokyo: Times Mirror Books, 1987), 29, cited in Janet Jenkins, *Disneyland: Illusion, Design, and Magic,* unpublished paper, New York University, Graduate School of Public Administration, 1993, 1.

18. Peter M. Wolf, *Eugène Hénard and the Beginning of Urbanism in Paris 1900–1914* (The Hague: Ando, 1968), 19–20.

19. So persuasive was the allure of ridding cities of cars that Jane Jacobs gave serious consideration to Gruen's proposals, although she was also starting to think through the consequences of all-pedestrian streets: Jacobs, *Death and Life,* 344.

20. Cartoon, Joseph L. Parish Jr., *Chicago Tribune,* 1946. Copyrighted © Chicago Tribune company. All rights reserved. Used with permission.

21. Andres Duany and Elizabeth Plater-Zyberk, "The Second Coming of the American Small Town," *Wilson Quarterly* 16 (Winter 1992): 19–32.

22. Esther B. Fein, "Caring at Home, and Burning Out," *New York Times,* December 19, 1994; Dolores Hayden, "Awakening from the American Dream: Why the Suburban Single-Family House Is Outdated," *Utne Reader* (May–June 1989): 64–67; Felicity Barringer, "Word for Word: The Adventures of Ozzie and Harriet, Dialogue That Lingers: 'Hi, Mom.' 'Hi, Pop.' 'Hi, David.' 'Hi, Rick,'" *New York Times,* October 9, 1994.

23. Pamela G. Kripke, "Oh, the Differences When Two People Work at Home," *New York Times,* December 31, 1992.

4. ALL IN A ROW

1. Samuel Hazard, "Instructions given by me, William Penn . . . to . . . my Commissioners for the settling of the . . . Colony," *Annals of Pennsylvania* (Philadelphia, 1850), 527–553, cited in Reps, *Urban America,* 160.

2. James, *American Scene,* 42.

3. Charles Moore, Gerald Allen, and Donlyn Lyndon, *The Place of Houses,* (New York: Holt, Rinehart & Winston, 1974), 11–14.

4. Garreau, *Edge City,* 470.

5. William Hening, *The Statutes at Large . . . of Virginia,* III, Chapter XLIII of the Laws of 1705, An Act Continuing the Act directing the Building of the Capitol and the City of Williamsburg (New York, 1823), 419–432, cited in Reps, *Urban America,* 110.

6. See Ada Louise Huxtable, "Inventing American Reality," *New York Review of Books,* December 3, 1992, 24–29.

7. Peets, *Designing Cities,* 161.

8. Wright's desire to be different as well as to fit within the context of Fifth Avenue was part of his larger ambivalence toward New York City. See Herbert Muschamp, *Man About Town: Frank Lloyd Wright in New York City* (Cambridge: M.I.T. Press, 1983).

9. Michael Pollan, "Grass Gardens," *Sanctuary,* Massachusetts Audubon Society, May–June 1995, 9.

10. Saul Padover, "Proceedings to be had under the Residence Act," November 29, 1790, *Thomas Jefferson and the National Capital* (Washington, 1946), 31, quoted in Reps, *Urban America,* 245–246.

11. Herbert Gans, *The Levittowners: Ways of Life and Politics in a New Suburban Community* (New York: Columbia University Press, 1967).

12. See Robert Venturi's discussion of the opposite problem, an "easy unity," in *Complexity,* 89.

13. Evelyn Nieves, "Wanted in Levittown: Just One Little Box with Ticky Tacky Intact," *New York Times,* November 3, 1995.

14. Venturi, *Complexity,* 76.

15. James, *American Scene,* 294, 409.

16. Kostof, *City Assembled,* 172.

17. Sitte, *City Planning* 105–106.

18. Venturi, *Complexity,* 133.

19. Moore, "You Have to Pay for the Public Life," 63.

20. Vincent Scully first used "hole in the wall" with reference to the Seagram Building in "The Death of the Street," *Perspecta 8: Yale Architectural Journal* (1963): 91–96.

21. Reyner Banham, *Age of the Masters: A Personal View of Modern Architecture* (New York: Harper & Row, 1962), 114–115.

22. For a discussion of the Seagram Building after its context had changed, see Kurt W. Forster, "Crown of the City: The Seagram Building Reconsidered," *Skyline,* February 1982, 28–29.

23. Venturi et al., *Las Vegas,* 1.

24. Scully, *American Architecture,* 160.

25. Witold Rybczinski, *City Life: Urban Expectations in a New World* (New York: Scribner, 1995), 89–93.

26. James, *American Scene,* 315.

27. Rybczinski has a similar reaction to a recessed hotel on a commercial street in Woodstock. *City Life,* 89–90.

28. Remarks by Philip Johnson at "New York 1960," symposium sponsored by the Architectural League of New York (February 2, 1995).

29. Moore, Allen, and Lyndon, *Place of Houses,* 10–11.

30. Ibid., 16–17.

31. Henry Hope Reed, *The Golden City* (New York: Doubleday, 1959; reprint, New York: Norton, 1971), 93.

32. For a more detailed discussion of the Yale campus see Stern, *Pride of Place,* 48–58.

33. James, *American Scene,* 93.

5. GATES AND UNINTENDED PAUSES

1. Venturi, *Complexity*, 29.
2. Ibid., 90.
3. William J. Miller, former director Delaware River and Bay Authority, telephone interview by author, October 30, 1993. See *Crossing the Delaware: The Story of the Delaware Memorial Bridge, the Longest Twin-Suspension Bridge in the World* (Wilmington: Gauge Corporation, 1990), 61.
4. Frank Lloyd Wright, *The Future of Architecture* (New York: Horizon Press, 1958; reprint, Mentor Books, 1963), 29–32.
5. Lewis Mumford, *The Highway and the City* (New York: Harcourt Brace, 1953; reprint, Mentor Books, 1964), 224–227.
6. Stuart E. Cohen, introduction to *Late Entries to the Chicago Tribune Tower Competition* (New York: Rizzoli, 1980), 9.
7. Zucker, *Town and Square*, 164.
8. Reps, *Urban America*, 111.
9. Paul Goldberger, *The City Observed: New York* (New York: Random House, First Vintage Books, 1979), 230.
10. Scully, *American Architecture*, 203.

6. AT THE CROSSROADS

1. Reps, *Urban America*, 124.
2. *Mourt's Relation: A Journal of the Pilgrims at Plymouth* (London, 1622; reprint, Cambridge, Mass.: Applewood Books, 1986), 42–44.
3. The pattern at Plymouth was first evidenced in settlements begun by the British in the decade previous in Londonderry, Northern Ireland. These settlements also featured a main street with buildings grouped on both sides. Unlike Londonderry, where some buildings were freestanding and others shared party walls, all buildings at Plymouth were freestanding on their own lots: James Baker, chief historian, Plimoth Plantation, telephone interview by the author, July 6, 1994.
4. Edward T. Hall, *The Silent Language* (Greenwich, Conn.: Fawcett, 1959), 153.
5. Boorstin, *Image*, 50.
6. Hegemann and Peets, *American Vitruvius*, 289–290.
7. Peets, *Designing Cities*, 90.
8. Deborah Howard, *The Architectural History of Venice* (New York: Holmes & Meier, 1981), 181.
9. Peets, *Designing Cities*, 51.
10. Ibid., 130.
11. Hegemann and Peets, *American Vitruvius*, 232.
12. Rotaries are relics of the early days of the automobile. Having long since been proven to cause traffic accidents, they are slowly disappearing.
13. Thomas S. Hines, *Burnham of Chicago: Architect and Planner* (New York: Oxford University Press, 1974), 147.
14. Scully, *American Architecture*, 59.
15. Herbert Muschamp, "Art and Science Politely Disagree," *New York Times*, November 16, 1992. See also Michael J. Crosbie, "Dissecting the Salk," *Progressive Architecture* (October 1993), 41–50.
16. Peets, *Designing Cities*, 131.
17. Christian Norberg-Schulz, *Existence, Space and Architecture* (New York: Praeger, 1971), 53.
18. Richard S. Simons, "White Elephant on the Circle," *Indianapolis Star Magazine*, December 21, 1952. See also Edward A. Leary, "Early Governors Shuddered upon

Seeing Mansion," *Indianapolis Star,* September 26, 1971.

19. Lynch, *Image of the City,* 114.
20. Zucker, *Town and Square,* 158.
21. Beverly O'Neill, past president, Patrick Thomas Properties, Houston, Texas. Interview by author, March 12, 1993.
22. Louis Kahn, "Order in Architecture," *Perspecta 4: Yale Architectural Journal* (1957): 61.

7. AROUND THE BEND

1. Peets, *Designing Cities,* 68.
2. Moholy-Nagy, *Matrix of Man,* 146.
3. Peets, *Designing Cities,* 42–43.
4. Reps, *Urban America,* 103–108.
5. Carl R. Lounsbury, "The Beaux-Arts Ideals and Colonial Reality: The Reconstruction of Williamsburg's Capitol, 1928-1934," *Journal of the Society of Architectural Historians* 49 (December 1990): 373–389.
6. Peets gives a fascinating account of why an oblique view of the statue is preferable: "It was only after coming into the statue hall that I felt the great size of the room and of the Lincoln. But still I could not easily read the statue or feel the disposition of masses. . . . The principal source of light was [in] back of me. I thus lost all but the fringes of shadow. . . . The remedy plainly was to find a sidewise view of the statue." *Designing Cities,* 102.
7. Hall, *Hidden Dimension,* 108–110
8. Lynch, *Image of the City,* 114–115; Donald Appleyard, Kevin Lynch, and John R. Myer, *The View from the Road* (Cambridge, Mass.: M.I.T. Press, 1964), 5.
9. Venturi, *Complexity,* 37–38.
10. Bloomer and Moore, *Body, Memory,* 104.
11. Sitte, *City Planning,* 87.
12. Anthony Bailey, "Manhattan's Other Island," *New York Times Magazine,* December 1, 1974.
13. Christopher Tunnard and Boris Pushkarev, *Man-Made America: Chaos or Control?* (New Haven: Yale University Press, 1963), 265. See also the discussion of the aesthetics of roadway design, 159–274.
14. One of the few other books to deal with this subject is by Donald Appleyard, Kevin Lynch, and John R. Meyer, *The View from the Road,* which chronicles the sequence of visual experiences on several highways in and around the Boston area. In so doing the tract demonstrates that neither planner, architect, nor highway engineer has the power to shape the aesthetics of these roadways in their entirety.
15. Sitte, *City Planning,* 64–65.
16. Brooks, "Jeanneret and Sitte," 264.
17. Tunnard and Reed, *American Skyline,* 156.
18. The building was once one of the largest on the New York skyline. See Christopher Gray, "A 1922 Facade That Hides Another From the 1880's," *New York Times,* March 26, 1995.

8. THE ENDLESS PROCESSION

1. Lynch, *Image of the City,* 99, 107.
2. Whitaker, "The Waterfront," 66–71.
3. Lynch, *Image of the City,* 99.
4. Charles Goodrum and Helen Dalrymple, *Advertising in America, the First 200 Years* (New York: Harry N. Abrams, 1990), 217. Also see Frank Rowsome, *The Verse by*

the Side of the Road: The Story of the Burma-Shave Signs and Jingles (Brattleboro, Vt.: Stephen Greene Press, 1965).

5. Mumford, *City in History,* 368.
6. James, *American Scene,* 38–39; Scully, *American Architecture,* 32.
7. Venturi, et al., *Las Vegas,* 4.
8. Venturi, *Complexity,* 59.
9. Ibid., 64–70.
10. William Styron, "In Praise of Vineyard Haven," in *On the Vineyard* (New York: Anchor Books, 1980), 38.
11. Benjamin Forgey, "Along the Avenue Made for a Parade," *Washington Post,* January 16, 1993.
12. Peets, *Designing Cities,* 71.
13. *Pennsylvania Avenue,* Report of the President's Council on Pennsylvania Avenue (Washington, D.C., 1964), 18.
14. Pennsylvania Avenue Development Corporation, *Historic Preservation Plan* (Washington, D.C., 1977), 10.
15. *Pennsylvania Avenue,* 19.
16. Rudolph, "View of Washington," 64.
17. For another view, see Paul Goldberger, "Washington Is Planning an Open Plaza to Ease Pennsylvania Avenue Clutter," *New York Times,* July 9, 1978.
18. Peets, *Designing Cities,* 18.

AFTERWORD: WHERE DO WE GO FROM HERE?

1. Scully, *Architecture and Urbanism,* 7.
2. See Ada Louise Huxtable, "Is Modern Architecture Dead?" *New York Review of Books,* July 16, 1981.
3. Manfredo Tafuri, *Architecture and Utopia: Design and Capitalist Development* (Cambridge: M.I.T. Press, 1976), ix.
4. Christian Norberg-Schulz, "Towards an Authentic Architecture," *The Presence of the Past: First International Exhibition of Architecture* (Venice: Edizioni La Biennale di Venezia, 1980), 21, quoted in Robert A. M. Stern with Raymond W. Gastil, *Modern Classicism* (New York: Rizzoli, 1988), 256.
5. Ayn Rand, screenplay, *The Fountainhead,* Warner Bros., 1949, based on the novel by Ayn Rand (Chicago: Sears Readers Club, 1943).
6. Andrew Saint put forward an excellent history of the architect's own self-image in *The Image of the Architect* (New Haven: Yale University Press, 1983).
7. Sitte, *City Planning,* 92.
8. Banham, *First Machine Age,* 329–330.

BIBLIOGRAPHY

Adams, Thomas, Harold M. Lewis, and Lawrence M. Orton. *The Building of the City*. New York: Regional Plan of New York and Its Environs, 1931.

Appleyard, Donald, Kevin Lynch, and John R. Meyer. *The View from the Road*. Cambridge: M.I.T. Press, for the Joint Center for Urban Studies, 1964.

Architecture Columbus. Columbus, Ohio: Columbus Chapter, American Institute of Architects, 1976.

The Architecture of Paul Rudolph. New York: Praeger, 1970.

The Architecture of Sir Edwin Lutyens. 3 vols. London: Country Life, 1950. Reprint, Antique Collectors' Club, 1984.

Argan, Giulio C. *The Renaissance City*. New York: George Braziller, 1969.

Ayoub, Mireille T. "European Travelers." *Architectural Forum* 139 (September 1973): 60–65.

Bacon, Edmund N. *Design of Cities*. Rev. ed. New York: Viking Press, 1974. Reprint, Penguin Books, 1976.

Banham, Reyner. *Theory and Design in the First Machine Age*. New York: Praeger, 1960.

———. *Age of the Masters: A Personal View of Modern Architecture*. New York: Harper & Row, 1962.

Barnett, Jonathan. *The Elusive City: Five Centuries of Design, Ambition and Miscalculation*. New York: Harper & Row, 1986.

Barzun, Jacques. *The Use and Abuse of Art*. Bollingen Series 35.22. Princeton: Princeton University Press, 1974.

Benevolo, Leonardo. *The History of the City*. Trans. Geoffrey Culverwell. Cambridge: M.I.T. Press, 1980.

Blake, Peter. *Form Follows Fiasco*. Boston: Little, Brown, Atlantic Monthly Press, 1977.

Blaser, Werner, ed. *Drawings of Great Buildings*. Basel: Birkhauser Verlag, 1983.

Bloomer, Kent C., and Charles W. Moore. Contrib. Robert J. Yudell. *Body, Memory, and Architecture*. New Haven: Yale University Press, 1977.

Boorstin, Daniel J. *The Image: A Guide to Pseudo-Events in America,* 1961. Reprint, 25th Anniversary Ed., New York: Atheneum, 1987.

Braudel, Fernand. *The Mediterranean and the Mediterranean World in the Age of Philip II*. 2 vols. Trans. Sian Reynolds. New York: Harper & Row, 1972–1973.

Brooks, H. Allen. "Jeanneret and Sitte: Le Corbusier's Earliest Ideas on City Planning." In *In Search of Modern Architecture: A Tribute to Henry-Russell Hitchcock,* edited by Helen Searing, 278–97. Cambridge: M.I.T. Press, 1982.

Bunting, Bainbridge. *Houses of Boston's Back Bay: An Architectural History, 1840–1917.* Cambridge: Harvard University Press, Belknap Press, 1967.

Castagnoli, Ferdinando. *Orthogonal Town Planning in Antiquity.* Trans. Victor Caliandro. Cambridge: M.I.T. Press, 1971.

Choay, Françoise. *The Modern City: Planning in the Nineteenth Century.* New York: George Braziller, 1969.

Collins, George R., and Christiane Craseman Collins. *Camillo Sitte and the Birth of Modern City Planning.* Columbia University Studies in Art History and Archeology, no. 2. London: Phaidon Press, 1965.

Cook, John W., and Heinrich Klotz, eds. *Conversations with Architects.* New York: Praeger, 1973.

Crosbie, Michael J. "Dissecting the Salk." *Progressive Architecture* (October 1993): 41–50.

Crouch, Dora P., Daniel J. Garr, and Axel I. Mundigo. *Spanish City Planning in North America.* Cambridge: M.I.T. Press, 1982.

Dennis, Michael. *Court and Garden: From the French Hotel to the City of Modern Architecture.* Cambridge: M.I.T. Press, 1986.

Didion, Joan. *White Albums.* New York: Simon & Schuster, 1974.

Duany, Andres, and Elizabeth Plater-Zyberk. "The Second Coming of the American Small Town." *Wilson Quarterly* 16 (Winter 1992): 19–32ff.

Dunlap, David W. *On Broadway: A Journey Uptown over Time.* New York: Rizzoli, 1990.

Fabos, Julius Gy., Gordon T. Milde, and V. Michael Weinmayr. *Frederick Law Olmsted, Sr.: Founder of Landscape Architecture in America.* Amherst: University of Massachusetts Press, 1968.

Finney, Jack. *Time and Again.* New York: Simon & Schuster, 1970.

Fitzgerald, F. Scott. *The Great Gatsby.* New York: Scribner's, 1925.

Forster, Kurt W. "Crown of the City: The Seagram Building Reconsidered." *Skyline* (February 1982): 28–29.

Franchina, Jennifer, trans. and ed. *Roma Interrotta.* Rome: Incontri Internazionali D'Arte, 1979.

Gallery, John, ed. *Philadelphia Architecture.* Philadelphia: Foundation for Architecture, 1984.

Gans, Herbert. *The Levittowners: Ways of Life and Politics in a New Suburban Community.* New York: Pantheon Books, 1967.

Garreau, Joel. *Edge City: Life on the New Frontier.* New York: Doubleday, 1991; Anchor Books, 1992.

Giedion, Sigfried. *Space, Time and Architecture.* 5th ed. Cambridge: Harvard University Press, 1967.

Giurgola, Romaldo, and Jaimini Mehta. *Louis I. Kahn.* Zurich: Artemis, 1975.

Goldberger, Paul. "Form and Procession." *Architectural Forum* 138 (January–February 1973): 32–53.

———. *The City Observed: New York.* New York: Random House, First Vintage Books, 1979.

Goodrich, Lloyd. *Edward Hopper.* New York: Harry N. Abrams, 1976.

Goodrum, Charles, and Helen Dalrymple, *Advertising in America; the First 200 Years.* New York: Harry N. Abrams, 1990.

Grove, Noel. "Greenways." *Land and People 6, Trust for Public Lands* (Fall 1994): 2–8.

Guinness, Desmond, and Julius Trousdale Sadler Jr. *Mr. Jefferson, Architect.* New York: Viking Press, 1973.

Gutkind, Edwin Anton. *International History of City Development.* Vol. 2.: *Urban*

Development in the Alpine and Scandinavian Countries. New York: Free Press of Glencoe, 1964.

Hall, Edward T. *The Silent Language.* Greenwich, Conn.: Fawcett, 1959.

———. *The Hidden Dimension.* Garden City, N.Y.: Anchor Doubleday, 1969.

Hawthorne, Nathaniel. *The Blithedale Romance.* 1852. Reprint, New York: Meridian Classic, 1981.

Hayden, Dolores. "Awakening from the American Dream: Why the Suburban Single-Family House Is Outdated." *Utne Reader* (May–June 1989): 64–67.

———. *The Power of Place.* Cambridge: M.I.T. Press, 1995.

Hegemann, Werner, and Elbert Peets. *The American Vitruvius: An Architects' Handbook of Civic Art.* 1922. Reprint, New York: Benjamin Blom, 1972.

Hibbert, Christopher. *The English: A Social History, 1066–1945.* New York: Norton, 1987.

Hines, Thomas S. *Burnham of Chicago: Architect and Planner.* New York: Oxford University Press, 1974.

Historic Preservation Plan Washington, D.C.: Pennsylvania Avenue Development Corporation, 1977.

Hitchcock, Henry-Russell. *In the Nature of Materials: The Buildings of Frank Lloyd Wright, 1887–1941.* New York: Hawthorn Books, 1942. Reprint, Da Capo, 1975.

Holland, Laurence B., ed. *Who Designs America?* Garden City, N.Y.: Anchor Books, Doubleday, 1966.

Homer. *The Odyssey of Homer.* Trans. T. E. Shaw [T. E. Lawrence]. New York: Oxford University Press, 1932.

Howard, Deborah. *The Architectural History of Venice.* New York: Holmes & Meier, 1981.

Huxtable, Ada Louise. "Inventing American Reality." *New York Review of Books,* December 3, 1992, 24–29.

Ison, Walter. *The Georgian Buildings of Bath. Bath,* England: Kingsmead Press, 1980.

Izenour, Steven, and David Dashiell III. "Relearning from Las Vegas." *Architecture* 79 (October 1990): 46–51.

Jackson, John Brinckerhoff. *Landscapes: Selected Writings of J. B. Jackson.* Amherst: University of Massachusetts Press, 1970.

———. *Discovering the Vernacular Landscape.* New Haven: Yale University Press, 1984.

———. *A Sense of Place, A Sense of Time.* New Haven: Yale University Press, 1994.

Jacobs, Jane. *The Death and Life of Great American Cities.* New York: Random House, 1961.

James, Henry. *The American Scene.* London: Chapman and Hall, 1907. Reprint, Bloomington: Indiana University Press, 1968.

Jencks, Charles. *The Language of Post-Modern Architecture.* New York: Rizzoli, 1977.

Jenkins, Janet. *Disneyland, Illusion, Design, and Magic.* Unpublished paper. New York University, Graduate School of Public Administration, 1993.

Johnson, Nunnally. Screenplay. *The Grapes of Wrath.* 20th Century–Fox, 1940. Based on John Steinbeck. *The Grapes of Wrath.* New York: Viking Press, 1940.

Jordy, William H. *The Impact of European Modernism in the Mid-Twentieth Century.* Vol. 5 of *American Buildings and Their Architects.* New York: Oxford University Press, 1972.

Kahn, Louis. "Order in Architecture." *Perspecta 4: Yale Architectural Journal* (1957): 58–65.

Kostof, Spiro. *A History of Architecture: Settings and Rituals.* New York: Oxford University Press, 1985.

———. *The City Shaped: Urban Patterns and Meanings throughout History.* Boston: Little, Brown; Bullfinch Press, 1991.

———. with Greg Castillo. *The City Assembled: The Elements of Urban Form through History.* Boston: Little, Brown, Bullfinch Press, 1992.

Krinsky, Carol Herselle. *Rockefeller Center.* London: Oxford University Press, 1978.

Kunstler, James Howard. *The Geography of Nowhere: The Rise and Decline of America's Man-Made Landscape.* New York: Simon & Schuster, 1993.

Lagerfeld, Steven. "What Main Street Can Learn from the Mall." *Atlantic,* November 1995, 110ff.

Late Entries to the Chicago Tribune Tower Competition. New York: Rizzoli, 1980.

Le Corbusier and Pierre Jeanneret. *Oeuvre Complète 1910–1929.* Zurich: Les Editions d'Architecture (Artemis), 1964.

———. *Oeuvre Complète 1929–1934.* Trans. A. J. Dakin. Zurich: Les Editions d'Architecture (Artemis), 1964.

———. *Oeuvre Complète 1934–1938.* Trans. A. J. Dakin. Zurich: Les Editions d'Architecture (Artemis), 1964.

Lemann, Nicholas. "Stressed out in Suburbia." *Atlantic,* November 1989, 34ff.

Liebs, Chester H. *Main Street to Miracle Mile, American Roadside Architecture.* Boston: Little, Brown, 1985.

Longstreth, Richard. *The Buildings of Main Street.* Washington, D.C.: Preservation Press, National Trust for Historic Preservation, 1987.

Lounsbury, Carl L. "The Beaux-Arts Ideals and Colonial Reality: The Reconstruction of Williamsburg's Capitol, 1928–1934." *Journal of the Society of Architectural Historians* 49 (December 1990): 373–89.

Lynch, Kevin. *The Image of the City.* Cambridge: M.I.T. Press, 1960. Reprint, 1964.

———. "The City as Environment." *Scientific American,* September 1965, 209 219.

Manson, Grant Carpenter. *Frank Lloyd Wright to 1910, The First Golden Age.* New York: Reinhold, 1958.

McAlester, Virginia, and Lee McAlester. *A Field Guide to American Houses.* New York: Knopf, 1989.

McShane, Clay. *Down the Asphalt Path: The Automobile and the American City.* New York: Columbia University Press, 1994.

Moholy-Nagy, Sybil. *Matrix of Man.* New York: Praeger, 1968.

A Monograph of the Works of McKim, Mead & White, 1879–1915. 1915. Reprint, New York: Benjamin Blom, 1973.

Moore, Charles W. "You Have to Pay for the Public Life." *Perspecta 9–10: Yale Architectural Journal* (1965): 57–97.

Moore, Charles W., and Gerald Allen. *Dimensions, Space, Shape, & Scale in Architecture.* New York: Architectural Record Books, 1976.

Moore, Charles W., Gerald Allen, and Donlyn Lyndon. *The Place of Houses.* New York: Holt, Rinehart & Winston, 1974.

Mourt's Relation: A Journal of the Pilgrims at Plymouth. London: 1622. Reprint, Cambridge and Boston: A Krusell Book, Applewood Books, 1986.

Mumford, Lewis. *The South in Architecture.* New York: Harcourt, Brace, 1941.

———. *The Highway and the City.* New York: Harcourt, Brace, 1953. Reprint, New York: Mentor, 1964.

———. *The City in History.* New York: Harcourt, Brace & World, 1961.

Muschamp, Herbert. *Man about Town: Frank Lloyd Wright in New York City.* Cambridge: M.I.T. Press, 1983.

Newby, Howard. *Country Life: A Social History of Rural England.* Totowa, N.J.: Barnes & Noble Books, 1987.

Norberg-Schulz, Christian. *Baroque Architecture*. New York: Harry N. Abrams, 1971.

———. *Existence, Space and Architecture*. New York: Praeger, 1971.

———. *Meaning in Western Architecture*. New York: Praeger, 1975.

———. *New World Architecture*. New York: Architectural League of New York and Princeton Architectural Press, 1988.

Peets, Elbert. *On the Art of Designing Cities: The Selected Essays of Elbert Peets*. Ed. Paul D. Spreiregen. Cambridge: M.I.T. Press, 1968.

Pennsylvania Avenue. Report of the President's Council on Pennsylvania Avenue. Washington, D.C., 1964.

Pevsner, Nikolaus. *A History of Building Types*. Princeton: Princeton University Press, 1976.

Rand, Ayn. Screenplay. *The Fountainhead*. Warner Bros. 1949. Based on the novel by Ayn Rand. Chicago: Sears Readers Club, 1943.

Rasmussen, Steen Eiler. *Towns and Buildings*. 1951. Reprint, Cambridge: M.I.T. Press, 1969.

Records of the Colony of New Plymouth of New England. Vol. 1. William White, 1861.

Reed, Henry Hope. *The Golden City*. New York: Doubleday, 1959. Reprint, Norton, 1971.

Reps, John W. *The Making of Urban America: A History of City Planning in the United States*. Princeton: Princeton University Press, 1965.

———. *Washington on View: The Nation's Capital Since 1790*. Chapel Hill: University of North Carolina Press, 1991.

Robertson, Jaquelin. "Rediscovering the Street." *Architectural Forum* 140 (November 1973): 24–31.

Rowsome, Frank. *The Verse by the Side of the Road: The Story of the Burma-Shave Signs and Jingles*. Brattleboro, Vt.: Stephen Greene Press, 1965.

Rudolph, Paul. "A View of Washington as a Capital—Or What Is Civic Design?" *Architectural Forum* 118 (January 1963): 64–70.

Rueda, Luis, ed. *Robert A. M. Stern: Buildings and Projects, 1981–1985*. New York: Rizzoli, 1986.

Rybczynski, Witold. *City Life: Urban Expectations in a New World*. New York: Scribner, 1995.

Rykwert, Joseph. *The Idea of a Town*. Princeton: Princeton University Press, 1976.

Saalman, Howard. *Haussmann: Paris Transformed*. New York: George Braziller, 1971.

Saarinen, Eliel. *The City*. New York: Reinhold, 1943.

Saint, Andrew. *The Image of the Architect*. New Haven: Yale University Press, 1983.

Scott, Geoffrey. *The Architecture of Humanism: A Study in the History of Taste*. New York: Norton, 1974.

Scully, Vincent, Jr. "Modern Architecture: Toward a Redefinition of Style." *Perspecta 4: Yale Architectural Journal* (1957): 4–11.

———. *Louis I. Kahn*. New York: George Braziller, 1962.

———. "The Death of the Street." *Perspecta 8: Yale Architectural Journal* (1963): 91–96.

———. *American Architecture and Urbanism*. New York: Praeger, 1969.

———. "American Houses: Thomas Jefferson to Frank Lloyd Wright." *In The Rise of an American Architecture*, edited by Edgar Kaufman Jr. New York: Praeger, 1970.

———. *Architecture: The Natural and the Manmade*. New York: St. Martin's Press, 1991.

Sharp, Dennis. *A Visual History of Twentieth-Century Architecture*. Greenwich, Conn.: New York Graphic Society, 1972.

Sharp, Thomas. *The Anatomy of the Village*. Harmondsworth, Middlesex, England: Penguin Books, 1946.

Shumway, Floyd, and Richard Hegel, eds. *New Haven: An Illustrated History*. Woodland Mills, Calif.: Windsor Publications, 1981.

Sitte, Camillo. *City Planning According to Artistic Principles*. Trans. George R. Collins and Christiane Craseman Collins. Columbia University Studies in Art History and Archeology, no. 3. London: Phaidon Press, 1965.

Smith, C. Ray. *New Attitudes in Post-Modern Architecture*. New York: Dutton, 1977.

Smith, G. E. Kidder. *A Pictorial History of Architecture in America*. 2 vols. New York: American Heritage, 1976.

Stein, Clarence S. "Toward New Towns for America." Radburn, *The Town Planning Review* 20 (October 1949): 219–51.

Stein, Susan R. *The Worlds of Thomas Jefferson at Monticello*. New York: Abrams, 1993.

Stern, Robert A. M. "With Rhetoric: The New York Apartment." *VIA* 4 (1980): 78–111.

———. *Pride of Place*. Boston: Houghton Mifflin; New York: American Heritage, 1986.

Stern, Robert A. M., with Raymond W. Gastil. *Modern Classicism*. New York: Rizzoli, 1988.

Stern, Robert A. M., Gregory Gilmartin, and Thomas Mellins. *New York 1930: Architecture and Urbanism between the Two World Wars*. New York: Rizzoli, 1987.

Stern, Robert A. M., Gregory Gilmartin, and John Montague Massengale. *New York 1900: Metropolitan Architecture and Urbanism, 1890–1915*. New York: Rizzoli, 1983.

Stern, Robert A. M., Thomas Mellins, and David Fishman. *New York 1960: Architecture and Urbanism between the Second World War and the Bicentennial*. New York: Montacelli Press, 1995.

Stern, Robert A. M., ed., with John Montague Massengale. *The Anglo-American Suburb*. New York: St. Martin's Press, 1981.

Stilgoe, John R. *Borderland: Origins of the American Suburb, 1820–1939*. New Haven: Yale University Press, 1988.

Styron, William. "In Praise of Vineyard Haven." In *On the Vineyard*. New York: Anchor Books, 1980.

Summerson, John. *Georgian London*. London: Barrie & Jenkins, 1962.

———. *The Life and Work of John Nash, Architect*. Cambridge: M.I.T. Press, 1980.

Thompson, Hunter. *Fear and Loathing in Las Vegas: A Savage Journey to the Heart of the American Dream*. 1971. Reprint, New York: First Vintage Books, 1989.

Tunnard, Christopher, "Design at the Scale of the Region." *Eye: Magazine of the Yale Arts Association* 1 (1967): 8–13.

———. *A World with a View*. New Haven: Yale University Press, 1978.

Tunnard, Christopher, and Henry Hope Reed. *American Skyline*. Boston: Houghton Mifflin, 1953. New York: Mentor, 1956.

Tunnard, Christopher, and Boris Pushkarev. *Man-Made America: Chaos or Control?* New Haven: Yale University Press, 1963.

Turner, Frederick Jackson. *The Frontier in American History*. Tuscon: University of Arizona Press, 1986.

Vale, Lawrence J. *Architecture, Power and National Identity*. New Haven: Yale University Press, 1992.

Venturi, Robert. *Complexity and Contradiction in Architecture*. New York: Museum of Modern Art, 1966.

Venturi, Robert, and Denise Scott Brown. "The Significance of A&P Parking Lots or Learning from Las Vegas." *Architectural Forum* 128 (March 1968): 36–43.

Venturi, Robert, Denise Scott Brown, and Steven Izenour. *Learning from Las Vegas*. Cambridge: M.I.T. Press, 1972.

Venturi, Robert, Denise Scott Brown, and Steven Izenour. *Signs of Life: Symbols in the American City.* Exhibition catalog. Washington, D.C.: Renwick Gallery, 1976.

Venturi, Scott Brown & Associates. *Venturi Scott Brown & Associates: On Houses and Housing.* Architectural Monographs 21. New York: St. Martin's Press, 1992.

Voltaire [François-Marie Arouet]. *Candide.* 1759. Reprint, New York: Random House, Literary Guild, 1929.

Voorhees, Walker, Smith & Haines. "Explanation of Commercial Bulk Regulations." *In Zoning New York City; A Proposal for a Zoning Resolution for the City of New York.* Submitted to the City Planning Commission August 1958, 127–31.

Webb, Bruce C., and William F. Stern. "Houston-Style Planning: No Zoning but Many Zones." *Cité: Architecture and Design Review of Houston* 32 (Fall 1994–Winter 1995): 14–15.

West, Nathanael. *The Day of the Locust.* 1939. Reprint, New York: New Directions, 1950.

Westmacott, Richard. *African-American Gardens and Yards in the Rural South.* Knoxville: University of Tennessee Press, 1992.

Whitaker, Craig. "Rouse-ing Up the Waterfront." *Architectural Record* 174 (April 1986): 66–71.

White, Morton, and Lucia White. *The Intellectual versus the City: From Thomas Jefferson to Frank Lloyd Wright.* Cambridge: Harvard University Press, 1962.

White, Norval, and Elliot Willensky. *AIA Guide to New York City.* New York: Collier, 1967.

Whyte, William H., Jr. *The Organization Man.* New York: Simon & Schuster, 1956.

Wilkinson, Jeff. "The Story of Porches." *Old-House Journal* 18 (July–August 1990): 30–37.

Wittkower, Rudolf. *Architectural Principles in the Age of Humanism.* London: Alec Tiranti, 1962. Reprint, New York: Norton, 1971.

Wolf, Peter M. *Eugène Hénard and the Beginning of Urbanism in Paris 1900–1914.* The Hague: Ando, 1968.

———. *The Future of the City.* New York: Watson-Guptill, Whitney Library of Design, 1974.

The WPA Guide to Washington, D.C. Washington: Government Printing office, 1937, as *Washington: City and Capital.* Reprint, New York: Pantheon Books, 1983.

Wright, Frank Lloyd. *The Future of Architecture.* New York: Horizon Press, 1958. Reprint, Mentor, 1963.

———. *The Living City.* New York: Horizon Press, 1958. Reprint, Mentor, 1963.

Wright, Gwendolyn. *Building the American Dream.* Cambridge: M.I.T. Press, 1981.

Wycherley, R. E. *How the Greeks Built Cities.* New York: Macmillan, 1962. Reprint, Anchor Books, 1969.

Zucker, Paul. *Town and Square: From the Agora to the Village Green.* New York: Columbia University Press, 1959. Reprint, Cambridge: M.I.T. Press, 1970.

ACKNOWLEDGMENTS

I am grateful to the Graham Foundation for Advanced Studies of the Fine Arts whose generous support made possible the large number of illustrations in the book. I must also thank The Sanborn Map Company of Pelham, New York, whose tax maps of many American cities were an invaluable tool, and Joseph Passonneau & Partners whose maps of Washington, D.C., were the basis for the plans of Pennsylvania Avenue.

Many people contributed thoughts and ideas that enriched (and sometimes challenged) my own. Former students Christopher Boone, Janet Jenkins, and Ralph McCoy broadened my understanding with their own research. Professor Steven Neuwirth's critique of the thesis strengthened my belief in the pervasiveness of our cultural values. John Rauch, my father, Elliot Whitaker, and Michael Wurmfeld read drafts of the work in progress and offered invaluable criticism at important junctures. Demetri Sarantitis and Victoria Rospond critiqued the photographs and drawings. Don Cantillo found many of the pictures, and he also developed a methodology for making the maps and plans legibile at various scales. Many of the actual plans were the work of Hui-Hua Annexstein. Michael Seymour, Geoffrey Spencer, and Robert Wollam lent frequent and patient logistical support, as did Monica Ann Wallach, who also edited the manuscript. Abigail Sturges's beautiful book design strengthened the pictorial narrative considerably. Roy Finamore, my editor at Clarkson Potter, believed this book should be published, and he and his assistant, Lenny Allen, worked tirelessly to shape the manuscript into a final product.

Two people in particular had much to do with the larger effort. My agent, Regina Ryan, encouraged me throughout. She edited the manuscript twice, strengthening it each time. My wife, Jennifer Seymour Whitaker, not only edited the manuscript several times, but listened patiently for several years as the ideas came into focus.

ILLUSTRATION CREDITS

1, Jim Bolenbaugh; 2, Craig Whitaker; 3, Photograph: Chester H. Liebs, *Main Street to Miracle Mile,* Johns Hopkins University Press, 1995; 4, Craig Whitaker; 5, Collection, M. Yvan Christ, Paris, uncredited photo, 1865; 6, Photograph: © Andreas Feininger; 7, *American Architect and Architectural Review*; 8, Ferdinando Castagnoli, *Orthogonal Town Planning in Antiquity,* The MIT Press, (von Gerkan, "Milet I"); 9, Ohio State University Libraries; 10, drawn and published by Augustus Koch, 1870, Library of Congress Map Division; 11, Jim Wilson/ NYT Pictures; 12, Engraving by Pierre Le Pautre, E. de Ganay, "Andre Le Notre," Editions Vincent, Freal & Cie., pl 18; 13, Regional Plan Association, *Regional Plan of New York and Its Environs: The Building of the City, 1931,* Volume 2; 14, Hui-Hua Annexstein; 15, Springer-Verlag; 16, Burton Historical Collection, Detroit Public Library; 17, Reps, John; *The Making of Urban America.* Copyright © 1965 by PUP. Reprinted by permission of Princeton University Press; 18, From the Collections of The New Jersey Historical Society, Newark, New Jersey; 19, Fairchild Aerial Surveys; Tunnard & Pushkarev, *Man-Made America,* Yale University Press © 1963; 20, Reprinted with permission from *Perspecta 6: The Yale Architectural Journal,* 1960; 21, Library of Congress; 22, Hui-Hua Annexstein; 23, Waldemar Kaden, woodcuts by A. Closs; 24, Washington State Historical Society, Tacoma, Washington; 25, Sharp, Thomas, *The Anatomy of the Village,* Penguin © 1946; 26, Reps, John, *The Making of Urban America.* Copyright © 1965 by PUP. Reprinted by permission of Princeton University Press; 27, Robert Cameron, Aerial Photographer; 28, Craig Whitaker; 29, Hui-Hua Annexstein; 30, *Civic Art*; 31, © Paramount Pictures; courtesy of Billy Rose Theatre Collection, The New York Public Library for the Performing Arts, Astor, Lenox and Tilden Foundations; 32, Manoogian Foundation; 33, Corbis-Bettmann.

34, Craig Whitaker; 35, Craig Whitaker; 36, Hui-Hua Annexstein, adaptation of drawing owned by Mr. W. R. Headley; 37, Old Sturbridge Village; 38, Craig Whitaker; 39, Photograph: © Yukio Futagawa; 40, Venturi, Scott Brown and Associates; 41, From *A Pictorial History of Architecture in America* by G. E. Kidder Smith; 42, Craig Whitaker; 43, The Library of Virginia; 44, Craig Whitaker; 45, Craig Whitaker; 46, Venturi, Scott Brown and Associates; 47, Craig Whitaker with the assistance of the Mount Vernon Ladies' Association, which owns and operates Mount Vernon; 48, Craig Whitaker; 49, Craig Whitaker; 50, The Library of Congress; 51, Craig Whitaker; 52, Craig Whitaker; 53, Craig Whitaker; 54, Craig Whitaker; 55, Craig Whitaker; 56, Photographic Archives, Ekstrom Library, University of Louisville; 57, Designer: Robert L.

Zion, Landscape Architect; 58, Library of Congress; 59, Craig Whitaker; 60, Venturi, Scott Brown and Associates; 61, Photograph: Jock Pottle/ Esto; © The J. Paul Getty Trust and Richard Meier & Partners; 62, Springer/ Corbis-Bettmann; 63, Craig Whitaker; 64, Aerial Viewpoint Photo Labs, Inc.; 65, John Hill, Craig Witaker; 66, Clarence S. Stein; 67, Gretchen van Tassel; 68, Craig Whitaker; 69, Craig Whitaker; 70, © 1996 FLW FDN; 71, *Anglo-American Suburb,* Academy Group Ltd.; 72, Craig Whitaker; 73, Ezra Stoller © Esto; 74, Fondation Le Corbusier, © 1996 Artists Rights Society (ARS), New York/ SPADEM, Paris; 75, Ezra Stoller © Esto; 76, Collection of The New-York Historical Society; 77, Craig Whitaker; 78, From *The City Shaped* by Spiro Kostof. Copyright © 1991 by Spiro Kostof. By permission of Little, Brown and Company; 79, Courtesy of the George S. Bolster Collection of the Historical Society of Saratoga Springs; 80, Gerald Allen, from *Place of Houses* by Charles Moore, Gerald Allen and Donlyn Lyndon. Copyright © 1974 by Charles Moore, Gerald Allen, Donlyn Lyndon. Reprinted by permission of Henry Holt and Co., Inc.; 81, © Curtis Publishing Company; 82, Craig Whitaker; 83, Craig Whitaker.

84, Regional Plan Association, Hui-Hua Annexstein; 85, Don Cantillo, Craig Whitaker; 86, Craig Whitaker; 87, Craig Whitaker; 88, Cassandra Wilday; 89, Craig Whitaker; 90, Michael Flanagan; 91, Gruzen Samton/ Beyer, Blinder, Belle, Master Planners-Architects; 92, Craig Whitaker; 93, Craig Whitaker; 94, Craig Whitaker; 95, Craig Whitaker; 96, Chicago Historical Society; 97, Steven Zane, Coalition for a Better Waterfront; 98, Craig Whitaker; 99, Craig Whitaker; 100, © Country Life Picture Library; 101, © 1996 FLW FDN; 102, Craig Whitaker; 103, Industrial Areas Foundation; 104, Fondation Le Corbusier, © 1996 Artists Rights Society (ARS), New York/ SPADEM, Paris; 105, Fondation Le Corbusier, © 1996 Artists Rights Society (ARS), New York/ SPADEM, Paris; 106, Photograph: John Donat; 107, Craig Whitaker, courtesy Linda N. J. Szymanski; 108, ICHi-26090, Chicago Historical Society; 109, Craig Whitaker; 110, Venturi, Scott Brown and Associates; 111, Craig Whitaker, used by permission from Disney Enterprises, Inc.; 112, Janet K. Jenkins, used by permission from Disney Enterprises, Inc.; 113, Courtesy of Peter Wolf; 114, Craig Whitaker; 115, Hui-Hua Annexstein; 116, Rantoul Collection, Harvard University Graduate School of Business Administration; 117, Hui-Hua Annexstein; 118, Hui-Hua Annexstein.

119, New Haven Colony Historical Society; 120, Wade Perry, from *Place of Houses* by Charles Moore, Gerald Allen and Donlyn Lyndon. Copyright © 1974 by Charles Moore, Gerald Allen, Donlyn Lyndon. Reprinted by permission of Henry Holt and Co., Inc.; 121, Craig Whitaker Architects; 122, Craig Whitaker; 123, Craig Whitaker; 124, © 1996 FLW FDN; 125, Photograph: Robert E. Mates; © The Solomon R. Guggenheim Foundation, New York; 126, © 1996 FLW FDN; 127, Craig Whitaker; 128, Craig Whitaker; 129, Craig Whitaker; 130, Craig Whitaker; 131, Craig Whitaker; 132, Library of Congress; 133, Fondation Le Corbusier, © Artists Rights Society (ARS), New York/ SPADEM, Paris; 134, *Civic Art*; 135, Craig Whitaker; 136, David W. Dunlap; 137, Craig Whitaker; 138, Art Color Card; 139, From Beers Atlas, courtesy of Terry Tyler; 140, Craig Whitaker; 141, Craig Whitaker; 142, Craig Whitaker; 143, Courtesy of Abramowitz Kingsland Schiff; 144, From *Design of Cities* by Edmund Bacon. Copyright © 1967, 1974 by Edmund N. Bacon. Used by permission of Penguin, a division of Penguin Books USA, Inc.; 145, Hui-Hua Annexstein, Craig Whitaker; 146, Craig Whitaker; 147, photograph: Tom Bernard, Venturi, Scott Brown and Associates; drawing: Venturi, Scott Brown and Associates; 148, Craig Whitaker; 149, Wade Perry, from *Place of Houses* by Charles Moore, Gerald Allen and Donlyn Lyndon. Copyright © 1974 by Charles Moore, Gerald Allen, Donlyn Lyndon. Reprinted by permission of Henry Holt and Co., Inc.; 150, Robert Cameron, Aerial Photographer; 151, *Civic Art*; 152, Craig Whitaker; 153, Bancroft Library, University of California at Berkeley; 154, Craig

Whitaker; 155, The Ohio State University Photo Archives; 156, The Ohio State University Photo Archives; 157, Craig Whitaker; 158, Craig Whitaker, Hui-Hua Annexstein; 159, Craig Whitaker; 160, Ohio Historical Society; 161, Joshua White, Frank O. Gehry & Associates.

162, Craig Whitaker; 163, Craig Whitaker; 164, Craig Whitaker; 165, A. Cartoni, Rome; 166, Venturi, Scott Brown and Associates; 167, Reprinted with permission from *Perspecta 4: The Yale Architectural Journal,* 1957; 168, Photograph: Louis Checkman; 169, Postcard Gallery; 170, G. E. Kidder Smith; 171, Published by Jasper Johns and Simca Print Artists, Inc. © 1996 Jasper Johns/ Licensed by VAGA, New York, NY; 172, Copyright © Estate of Diane Arbus, 1971; Courtesy Robert Miller Gallery, New York; 173, Photograph Collection, Art & Architecture Library, Yale University; 174, American Institute of Steel Construction, Inc.; 175, New York State Department of Transportation, Tunnard & Pushkarev, *Man-Made America,* copyright © 1963 Yale University Press; 176, From *The City Shaped* by Spiro Kostof. Copyright © 1991 by Spiro Kostof. By permission of Little, Brown and Company; 177, Blaser/ Hannaford (eds.), *Drawings of Great Buildings*, Birkhauser Verlag AG, Basel, 1993; 178, From *A Pictorial History of Architecture in America* by G. E. Kidder Smith; 179, Ezra Stoller © Esto; 180, *Louis I. Kahn,* Les Editions d'Architecture, Artemis, Zurich; 181, From *The City Shaped* by Spiro Kostof. Copyright © 1991 by Spiro Kostof. By permission of Little, Brown and Company; 182, Photograph: Harry Hartman, courtesy Merchant's House Museum; 183, Craig Whitaker; 184, Paul D. Spreiregen; 185, The Connecticut Historical Society, Hartford, Connecticut; 186, Robert Cameron, Aerial Photographer; 187, © FVN Corporation; 188, NYT Pictures; 189, Leonardo Benevolo, *The History of the City*, The MIT Press; 190, *McKim Mead & White: 1879–1915;* 191, Craig Whitaker; 192, Michael Flanagan; 193, Photograph: Wolfgang Volz; Copyright © Christo 1976; 194, Photograph: Harry Shunk; Copyright © Christo 1972; 195, Craig Whitaker; 196, Craig Whitaker; 197, New York State Thruway Authority; 198, Craig Whitaker; 199, Craig Whitaker; 200, Photograph © 1996: Whitney Museum of American Art, New York; 201, Craig Whitaker; 202, Craig Whitaker; 203, Photograph: William Beuke; ICHi-05780, Chicago Historical Society; 204, Craig Whitaker; 205, Craig Whitaker; 206, Hui-Hua Annexstein, Craig Whitaker; 207, Hui-Hua Annexstein, Craig Whitaker; 208, Edizione SACAT, Turin; 209, Hui-Hua Annexstein; 210, Massachusetts Department of Commerce, Tunnard & Pushkarev, *Man-Made America,* Copyright © 1963 Yale University Press; 211, Swem Library, College of William and Mary; 212, Craig Whitaker; 213, Craig Whitaker; 214, Craig Whitaker; 215, Negative 60215, frame 28, Courtesy Department of Library Services, American Museum of Natural History; 216, Craig Whitaker, Hui-Hua Annexstein; 217, Craig Whitaker; 218, Craig Whitaker; 219, Hui-Hua Annexstein; 220, Drawing by Paul Rudolph; 221, Craig Whitaker; 222, Collection of The New-York Historical Society; 223, The Wurts Collection, Museum of the City of New York; 224, Collection of The New-York Historical Society; 225, Craig Whitaker, Hui-Hua Annexstein.

226, Courtesy of Plimoth Plantation, Inc., Plymouth, Massachusetts; 227, drawn and published by William Birch, Library of Congress, Map Division; 228, Collection of Craig Whitaker; 229, *Civic Art;* 230, The Library of Congress; 231, Craig Whitaker; 232, Craig Whitaker; 233, Photograph: Adam Woolfitt; Copyright © Robert Harding Picture Library; 234, I.N. Pillsbury. Journal of the Association of English Societies, Library of Congress Map Division; 235, Ohio Historical Society; 236, Map Collection, Olin Library, Cornell University; 237, Nicholas Tassin, Les Plans et Profils de Toute les Principales, Library of Congress Map Division; 238, *Civic Art;* 239, Steen Eiler Rasmussen, *Towns and Buildings,* The MIT Press; 240, *Civic Art;* 241, *Civic Art;* 242, Reps, John, *The Making of Urban America.* Copyright © by PUP. Reprinted by permission of Princeton University Press; 243, Permission for use granted by *Architectural Record;* 244, Paul D.

INDEX